teleparody

predicting/preventing the tv discourse of tomorrow

D1314130

teleparody

predicting/preventing the tv discourse of tomorrow

**EDITED BY
ANGELA HAGUE & DAVID LAVERY**

WALLFLOWER PRESS
LONDON AND NEW YORK

First published in Great Britain in 2002 by
Wallflower Press
5 Pond Street, London NW3 2PN
www.wallflowerpress.co.uk

A catalogue for this book is available from the British Library

ISBN 1-903364-39-6 (paperback)
ISBN 1-903364-40-X (hardback)

Design by Piers Parlett

Printed in Great Britain by Antony Rowe, Chippenham, Wiltshire

contents

how to read this book

Teleparody may be read in a variety of ways. Below you will find both a generic table of contents, in which teleparodies are grouped according to the generic similarities of their subjects (hence, those pieces devoted to sitcoms congregate together; those pieces which are heavily theoretical are segregated, et cetera) and an alternative menu, in which teleparodies are arranged by 'degree of difficulty'. Using the index, you could, of course, choose instead to read only those passages dealing with the TV shows or theorists that interest you. By consulting the book's website (www.teleparody.com) you will discover additional entrances and exits (including the invitation to write and submit for online publication your own teleparody). We certainly do not presume to dictate how you read this unorthodox book, but we feel certain that whether you follow a linear course, graze, or surf, you will agree – with apologies to Comedy Central's *The Daily Show* – that it may be 'the most important ever'.

generic table of contents

the sitcom

drama

children's tv

gender

theory

alternative menu

lite (easily read even by amateurs)

medium (requiring somewhat more esoteric/trivial knowledge)

heavy (for sophisticates and pseudo-sophisticates)

contributors

Will Brooker is Assistant Professor of Communication at the University of Richmond, London. He is the author/editor of *Postmodern After-Images: A Reader in Postmodern Film, Television and Video*; *Teach Yourself: Cultural Studies*; and *Batman Unmasked: Analyzing a Cultural Icon*.

Jeremy Brown recently completed his M.A. degree in English at Middle Tennessee State University.

Mark J. Charney is Professor of English and Director of Undergraduate Studies in English at Clemson University and chair of the American College Theatre Festival, Region IV. He is the author of a monograph on Barry Hannah.

Marc Dolan is Associate Professor of English and American Studies at the City University of New York. He is the author of *Modern Lives: A Cultural Re-Reading of 'The Lost Generation'* and is currently working on a history of creativity in the mass media between the two World Wars.

Michael Dunne teaches at Middle Tennessee State University, where he is the co-editor of *Studies in Popular Culture*. He is the author of numerous articles and three books, *Metapop: Self Referentiality in Contemporary American Pop Culture, Hawthorne's Narrative Strategies,* and *Intertextual Encounters in American Fiction, Film, and Popular Culture.*

Bill Freind teaches at Providence College. He is currently at work on a book examining the role of history in twentieth-century poetry.

Kenneth Gillam is a doctoral candidate in English at Illinois State University.

Charles A. Goldthwaite, Jr. is a doctoral candidate in English at the University of Virginia.

Allison Graham is Professor of Communication at the University of Memphis. The co-producer of the Emmy-nominated documentary *At the River I Stand,* she is the author of numerous articles and two books, *Lindsay Anderson* and *Framing the South: Hollywood, Television, and Race During the Civil Rights Struggle.*

Angela Hague is Professor of English at Middle Tennessee State University. The author of *Iris Murdoch's Comic Vision* and *Fiction, Intuition, and Creativity: Studies in Bronte, James, Woolf, and Lessing* and co-editor of *Deny All Knowledge: Reading The X-Files*, she is currently writing a book on alien abduction.

Dennis Hall teaches English and is a utility infielder at the University of Louisville, who writes pieces on general popular culture and (with M. Thomas Inge) is co-editor of the third edition of *The Handbook of American Popular Culture* which he desperately hopes will be in your library if not your neighborhood bookstore soon. Although he does not own any pets, he is conspicuously kind to his wife and children.

Eugene Halton is Professor of Humanities at the University of Notre Dame and the author of several books including *Bereft of Reason: On the Decline of Social Thought and Prospects for Its Renewal.*

Richard Henry is Assistant Professor of English at SUNY Potsdam. He is the author of *Pretending and Meaning: Toward a Pragmatic Theory of Fictional Discourse; Contributions in Philosophy* and (with Deborah Rossen-Knill) of two articles on parody.

Matthew Hills teaches at Cardiff University, is the co-editor of *Intensities: The Journal of Cult Media,* and is the unapologetic author of *Cult Media and Fan Cultures.*

Robert P. Holtzclaw is Associate Professor of English at Middle Tennessee State University, where he directs the program in Film Studies.

Kevin Kehrwald recently earned his PhD at Purdue University. He teaches film studies at Frostburg State University in Maryland.

David Lavery is Professor of English at Middle Tennessee State University. He is the author of numerous articles and the author/editor of six books, including *Fighting the Forces: What's at Stake in Buffy the Vampire Slayer* and *This Thing of Ours: Investigating The Sopranos*.

Paul Malone is Assistant Professor in the Department of Germanic and Slavic Studies at the University of Waterloo, Canada. He has published articles and book chapters on film versions of Kafka's *The Trial*, computer-generated celebrities, and performance theory, and is the editor of *Germano-Slavica: A Canadian Journal of Germanic and Slavic Comparative and Interdisciplinary Studies*.

'Clifford Mapes' (Professor of English at West Central Biotechnical Institute) is a pseudonym for Warren Tormey, who was originally reluctant to have his name connected with this collection. He has, however, come around, and invites any reader to identify all of the baseball references buried in his review. A lifelong fan of the Arizona Diamondbacks, he has two cats: Julius and Thea, and is completing his doctorate at Middle Tennessee State University.

Ben Picken-Schnozzle is the post-rational identity of the melancholy Jimmie L. Reeves, who suffers from post-tenure guilt as an Associate Professor of Mass Communications at Texas Tech University. In addition to articles on subjects ranging from Mr. T to *The X-Files*, Dr. Reeves is the co-author of *Cracked Coverage: Television News, the Anti-Cocaine Crusade, and the Reagan Legacy*.

Jim Riser is Assistant Professor of English at the University of North Alabama.

Robert J. Thompson is the author/editor of five books on popular television, including *Prime Time, Prime Movers* (with David Marc) and *Television's Second Golden Age*. He directs the Center for the Study of Popular Television at Syracuse University.

Stephen Tompkins is a doctoral candidate at Lehigh University.

Greg A. Waller is Professor of English at the University of Kentucky. He is the author/editor of *American Horrors: Essays on the Modern American Horror Film*, *Main Street Amusements: Movies and Commercial Entertainment in a Southern City, 1896–1930* and *Moviegoing in America: A Sourcebook in the History of Film Exhibition*.

Brenda R. Weber teaches in the Honors and Women's Studies Programs at the University of Kentucky. She holds a doctorate from Miami University of Ohio and specialises in Anglo-American Victorian writing. The author of recent articles on nineteenth-century education for women and the *Avonlea* novels, she is presently composing *Writing the Woman Writing: The Ethos of Authorship in the Anglo-American Literary Marketplace, 1850–1900.*

'Krystal Whitecastle' (Assistant Professor of Media Studies at Impoverished State University) is the distaff side of Pete McCluskey, Assistant Professor of English at Middle Tennessee State University, where he teaches classes in Shakespeare and Renaissance drama.

Rhonda V. Wilcox is Professor of English at Gordon College in Barnesville, GA. The author of numerous essays on popular culture, she wrote the chapter on television for the *Handbook of American Popular Culture* (Third Edition). With David Lavery, she is the editor of *Fighting the Forces: What's at Stake in Buffy the Vampire Slayer.*

Shannon R. Wooden is a PhD candidate in the Department of Social Medicine at the University of North Carolina School of Medicine.

In memory of Jerry Stern (1938–1996)
who always wanted to write a book on *Mister Ed*
and now has.

introduction

'This is parody's mission: it must never be afraid of going too far.
If its aim is true, it simply heralds what others will later produce,
unblushing, with impassive and assertive gravity.'

Umberto Eco, *Misreadings*

'The writing of a novel is a form of the loss of creative liberty.
In turn, the reviewing of books is a servitude still less noble. Of the writer
one can at least say that he has enslaved himself – by the theme selected.
The critic is in a worse position: as the convict is chained to his wheelbarrow,
so the reviewer is chained to the work reviewed. The writer
loses his freedom in his own book, the critic in another.'

Stanislaw Lem, *A Perfect Vacuum*

1

Prehistory by David Lavery

Every great writer, Borges once noted enigmatically in an essay on Franz Kafka, '*creates* his precursors' (1999: 365; emphasis in original). But does not every new art form as well? Every new critical form? Whatever the fictions that make up this volume actually are (and even the editors will admit they are not entirely certain, though as a gloss we have thought of them as 'prophetic/prophylactic' criticism), they are not without precedent. They have not only cursors/cursers — those colleagues who complained, at a national conference where some of them were presented, that we had 'gone too far!' (and by complaining confirmed that, in Eco's characterisation, we were doing parody just right) — but precursors.

As parodies, after all, they partake of a long tradition. As early as the Greek comic playwright Aristophanes and the Roman rhetorician Quintillian, parody, a word derived from Greek roots meaning 'to sing' and 'alongside of/subsidiary to,'[1] was already considered, in theory and in practice, 'pejorative in intent and ridiculing in its ethos or intended response' (Hutcheon 1985: 51). Writing in 1962 Gilbert Highet speaks of parody's range as 'amusement, derision, and sometimes scorn' (1962: 69). More recently, Linda Hutcheon, in *A Theory of Parody: The Teachings of Twentieth-Century Art Forms* (1985), argues for the centrality of parody to Postmodernism: in the age of 'the already said' (Eco's phrase — see the Afterword to *Name of the Rose*), parody — whether derisive, playful, or reverent — has naturally become ubiquitous. Further, Hutcheon argues, it should be thought of as 'a form of imitation, but imitation characterized by ironic inversion, not always at the expense of the parodied text' (1985: 6). The teleparodies that follow — mostly taking the form of reviews[2] — continue parody's grand tradition, embodying all its inherent contradictions, but they evoke as well a somewhat more esoteric, and more difficult to identify, lineage.

If, for example, some of the following make fabulous use of the pedant's tools — the footnote, the bibliography, and the scholarly commentary — as discursive forms, did not Vladimir Nabokov pave the way in *Pale Fire* (1962), a 'novel' comprised of a 30-page poem followed by over 150 pages of mock-arcane annotation?

If our supposedly academic volume, taken as a whole, strains credulity and fails to pass the 'duck test', it is not the first. In the 25 June 1996 issue of *The Village Voice* was it not possible to read an announcement of a forthcoming already published tome (assembled by SWISH [The Society for the Withering Investigation of Sports]) very much in the same spirit as the present one?

Re/Bound: Slavery and Liberation in the Work of Dennis Rodman. To be published last year by Routledge. Contents: Lisa Jones, 'The Afro-American: A History of Hair as Canvas'; Eugene Genovese, 'Roll Over Jordan, Roll Over: Defense as an Offensive Trope'; Stanley Aronowitz, 'Globe-Trotsky: A Survey of Basketball's Worldwide Revolution'; Jacques Derrida, 'De-Center and Dis-Senter; or Logos and *Logos*'; bell 'sky' hooks, 'Madonna and Manchild: Transgression and Aggression in the Theater of Dennis Rodman'; Francis Fox Piven, 'Hoop Schemes: The NBA and the Dismantling of the Welfare State'; Judith Butler, 'Naming the Rim: Clarence Thomas, Faye Resnick, and the End(s) of Jurisprudence'; Slavoj Zizek, 'Double Dribble: Toward a Politics of the *Doppelgänger* in the Televisual Realm of Professional American Basketball'; Tom Frank, 'City of Big (Tattooed) Shoulders: Licensing, Labor, Layups, and Layoffs'.

'Essays' for *Re/Bound,* we are told in a concluding whimsical note, 'must be submitted in accordance with *The Chicago Bulls Manual of Style*.'

If these pages contain occasional enigmatic references to other non-existents – books, for example, that will not be published for several decades, or futuristic media developments – in a strange loop of interconnecting fictions, they are in good company. For do we not find in Douglas R. Hofstadter's award-winning *Gödel, Escher, Bach: An Eternal Golden Braid* (1979) an equally loopy, vaguely familiar annotated bibliography entry?

> Gebstadter, Egbert R. *Copper, Silver, Gold: An Indestructible Metal Alloy.* Perth: Acidic Books, 1979. A formidable hodge-podge, turgid and confused – yet remarkably similar to the present work. Professor Gebstadter's Shandean digressions include some excellent examples of indirect self-reference. Of particular interest is a reference in its well-annotated bibliography to an isomorphic, but imaginary, book (p. 748).

If *Teleparody*'s reviewers have read and critiqued books that are not yet, they imitate genius.[3] For has not the impossibly polymathic Polish science fiction mastermind Stanislaw Lem authored two entirely comparable books: *A Perfect Vacuum* (1971), a collection of 'perfect reviews of non-existent books' (books, Lem implies, he had always meant to write but had not gotten around to), and *Imaginary Magnitude* (1981), prefaces for books that will be written in the twenty-first century?[4] 'Literature to date has told us of fictitious *characters*,' Lem explains. 'We shall go further: we shall depict fictitious *books*' (Lem's emphasis). In such a development Lem discerns 'a chance to regain creative liberty, and at the same time to wed two opposing spirits – that of the belletrist and that of the critic' (1971: 4).[5]

If these teleparodies play matchmaker to artistic and critical/scholarly impulses through the medium of television, the following nuptials are not the first of their kind. Nor are they the first to blur the boundary between real scholarship and parody. The reader will no doubt recall the grave commotion caused several years back by the publication in the cultural studies journal *Social Text* of an article titled 'Transgressing the Boundaries: Toward a Transformative Hermeneutic of Quantum Gravity' by NYU physicist Alan D. Sokal. When Sokal subsequently revealed in *Lingua Franca* that his essay was in fact a parody, a hoax intended to expose the nakedness of postmodern critical emperors, all hell broke loose.

Sokal was not the only scholar at play in the 1990s. Lawrence Douglas and Alexander George authored an hilarious put-on called 'Freud's Phonographic Memory and the Case of the Missing Kiddush Cups' (published in *Tikkun*), a send-up of scholarly discourse that includes a footnote citing an essay by Father Terence McFeely, S.J., entitled 'The Mammary of Things Past: What is Beneath Freud's Slip', (published in *The Journal of Genital Theory*). As Douglas explained in a back page piece in *The Chronicle of Higher Education*, their attempt at humor, immediately recognised as such by his own mother, who found it hilarious, was subsequently cited with great seriousness by several scholars (with tin ears equal to those of *Social Text*'s editors) who had not gotten the joke.

Teleparody, too, has bred some confusion. When this book was in development, the editors posted for a time some of these teleparodies on the web to facilitate editing. One of the internet search engines discovered the otherwise blind site, and a surfer who discovered my own contribution to this book (a review of a book on *Baywatch*) called attention to the supposed author, a former acquaintance of mine, of one of the essays in that book.[6] My colleague, congratulated on his recent publication, e-mailed me to inquire how he had come to publish an essay that he did not remember ever having written. With ease I explained that I had merely appropriated his real name as the fictional author of a make-believe essay in an imaginary book which I was pretending to review. He was not amused, and I removed his name.

Nor are we the first to send-up television. Perhaps television lends itself to parody. After all, as Mark Crispin Miller argues, the medium 'does not elicit our rapt absorption or hearty agreement, but ... actually flatters us for the very boredom and distrust which it inspires in us.' Television, in Miller's deeply cynical view, 'solicits each viewer's allegiance by reflecting back his/her own automatic skepticism toward TV' (1987: 194). If TV 'derides and conquers' – if, that is, it is inherently inclined toward self-parody – it is possible that any serious (or mock-serious) consideration of it will seem to be a put-on.

I grew up reading the brilliant television parodies in *Mad Magazine* recently collected in book form. Today, the always hilarious online humor newspaper *The Onion* masterfully parodies television scholarship. In one piece, 'Report: Mankind's Knowledge of TV Trivia Doubling Every Three Years,' we learn that research conducted by Rutgers University's Center for Media Studies indicates that 'species familiarity' with television minutiae is rapidly increasing and improving in quality. *The Onion* quotes Mark Bennett: 'It's no longer all that impressive to know that two different actors played Darrin on *Bewitched* ... To impress these days, you'd have to know that there were two Mrs. Kravitzes. Or two Louise Tates. Or that Jerry Seinfeld was on the first season of *Benson*.'[7]

But it hasn't just been humor zines that have parodied television. In pieces that might well be included in this volume, we find such a major intellectual as the Italian semiotician and novelist Umberto Eco parodying television scholarship in such journalistic pieces as 'How to Be a TV Host' and 'The Phenomenology of Mike Bongiorno'.[8] As original as we have tried to be, we too suffer the anxiety of influence.

As Geraghty and Lusted have observed (a passage also quoted by Matt Hills later in this volume): 'Criticisms of Television Studies are often based on a confusion between what is studied and the act of studying, and so it is assumed that because some television is sloppy, badly researched and offensive so too is its study' (1998: 5). Our anomalous contribution to Television Studies, a book whose genesis was (as my co-editor will explain in the following section) in the (too) serious consideration of bad television, *Teleparody* was, in a sense, spawned by the very confusion Geraghty and Lusted delineate. Beyond its humble beginnings, however, it became (we hope you will agree) something substantially more.[9]

Lawrence Douglas' perplexing experience with scholarly fiction led him to a surprising conclusion: 'For all our savvy and theoretical sophistication, we have lost the capacity to make very simple judgments about a text – such as, for example, whether it claims to be true or intends to make us laugh.' We trust *Teleparody* will produce no such confusion.

Notes

1 The ambiguous meaning – designating both 'beside' and 'opposite' – of the root word 'para' almost predicts the dual nature of parody as both criticism and homage (Rose 1993: 46).

2 Hutcheon quotes W. H. Auden's wishful thinking – in his concept of a 'daydream College for Bards' – that literary criticism, per se, be banned, replaced by 'the writing of parodies' as the 'only criticial exercise required of students' (1985: 51). Though by no means poets, our teleparodists all seem to have been schooled in Auden's academy.

3 Although the precedent I am about to cite is Polish, and more than one of our teleparodists is English, there may be something distinctly American about our enterprise. As the historian Daniel Boorstin has observed, American discourse is characterised by a way of speaking about things 'which had not yet gone through the formality of taking place' (1965: 98). Our book dispenses with formalities.

4 'Reviewing non-existent books is not Lem's invention,' he admits; 'we find such experiments not only in a contemporary writer, Jorge Luis Borges (for example his 'Investigations of the Writings of Herbert Quaine'), but the idea goes further back – and even Rabelais was not the first to make use of it' (1971: 3).

5 Elsewhere Lem wonders aloud: "If no philosopher named Schopenhauer had ever existed and if Borges had invented in a story a doctrine called 'The World as Will', we would accept this as a bit of fiction, not of the history of philosophy. But of what kind of fiction, indeed? Of fantastic philosophy, because it was published nonassertively. Here is a literature of imaginary ideas, of fictional values, of other civilizations – in a word, the fantasy of the 'abstract'" (1984: 220). Our teleparodists, we might suggest, are practicing 'fantastic criticism.'

6 As the reader will soon discover, our authors sometimes use real names (though only with permission), and sometimes change names to protect the innocent.

7 In another hilarious spoof ('Report: TV Helps Build Valuable Looking Skills' – this time from NYU's Center for Media Studies), we learn that adults 'who grew up in homes without television' have 'difficulty staring blankly at things for longer than a few seconds.' In fact, 'they frequently shifted their gaze and focus around the testing environment, often engaging others in the room in conversation and generally making a lot of disruptive noise and movement. Television-enriched adults, however, could sit and look at anything: a spot on the ceiling, a fire-alarm box, a stack of magazines on a table.' As we write, yet another delicious parody has just appeared in *The Onion*. Its first paragraph reads: 'WASHINGTON, DC – Pressure is building for the nation's TV networks to offer a formal apology and reparations to the four generations of Americans who lost millions of hours to inane sitcoms.'

8 Bongiorno is an Italian TV celebrity, best known as the host of quiz shows.

9 As this book was in development, our colleague Charles Wolfe, perhaps the foremost contemporary scholar of American popular music, passed on to us an essay he had written (but never published) in the late 1960s called 'Bilko's Plots and the *Bilko* Plots: Toward a Structural Definition of Television Situation Comedy'. He thought it might be appropriate. A brilliant exercise in what would eventually be called 'narratological criticism', it is, however, anything but a parody and can only be thought of as such because it takes seriously a sitcom high-brow thinking would deem not worthy of another thought. (We have placed Dr. Wolfe's essay on the *Teleparody* website.)

History by Angela Hague

This book has a curious origin. A few years ago I attended a women's study conference with several colleagues, a yearly ritual some female members of the department used to escape from the intellectual rigours of the English Department at Middle Tennessee State University. Before joining my friends at a session titled 'Women and Film,' I stopped by the book display room to kill some time and meandered around the several tables covered in books, idly picking them up and skimming their covers and tables of contents. At a certain point I realized they were all essentially the same book, with barely discernible differences packaged in identical jargon and critical 'assumptions' – each one, of course, proclaiming itself a radical new way of rethinking whatever hackneyed topic it pretended to enlighten. I had experienced this sense of the eternal recurrence of postmodernist thought before, but for some reason this time it struck me as comical. I didn't laugh, of course; I was surrounded by depressed-looking middle-aged women academics who looked as if they wouldn't appreciate a snicker, so I kept silent, rifling through studies of oppression, aging, healing, transformation, empowerment, and gender conflict.

Alas. The laughter I repressed was biding its time, waiting for the appropriate catalyst, which turned out to be the first paper of the session we all dutifully sat down to hear – fortunately in the back row, as it turned out. I have no memory of what the paper was actually about, except for the fact it concerned some kind of female problem in *The Piano* – pronounced 'pianer' because of the reader's unfortunate accent. But the accent wasn't the problem, for I'd been hearing it for all too many years to be offended, nor was the sex of the reader: I firmly believe that men have a right, and perhaps even an obligation, to read papers at women's studies conferences. It was the slightly hesitant earnestness of the delivery coupled with the hint of a daring piety: the author of this piece clearly thought he was breaking new ground and felt very pleased with himself as a result. I whispered to Charisse Gendron, who sat to my right, that 'his voice is driving me crazy.' Apparently she agreed, because she chuckled and then laughed aloud, hastily clapping her hand to her mouth. And then he said the word *phallogocentrism*.

Now we'd heard the word before (we were adults after all), but uttered at that particular moment and in that particular accent *phallogocentrism* took on a whole new absurd life of its own, exacerbated by the fact that the reader had apparently failed to determine its pronunciation before beginning to read the paper. He loved that word, you could tell, and hadn't realized its existence until quite recently, and he was determined to use it over and over and over again – each time with a different pronunciation. Who could have guessed how many different ways *phallogocentrism* can be pronounced? Charisse and I began laughing quietly at first, turning to look at each other every time the speaker brought forward a new and more creative version of *phallogocentrism*, and at some point our amusement mutated into mutual hysteria. We'd subside for a moment and then something – a dramatic pause or self-satisfied smile at the end of a sentence, or, more frequently, the emergence of a new variant of *phallogocentrism* – would set us off again.

We soon discovered that we couldn't stop laughing and were incapable of laughing quietly; the more we tried to smother our hilarity the funnier the situation became. Regrettably, the seats in each row of this small auditorium were connected to one another, and our increasingly failed attempts to control our laughter began to cause the entire row of seats to shake and wobble – at which point Charisse and I (by this time we had stuffed Kleenex in our mouths in yet another try at silencing ourselves) dived down onto the floor, perhaps hoping to remain unseen if not unheard. The illusion of being hidden apparently helped, for after a few moments we managed to stop laughing and sat back in our seats. I remember I suddenly realized that I was in terrible physical pain from repressing (and failing to repress) so much laughter and had begun to congratulate myself on finally re-establishing some self-control. Later I wondered how the people in front of us had managed not to turn around to see what those smothered gasps and moans were about; perhaps they speculated that certain members of the audience, unduly stimulated by the repetition of *phallogocentrism*, had begun to copulate frenetically in the aisles.

To my left sat Linda Badley, who throughout the entire performance had maintained an admirable stony-faced equanimity interrupted by occasional sympathetic sideways glances at the two of us. At the very moment Charisse and I regained the imitation of a professional demeanor, Linda emitted a very loud monosyllabic bark of laughter that was probably heard in the next room. That did it. As I fell forward in a new seizure of hilarity, I heard Charisse, again overcome with gales of laughter, jump up and start to move. With lightning speed she managed to get out of the row of seats and began to head toward the door. My last vision of her is etched forever in my memory: a woman bent over almost double, choking with laughter, determined to leave the scene of the crime. In a very real sense that was Charisse's exit from academe; a year later she resigned a tenured full professorship and moved to Minneapolis to work in a boutique. My own departure has been less official. Once Charisse left the room our *folie à deux* was over, and I was able to finish listening to the story of the silenced female in *The Pianer* without even smiling. However, since that time I have been unable to read any kind of 'serious' paper at a scholarly conference, a situation that has limited me to reading ironic essays on alien abduction at popular culture conventions. (Alien abduction as an area of research has its joys, let me assure you, for while I'm convinced the aliens are as centered on their collective logos as the rest of us, they are rumored to sport no phalli.) I have also developed a dangerously allergic sensitivity to many words and phrases used in theory and criticism, among them all forms of the infinitives 'to silence', 'to marginalize', 'to gesture', and 'to transgress'. 'Inscribe', 'encrypt', and 'iterate' are also out, as are most words connected by slashes or interrupted by parentheses. Even two such apparently innocuous words such as 'site' and 'space' are suspect.

One Saturday afternoon, having just finished editing the manuscript of *Deny All Knowledge: Reading The X-Files* (a collection of essays edited with David Lavery), I began to wonder how the frail vessel of that particular television show could possibly carry the weight of all that agonized theorizing the authors had expended upon it. I had recently begun watching reruns of *Simon and Simon* for their soporific effects (I heartily recommend this to anyone who fears becoming dependent upon Ambien) and began musing about how long it would be until a show that inane would become the battleground for cultural studies debates. What English teachers will do to avoid grading papers: I turned on my laptop and decided to write the review of the book before anyone (David Lavery?) got around to commissioning the essays for it. The result is the review of *Boys Will Be Boys* that follows. When in the interests of full disclosure I showed the 'review' to Professor Lavery, he immediately contacted Allison Graham and Rhonda Wilcox to write their own 'reviews', and the four of us presented the parodies that appear in this book at the Popular Culture Convention in Las Vegas in 1996.

Three other people who appear in *Teleparody* were in the audience: Robert Thompson, who contributed the Afterword; Dennis Hall, who does to *Mr. Ed* what should have been done long ago; and Jimmie Reeves (aka Ben Picken-Schnozzel), who accomplishes the same mission in relation to Homi Bhabha and a legion of other post-thinkers. They got the joke. Some others didn't; I suppose they were the ones who walked out rather huffily. So well received were the 'reviews' (and under that rubric I include the people who were offended) that we decided to turn it into a book of parodies of television scholarship. What we soon learned was how eager academics are to mock themselves – and how well they do it. We also discovered that a number of university presses were not amused; my favorite rejection letter reads that 'because we publish in the area of television and popular culture studies we do not believe that this collection would be appropriate for our list.' Which brings me back to the sound of muffled laughter and *phallogocentrism*.

Charisse, this one's for you.

Boys Will Be Boys: Critical Approaches to Simon and Simon
edited by David Lavery
Bucksnort, Tennessee: Middle Tennessee Normal University Press,
1996

reviewed by Angela Hague

In his fulsome and self-congratulatory introduction to *Boys Will Be Boys: Critical Approaches to Simon and Simon*, editor David Lavery calls the now-defunct television series 'the most significant event in media history in the past two decades.' Lavery also makes it clear that he believes that this collection of essays more than equals its subject, and while this claim initially appears to be exaggerated, a reading of the articles in the collection certainly lends credence to his assertion.

The first essay, by occult activist Artemis Bell, sets the tone of the book. In 'Boys Just Wanna Have Fun' Bell insists that the relationship between the two 'brothers' is in fact a sexual one, that Rick Simon (played by Gerald McRaney), supposedly A. J. Simon's older brother, is in fact his lover posing as his sibling, a pretence encouraged by A. J.'s mother, who prefers her son's homosexual relationship to a heterosexual one. Bell focuses on some of the more ambiguous moments in *Simon and Simon*, including Rick's singing of a mock country love song to A. J. (played by Jameson Parker) in one episode, both brothers' repeated attempts to prevent women from emerging as a significant issue in almost every episode, and the brothers' undivided interest in one another throughout the series. 'No women sully the amusement-park world of Rick and A. J.,' says Bell, 'and nothing interferes with the erotic maneuverings of the two men who flaunt their sexuality while thumbing both their noses at the gullible viewers who believe they are watching just another detective series.' Bell also exhaustively analyzes the series' theme song, with its incantation of 'Because they're not just brothers; they're best friends too' in order to prove her point, noting that the song was dropped after the first season as the homosexual subtext became more blatant. She concludes by stating that: 'The importance of *Simon and Simon* as a cultural artifact cannot be understated. While pretending to be an innocuous – and sometimes fatuous – television show about two harmlessly inept brothers attempting to solve pointless crimes, in reality the series presented the first gay couple in television history. And no one noticed.'

In 'Romancing the Family Simon' Charisse Gendron subjects the show to a no-holds-barred Lacanian reading, persuasively contending that A. J.'s relationship with his mother is simultaneously symbiotic and post-Oedipal. 'Jack Simon is dead, and A. J. now occupies the Father's space,' she says succinctly, adding that A. J.'s inability to break free from his strong bond with his mother renders him unable adequately to become the Father. Instead, it is Rick Simon who functions as the symbolic Father, but his second-class status is revealed in his inability to speak the Word that can command both Mrs. Simon and A. J. (Here Gendron analyzes at some length the roots and results of Rick's inarticulate, truncated use of language, also incisively deconstructing the famous 'incompleted kiss' of the credit sequence, in which Mother Simon, seated behind a birthday cake, is lovingly kissed by A. J.; as careful viewers of the series know so well, the scene is cut before Rick can complete his kiss.) Consequently, Mother Simon turns to A. J. for support and affection, forcing Rick into the role of an embittered voyeur. Gendron concludes by noting that 'the Simons are a family in deep emotional turmoil, a family that delineates a kind of sexual pathology rarely seen on American television.'

Will Brantley's coyly named 'Eroteneutics' turns a more technical eye upon the series. Premising that the narrative of *Simon and Simon* endlessly eroticizes the San Diego landscape the brothers move through, Brantley goes on to detail how the repeated low angle shots of skyscrapers (he counts 45 examples in the first season alone) confront the viewer with an external phallic world of monolithic barriers that simultaneously threaten and beckon. Conversely, interior spaces such as A. J.'s car and house and Rick's boat are rendered claustrophobic and ominous by a static camera that underscores the two detectives' inability to break out of the vaginal interstices of a narrative that denies them movement and freedom, just as the lingering establishing shots of A. J.'s house reinforce the womblike environment that both nourishes and constricts him. Although the essay depends upon a great deal of technical analysis that is difficult to paraphrase, it leaves the reader convinced of the brilliantly self-conscious yet deft filmic style of the series.

Interpretation takes a more political turn in Allison Graham's 'What Did You Do in the War, Rick?' Assuming the impassioned political stance that has become the signature of all her forays into cultural criticism, Graham insists that the repeated allusions to Rick Simon's Vietnam experience provide the only prism through which the series can be understood. Vietnam, she observes, throws its dark shadow across the entire series and results in Rick's inability to connect with anyone other than his family, truck, boat, and dog. 'Rick's immaturity and ironic detachment are emblematic of the emotional cauterization caused by his Vietnam past,' says Graham, going on to remark that 'his younger, blonder brother represents an *alter ego* untainted by the horrors of Vietnam, an *alter ego* who is a painful reminder of what might have been.' Rick's refusal to take the brothers' investigative business as seriously as does A. J. and his insistence upon living in a boat rather than a house are yet further examples of his inability to re-enter a culture that has damaged and then denied his identity as a Vietnam veteran. 'Rick Simon,' Graham warns, 'is a pressure cooker about to explode. His mother and brother are all that stand between him and potential catastrophe.' Graham's ruthless yet profoundly compassionate analysis of Rick Simon's difficulties is not simply cultural criticism at its best; rather, her article constitutes an ode for an entire generation.

But it is Lucia ReSalvo's brilliant '"Don't Tell Anybody": The Effect of Childhood Sexual Abuse upon A. J. Simon' that finally unveils the nasty secret the series so deceptively hides. In her characteristically blunt style, ReSalvo begins by announcing that 'A. J. Simon was sexually abused by his older brother as a child. As an adult the abuse continues. *Simon and Simon*, perhaps the most courageous television series ever aired, weekly presented American viewers with an incest victim's inability to resist the sexual demands of an older brother and his mother's complicity in the relationship.' These are not idle assertions, for ReSalvo, with the precision and attention to detail that have made her an internationally acclaimed literary critic, must finally persuade anyone who initially doubts her thesis. A. J., she maintains, exhibits the typical behaviors of the sexually abused individual, including uncertain and clumsy body language, an over-attention to grooming and dress, verbal hesitancy, fear of firearms, and, most telling, caution in business transactions. Rick Simon, on the other hand, assumes the classic stance of the sexual perpetrator, revealing his proclivities in his loose-limbed, assertive body language, his love of 'taking chances' that often physically endangers both brothers, careless attitudes toward investment and finance, and the wearing of his signature cowboy hat and tight jeans. Indeed, ReSalvo believes that the clothing of the brothers provides the most efficient method to sexually de-code the series. Rick's casual style reinforces his dominant role in the relationship, while A. J.'s insistence upon always wearing a suit and tie signals his need for a protective covering that symbolically – though not actually – will protect him from his brother's advances. The wearing of the tie becomes, for A. J., 'an understandable but pitiful assertion of a phallic identity that has been wrested from him by his brother.' Rick Simon, ReSalvo pointedly notes, 'does not need to wear a tie.' The essay concludes with an examination of the role of Mother Simon, noting (as do several of the other contributors) her very close relationship with her younger son. 'But this relationship has not caused her to protect him from Rick,' ReSalvo cogently argues. 'Instead, the relationship between A. J. and his mother has been initiated and maintained by A. J., who in his thirties is still hoping that his mother will intervene and put a stop to the sexual degradation that destroyed his childhood and blights his adult years.' ReSalvo is not sanguine about A. J.'s future, however, for she believes that 'his inner child has been so damaged it is unlikely that recovery is possible. For the Simon family, there can be no healing.'

Boys Will Be Boys does not end, however, with the ReSalvo essay but instead concludes with a very curious coda indeed, a long and for the most part vitriolic essay by former Christian Collusion leader Rafe Rood. Rood, who apparently was given access to all the other essays in the collection in order to write his rejoinder, uses the book, and particularly articles by Bell, Brantley, and ReSalvo, to mount an attack upon what he calls 'the obscene ramblings of demented academics desperately searching

11

for a worm in a perfectly healthy apple.' Attempts to pathologize the Simon family will ultimately fail, he contends, because the truth is that the two brothers and their charming mother represent the best television – and indeed the entire culture – has to offer. 'Warm, loving, unselfish, and polite people,' Rood piously intones, 'and the strong bonds that unite them will always prove victorious over the sleazy theoretical meanderings of overpaid, underworked intellectuals.' After declaring Victory Over Sleaze, Rood concludes his essay by describing *Simon and Simon* as 'the centerpiece of the Reagan era, a luxuriant flowering of family values, mother love, and business acumen that we may not be privileged to see again.'

One can only speculate what was in editor Lavery's mind when he chose to include Rood's essay in the collection, but a recent article in *The American Thinker* by Edward Sherwin, a widely respected George Herbert scholar, sheds some light upon the traditional academic response to the recent spate of books on television criticism. In 'Requiem for a Lightweight' Sherwin denounces *Boys Will Be Boys* and its compatriots as 'shallow, ignorant, farcical works that serve only to undermine the academic integrity of real scholarship.' Naming Lavery the 'Roger Corman of critical theory' and denouncing what he calls 'The Popular Culture Agenda,' Sherwin issues a stinging challenge to university presses to, in his phrase, 'stop the bleeding' and get back to the real business of academic publishing (it should be noted that Sherwin does not specify what this real business is). Whatever may be one's responses to 'television scholarship,' however, it cannot be denied that after reading *Boys Will Be Boys* one can only watch *Simon and Simon* with a darkened vision and ominous sense of the series' labyrinthine subtexts. Like James Joyce's *Ulysses*, the show would seem to have exhausted both its generic form and conventions *and* all critical attempts at interpretation.

the sitcom

Visual Pleasure and Nasal Elevation: A Television Teleology
by Taryn P. Cursive-Waters
Boise, Indiana: Proboscis Books, 2000

reviewed by Rhonda V. Wilcox

For over twenty years Laura Mulvey's essay 'Visual Pleasure and Narrative Cinema' has been fervently and ubiquitously applied by scholars of the celluloid arts. Her focus on the eye as the center of the viewing experience – through the gaze of character, cameraman, and audience – has served as an explicatorial key for hundreds of authors of hundreds of books and articles on film and television. One such scholar has boldly asked the question: 'If the eye, why not the nose?' The resultant work is *Visual Pleasure and Nasal Elevation* by Taryn P. Cursive-Waters. Oxford scholar Cursive-Waters has written a work which is eclectic in approach and sweeping in scope. This soon-to-be-seminal text covers applications which are sociological, Freudian, and Lacanian; Jungian, Bakhtinian, and Baudrillardian; of course, Feminist; and, to conclude, she offers an audience study which, in its sheer inventiveness, offers a retroactive construct of the ordered nature of television – in effect, a television teleology.

Visual Pleasure and Nasal Elevation begins with a sociological analysis of the straightforward nasal presentation of *Dragnet*'s Joe Friday. The raised nostrils of his cohort Detective Gannon (played by Harry Morgan) expose a sublimated primitive masculine contest for place which, in the case of Frank Gannon, is merely failed display. While Gannon is in one sense Friday's cohort on the series, the sociological cohort Gannon represents – those men who have never made it to the level of supervisor, to the ranks of control, to the top rung of the corporate ladder, to the heights of the hierarchy – this sociological caste can only aim their noses at higher places, as Gannon lifts his toward his taller partner. Sergeant Joe Friday – the man named after the last day of the work week, a time which hints at freedom, which forecasts autonomy for workers – represents that socio-economic group which controls workers. His 'full frontal nasality', as Cursive-Waters has termed it, is a blunt representation of one who has nothing to hide and nothing to fear.

A more recent police drama presents a similar pairing. In *Hill Street Blues*, Captain Frank Furillo is aided by Lt. Henry Goldblum. Whose is the more prominent nose? Again, the naso-sociological correlation is clear: Furillo's nose is unquestionably more prominent. And, indeed, he offers his own variation on 'full frontal nasality'; often when he addresses his men, he raises his eyes but flattens his voice while making sure not to thrust his nose forward, carefully avoiding the primitive contest for place that, in *Dragnet*, Gannon's nostrils unsuccessfully gesture towards; thus Furillo disarms his men and maintains his place in the sociological scheme. Cursive-Waters notes in passing an intertextual irony: Frank (the Failure) Gannon's name is echoed in the name of the man who always ends up on top despite successive power struggles – Captain Frank Furillo. Can this be coincidence? When one considers the fact that Harry is traditionally a nickname for Henry, and that therefore Harry (Henry) Morgan's name is recalled by the name Henry Goldblum, the likelihood of coincidence seems miniscule. But the names merely reinforce the overarching nasal pattern.

In contrast to Gannon's false naso-sociological elevation, Cursive-Waters applies Freudian analysis to the frequently elevated proboscis of *Star Trek*'s Vulcan Mr. Spock, which (in parallel to the famous raised eyebrow) represents genuine intellectual and physical superiority over the stereotypically masculine Captain Kirk, whose response of frequent retractive facial gestures (or 'nasal retreats') suggests to Cursive-Waters a classic castration fear. The traditional equation of nose and phallus plays a large part in Cursive-Waters' analysis. Given that Vulcans are not only twice as strong as humans but also intellectually more well-endowed, the Captain's subliminal reaction to Spock's nasal elevation is understandable. The underlying elements of the 'nasal retreat' are perhaps most blatantly displayed in the episode 'Amok Time'. The normally restrained, logical Vulcans are not only immensely strong and intelligent; they also, every seven years, turn into sexual maniacs. When Kirk unintentionally comes between the sex-mad Spock and his betrothed, Spock wields a Vulcan lirpa, a combination slicing and smashing device, in direct sexual contest; and Kirk, in shock, retracts his nose as he attempts to avoid Spock's weapon and, almost simultaneously, looks down at his own chest to see that Spock has indeed drawn blood (some of you may remember the scene). In terms of phallus, weapon, and nasal elevation, Spock is dominant. He ritually 'kills' Kirk, conquers him. The fact that Spock later feels guilty for doing so, the fact that ship's doctor Leonard McCoy had 'faked' the captain's death to ensure his survival, does not palliate Spock's genuine and dangerous triumph. Just as the female elements of *Star Trek* fandom tended to focus on Spock as a sexual object, so this episode plays out the sexual power which at most times in the series is sublimated in the apparently supercilious gesture of nasal elevation.

Thus, just as Mulvey concentrates on the male gaze as the normal delimiter of visual pleasure, so Cursive-Waters codes nasal elevation as, in most cases, essentially masculine. In one chapter, however, she indulges in a daring variation on her pattern. In the section entitled 'The Warlock Lacan', Cursive-Waters cites the vertical '*frisson de nez*' of Samantha the witch as a recurrent Lacanian epiphany of identity: in Samantha's case, the Lacanian mirror is constituted by the glazed eyes of her husband Darrin, eyes which are themselves objectified by Samantha's insistence on her own essence. The fact that Samantha is always emerging, and never completely emerged, from the infantile state is indicated by her frequent appearance in nightgowns or negligees. As Jane Gaines says, clothing can be an 'emblematic restatement of character traits' (1990: 21); and Anne Hollander points out that the traditional garment of the female intellectual is the black turtleneck. In contrast, Samantha dresses in pallid pastels. Far from being sensual or sexual, this clothing is the apparel of one who is not yet ready to leave the sheltered world of home and enter the outer world, Darrin's world of business. Like Kim Novak in *Bell, Book, and Candle*, Samantha has chosen to inhabit the infantile interior domestic world here represented by the Darrin Stephens household, the womb of becoming. Nonetheless, the infantile Samantha engages in a fantasy of complete power, changing the laws of time and space through her private nasal gestures. And it should be noted that her evil twin cousin, the ironically named Serena (of whom more later), does dress in black turtlenecks, does hint at sexuality, and does also exercise her own brand of nasal elevation – the brief, intermittent elevation of the '*frisson de nez*'.

Psychological criticism would not be complete without Carl Jung, and Cursive-Waters once more proves her theory's pertinence. In a study of the precedents for nasal interplay in television, she returns to the age of radio drama. This reviewer must note that in a work which purports to be about nasal pleasure, a discussion of radio drama must perforce be classified as a digression. However, Cursive-Waters does make a case for the intellectual evocation of the visual nose for what she calls 'virtual nasality'. In a complex argument based on a comparison of Jung's dream analysis to the response of radio audiences to auditory stimuli, she explicates the radio mystery drama called *The Shadow*. With the dark and brooding hero of this drama, the importance of Jung's concept of the Shadow Self could hardly be more strikingly displayed. And 'who knows what evil lurks in the hearts of men? The Shadow knows/nose'.

Another diversion into auditory explication is perhaps more justifiable in terms of the overall text and the history of scholarship. Taryn Cursive-Waters has long been an admirer – indeed, one might say a follower – of Kaja Silverman, whose well-known work *The Acoustic Mirror* discusses the representations of and reactions to the female voice in cinema. It is perhaps not inappropriate for this reviewer to reveal that, as a result of informal collaboration with Cursive-Waters, Silverman is rumored to be about to publish a sister volume to *The Acoustic Mirror*, a new book entitled *The Acoustic Nostril*. The central text which the book studies is the work of Howard Cosell. Given that Cosell's work has been disseminated in a very erratic fashion, the simple establishment of the text has been almost Shakespearean in difficulty. Once past the textual difficulties, however, the application to Cursive-Waters' thesis is apparent, and she takes advantage of her prior knowledge of Silverman's work to offer a brief discussion. The indirect aggression of Cosell's expansionist vocabulary, the occasional forays into social commentary (e.g. Muhammad Ali and military service), the intrusively rhythmic cadence, and, above all, the sheer nasality of Cosell's tones, make him the epitome of the masculine sound. His is the elevated voice of nasality.

In contrast to the lonely sonority of Cosell, Cursive-Waters decries a multiplicity of tongues – in fact, a version of Bakhtinian heteroglossia – represented by the nasal variations of the sitcom *Barney Miller*. This series made perhaps a more thorough-going attempt to include various racial and ethnic types than any other, possibly even including *Star Trek*; indeed, it might even be said that *Barney Miller* is the *Star Trek* of comedy. Incidentally, while *Barney Miller* can be considered ethnically heteroglossic, a socio-economic heteroglossia can be perceived in the characters of *Gilligan's Island*, ranging from the millionaire Thurston Howell III to the deck-hand Gilligan. Readers of the internet essay 'L'Isle du Gilligan' are likely to have already made this inference. Those familiar with Bakhtin's theories will understand that he argued that the novel was a breakthrough genre because it could contain within itself the voices of many worldviews, many sociological entities. This heteroglossia, Cursive-Waters maintains, is visually signified by *Barney Miller's* nasal variations. The Asian nose of Jack Soo's Nick Yemana is countered by the Aryan nose of Steve Landesberg's Arthur Dietrich; Abe Vigoda's Jewish 'Fish' is balanced by Ron Glass's African-American Ron; Gregory Sierra's Chano; Max Gail's Wojohowicz; and so on. There is even an echo of the Harry Morgan/Henry Goldblum type in the short-nosed Ron Carey's Carl. But Cursive-Waters rightly notes that, rather than being genuinely variant voices of the people, these characters offer only the claymation of stereotype. On *Barney Miller*, no nose has a genuine encounter with another. Ironically, this dissociation of real nose from stereo-typical nose may be the correct way to finally valorize the text: as Cursive-Waters points out, knowledgeable viewers would realize that the whitebread Barney Miller, the representative of the WASP head of the hierarchy, was in fact portrayed by the Jewish Hal Linden. The visual stereotype which Cursive-Waters terms 'the Vigoda Nose' is undercut by Linden's nominally mainstream sniffer. And in the distinction between the actors' noses and the characters' noses resides the true heteroglossic element. One must distinguish between the private nose and the public nose – in Cursive-Waters' words, the 'Publius Naso'.

In another of her many erratic vectors of organization, Cursive-Waters proceeds to advance her nasal thesis by further pursuing the Barneys of television. Having discussed *Barney Miller*, she moves on to analyze the trembling nasal intrusions of Barney Fife, another of the Frank Gannon cohort of failed nostrils. She plunges deep into Freudianism once more with her discussion of children's television hero Barney the Dinosaur. She notes first that, in a gesture of self-deprecation, Barney frequently raises his stubby hands to his face, in the process pawing his nose. She then recalls the phallic-nasal correlation and points out that, despite the purported restraint of the hand gesture, the whole figure of the dinosaur can be seen as phallic: purple, trembling Barney hops up and down on stage and changes in size from small to large and back again. Your reviewer must here venture an aside: self-deprecating nasal gesture or no, do we really want our children watching this?

In her next chapter, Cursive-Waters examines more benign television texts. She identifies a tacit acknowledgment of Baudrillard in the nasal simulacra of the Olsen Twins of *Full House*. She grants that nasal simulacra have had their roles in earlier series; for instance, *The Patty Duke Show*'s Patty and Cathy clearly played on the unre-ality of their nasal identity. Samantha and Serena of *Bewitched*, mentioned earlier, also serve as simulacra, with focus on their essential nasal gestures. But Cursive-Waters argues that, in such series, the overt admission of the existence of simulacra weakens the ultimate power of the audience's own recognition of the pairs. In con-trast, she says, there is a much subtler intercourse of signifier with signified in the text known as *Full House*. While for many television series young children are played by twins, in most cases the audience is unaware of that fact. The Olsen Twins of *Full House*, however, have become celebrities in their own right; and the audience's cognizance that the supposedly singular character 'Michelle' is actually two entities, two entities which deny their own Saussurean 'difference' while they attempt to serve interchangeably as signifiers of an unreal signified – such cognizance immeasurably enriches the text for the millions of *Full House* viewers. We are all aware of the distinction; but who among us can really tell those two noses apart?

In her final section of textual analysis, Cursive-Waters makes clear (if she had not done so already) the feminist applications of her theory. In this chapter, she deals with a variation on nasal elevation which she terms 'nasal extension'. Why is it, she asks, that a strong woman character like Barbra Streisand – and she does claim to deal with Streisand as a character, as a public persona – appear only in so-called 'specials'? A woman of extensive talent whose power can unquestionably be seen to be represented nasally is a threat to patriarchy, Cursive-Waters argues; hence Streisand must be ghetto-ized as different. As women at large have been restrained by the supposed compliments of men, the purportedly complimentary term 'special' is revealed to hide a reality of merely token representation. Where is the woman with a nose of power? When she appears at all, she appears as a figure of mockery. Compare *The Brady Bunch*'s Ann B. Davis with Florence Henderson, and ask yourself, 'How long is Florence Henderson's nose?' And who is cupped within the hand of patriarchy? Clearly, the restricted nasality of the short-nosed woman represents her restricted place in the world. And the story of nasal dominance can be read again and again. Is Mary Tyler Moore's nose longer than Dick Van Dyke's? Is Cybill Shepherd's nose longer than Bruce Willis's? Can we even say that Scully's nose is longer than Mulder's? The pattern, as Cursive-Waters declares, is clear.

In the final segment of *Visual Pleasure and Nasal Elevation*, Cursive-Waters confronts the teleology of television. In what others have seen as a haphazard concomitance of patterns, Cursive-Waters has discovered a design which represents the whole of our culture in any given television series – a design which may not be conscious but, like Kant's forms of perception, is so elementally part of our existence as to be organically part of our natures; or, in Cursive-Waters' pithy phrase, 'as plain as the nose on your face'. Yet her audience study takes a surprising direction. Ethnographic audience scholars such as the pioneering Camille Bacon-Smith, author of *Enterprising Women*, have spent years coming to know and carefully to record the audience of a particular series. Cursive-Waters, in contrast, has chosen to speak to no viewers whatsoever. She asserts that audiences do not know themselves and that, further, this refusal of knowledge is part of their essential relationship to the television text as well. This 'aesthetic agnosticism', as she puts it, defines the nature of the television experience. I conclude this review with her own final words: 'Viewers, in fact, abort the signifying nature of the medium by their own chosen distance from the text, by their refusal to press their noses against the screen of meaning.'

From Gidget to the End of History: Sally Field and the American Century, volumes I and II
by James Di Turno
New York: Situation Press, 2005

reviewed by Bill Freind

As most readers are surely aware, James Di Turno rocketed to fame with the publication of *Timmy's Down the Well, Again: The Life of the Lassies*, a metafictional biography/ethnography of the dogs who played Lassie. This text led to the development of what has come to be known as Post-Domestication Studies (or, more pejoratively, Critter Crit). Di Turno quickly became a major force in cultural studies, holding positions at the University of Florida–Key West and the École Normale Mediocre before receiving the prestigious Hanna-Barbera Chair of Media Studies at UCLA.

However, Di Turno's academic success was qualified by his increasingly erratic behavior. Rumors circulated that he believed that, like Doctor Doolittle, he really could talk to the animals, and in an interview published in *Lingua Franca* Di Turno suggested that he had 'channeled' the ghosts of the various Lassies to write *Timmy's Down the Well, Again*. At the 1999 Modern Language Association National Conference, Di Turno impersonated Chantal Mouffe, faking a French accent while dressed in a stylish if somewhat ill-fitting suit as (s)he delivered a paper suggesting that the theories of former Senator Huey Long offered the groundwork for a new revolutionary socialism. The nadir (or, perhaps, zenith) of this behavior was his now-infamous fistfight with Jean Baudrillard in a parking lot at Eurodisney. Witnesses claim that Di Turno donned a pair of Mickey Mouse ears and followed the aging French theorist for hours, taunting him in an accent apparently based on Pepé Le Pew, the famous cartoon skunk. Rather than attempting to bury this episode, Di Turno began to brag about it, even listing it on his *curriculum vitae*. (This seems to have been instrumental in his successful bid for tenure at the University of Florida, Palatka.) Di Turno claimed that these events, and others just as peculiar[1] were a type of performance art inspired by Dada, Surrealism, and the Fluxus movement. Some observers, however, remained unconvinced.

In a speech given to over 5,000 people at the Annual Convention of Adjunct Professors of Composition, Di Turno called for what he named 'Engaged Viewer Studies,' that is, a type of criticism that aspires to erase the distinction between life, television, and film. This is precisely what Di Turno seeks to do in *From Gidget to the End of History*. Simply stated, his argument is that Sally Field's career in television and cinematic history parallels that of American history in the second half of the twentieth century. What makes this claim especially provocative is Di Turno's insistence that Field's performances are themselves a type of cultural *zeitgeist avant le lettre*, that is, a way of not merely reflecting but anticipating – and even directing – the political and social trends that lay just over the horizon. Sally Field, then, becomes perhaps the most important figure in America in the last forty years, if not longer. It's a bold claim, but in this massive study Di Turno provides ample support for it.

In a discussion of her role as Gidget in the television series of the same name, Di Turno suggests that Field engages in a kind of 'libidinal guerilla warfare,' presenting the dormant sexuality that the role demanded while 'sublating that naïveté with a smoldering eroticism that joins with the chants and drumbeats of the sexual revolution that was already threatening to collapse the libidinal Bastille of Anytown, USA'. Viewers of the *Gidget* series might question the 'smoldering sexuality' that Di Turno sees in Field's character, and contentions such as that perhaps suggest a problem with the book: in spite of the impressive readings and sophisticated theoretical perspectives, Di Turno sometimes seems to write more as a fan than a critic. (It may be worth noting that Field took out a restraining order against Di Turno, noting that he had sent her over sixty-five rambling, handwritten letters and had slept in a car outside her house for ten days. Di Turno has said that that was part of his research for the book. Legal action is still pending.)

Di Turno shows his flare for original approaches in his analysis of Field's role in *The Flying Nun*. Eschewing conventional biography, he presents an account which might be indebted to *Dutch*, Edmund Morris' semi-fictional biography of Ronald Reagan. Di Turno writes:

> Eventually, Gidget grew restive in the empty hedonism of the California beach scene. She drifted up to the Bay Area, living for a time in a commune whose members included two of the people who would later found the Symbionese Liberation Army. Still sensing a type of spiritual vacuity, Gidget decided to enter the novitiate, taking the name of Sister Bertrille and joining the convent of San Tanco in San Juan, Puerto Rico.

Here Di Turno invents a narrative based not on Sally Field but on her characters, offering an imaginative and critical *tour de force* that challenges and ultimately effaces the bugbear of biographical identity. At the same time, however, one feels that perhaps a little standard biography would be helpful.[2]

Di Turno's reading of the show itself is more conventional, yet no less insightful. He reminds us that the basis of the show is essentially the *frisson* of sexual attraction between the younger nuns and Carlos, the suave and wealthy discotheque owner, and sees the tropical setting as a type of island paradise 'which aspires to return to Edenic days before sin and sexuality were so disastrously coupled, so to speak'. At the same time, he notes that the choice of Puerto Rico was significant, presenting a type of marginal space which both is and is not 'America'. Combining these two insights, Di Turno demonstrates that Sister Bertrille is both 'pushed to a liminal area and constrained by the habit of her order,' so that 'the woman who was once Gidget now recognizes freedom lies in restriction'. Thus, Di Turno argues, her ability to fly represents 'a symbolic reference to nascent female sexuality, and in particular, masturbatory orgasm, thus presenting a liberatory view of individual feminist sexuality'.

The second volume begins with a 180-page treatment of Field's performance in *Sybil*, a made-for-TV film about a woman suffering from multiple personality disorder. In this section, Di Turno employs a risky yet ultimately successful strategy, writing the entire chapter as a type of experimental poem:

```
closet        daddy         darkness         hurt hurt ouch
nearing no one yes no no no go fish      eggplant? thanks.four
hurt cheese steeping Burt? Burt?         bent pail, Trixie
nearing nearing nearing past     banjo dumptruck guppy
me I me I me not me me not me not même my memo
always? always? huh? lost.
```

Employing a relentless intertextuality, bilingual puns and an embrace of absurdity that recalls the best work of Beckett, Tzara, and Seuss, this section is a wrenching *cri de coeur*. It also provides a point of departure for the rest of the volume, which charts the movement of both Field and the United States as a whole away from the schizophrenia (literal and metaphorical) of the post-Watergate era and toward a type of reunification and even redemption.

Di Turno next turns to the film *Not Without My Daughter* (1991), in which Field plays a mother trying to secure the return of her child from an ex-husband who has brought the girl to Iran. He demonstrates that beneath its sentimental and even schmaltzy surface, the film is a coded presentation of the fear of family breakdown in both the home and in the country at large during the energy crisis and hyperinflation of the late 1970s.

But the climax to which the book builds is a Kojèvian reading of *Forrest Gump*, in which Di Turno argues that the title character is an allegory for Reaganomics, an economic system which, Di Turno suggests, offers such unprecedented opportunities that even the dim-witted can achieve success. This is a clear indication that we have reached Hegel's 'end of history': American-style capitalism, as metonymically depicted in *Gump*, has won the Cold War, thus making Field the figurative mother of that victory. No doubt some will be startled by this reading, since the politics of the American academy is generally left-of-center, and Di Turno's unapologetically patriotic conclusion would seem to conflict with that orientation. Yet his prose and argumentation are so compelling that even many of his detractors will be forced into grudging admiration by the power of his final lines:

A remarkable consensus concerning the legitimacy of liberal democracy has emerged throughout the world over the past few years, as it conquered rival ideologies such as hereditary monarchy, fascism, and most recently communism. More than that, I would suggest that liberal democracy may constitute the end point of mankind's [sic] ideological evolution and the final form of human development. This endpoint is fully figured in the career of Sally Field, one of the nation's greatest actors and, in many ways, cinematic mother of the end of history.[3]

There are, of course, problems with the book. One minor irritation is that Di Turno spends nearly ninety pages analyzing the dresses that Field has worn to various Academy Awards ceremonies. He also informs us of Field's favorite color (green) and her favorite food (steak fajitas). A problem that is perhaps more substantial has arisen since the book's publication. Field is currently filming a sitcom for the Fox network called *Madam, I'm Adam*, in which she plays the proprietor of a brothel. Operating from a premise similar to that of *She's the Boss* (the series in which Tony Danza played a domestic worker in the service of the affluent and attractive Judith Light), the show is centered upon the sexual and emotional tensions between Field's character and her handyman Adam, played by former New Kid on the Block Jordan Knight. The series is also set in San Juan, Puerto Rico, which seems to be a nod to the location of *The Flying Nun*; apparently Field has now got herself to a different kind of nunnery. Additionally, there are unsubstantiated rumors that Field has converted to Islam, which she first became interested in while filming the as-yet unreleased sequel to *Not Without My Daughter* (entitled *Not Without My Granddaughter*) in Teheran. Some readers who seek to advance their own political agendas might suggest that these developments call into question Di Turno's claim that we have indeed reached the end of history, yet these are relatively minor quibbles in a masterwork that promises to change the face of cultural studies.

Notes

1 For instance, on a variety of e-mail listserves, Di Turno dropped hints that he was Maurice Blanchot's illegitimate grandson, and at UCLA he taught a class on the history of pastrami. The class was surprisingly well-attended, and one of Di Turno's graduate students is now writing a doctoral dissertation on the politics of coleslaw.
2 What makes Di Turno's invented biography more problematic is the fact that he himself does not always seem to recognize the distinction between actor and character. Many of the letters he sent to Field were addressed not to her but her characters, as well as the other characters on her shows. In one letter sent to the sisters of San Tanco, he urges them to overthrow the Mother Superior, using violence if necessary, and to establish their own order.
3 Some readers may note an uncomfortably close similarity to Francis Fukuyama's *The End of History and the Last Man* (New York: The Free Press, 1992).

Equinicity: Contending Discourses in Mister Ed
by Jerome Stern
Murfreesboro, Tennessee: The Augean Press, 1996

reviewed by Dennis Hall

The confluence of events in the cultural gestalt of the 1960s, as Jerome Stern's exhaustively researched and carefully argued study demonstrates, inevitably led to the production and overwhelmingly popular reception of the television series *Mister Ed*, which aired on CBS from October 1961 through September 1965.

Some in academe have attributed Stern's long-standing and widely-known interest in what the standard reference works describe as one of the more nonsensical TV comedies to chronic insomnia or (less generously) to weakness of wit. Readers of Stern's incisive account of *Mister Ed*, however, will discover the ineluctable historicity of this mythic tale of intimacy between architect and suburbanite Wilbur Post (played by Alan Young) and Ed, a talking sorrel stallion (played by a roan gelding with the voice of retired cowboy film star Allan 'Rocky' Lane) who has pretensions to the title of 'playboy horse of Hollywood.' Moreover, Stern elucidates – admittedly more convincingly in some instances than in others – the cultural multivalence of this unique text, a ganglion of discourses that subtly, almost imperceptibly, mapped the course of postmodern culture in America fully twenty years prior to its general awaking.

Equinicity opens with a long chapter on the origins and production of the show, detailing the herculean struggle, begun in 1954, of Arthur Lubin, who had achieved distinction as director of the *Francis the Talking Mule* movies, to bring an articulate quadruped to the small screen and into lives of more people than Francis could have imagined. (In a digression that reveals Stern's as well as Lubin's extensive classical and canonical learning, the debt of these early scripts to the conversations between Bucephalus and Alexander, Incitatus and Caligula, Dapple and Sancho Panza, the Houyhnhnm master and Gulliver, Grizzle and Dr. Syntax, among others too numerous to mention, is made plain in the best New Historical fashion.) Initially rebuffed by network kingpins, Filmways Productions was accused of flogging a dead horse, as the media at the time could not resist describing the effort to syndicate *Mister Ed*.

Lubin, undaunted, forged ahead, creating episodes that mark a significant paradigmatic shift from the filmic point of view to the televisual point of view in complex multi-sense textual encoding, a technical and artistic breakthrough, the results of which now may be seen in television shows as diverse as *The Simpsons*, *Nature*, *NYPD Blue*, and *Seinfeld*.

Mister Ed constructed its own large and enthusiastic audience. While Stern's own fervor on this point perhaps obtrudes a bit upon the book's otherwise scholarly demeanor, he makes a convincing case. It is easy to see why CBS, formerly the most vehement of the project's detractors, relented and so contributed, doubtless unwittingly, to the formation of postmodern culture by imposing the series upon the mass audience for five viewing seasons. While Stern endearingly relates the foaling of *Mister Ed*, he at the same time writes one of the master narratives in the chronicle of the most significant medium on the cusp of the two most significant decades in American cultural history.

Of greater significance, however, is *Equinicity*'s attention to the cultural interpretation of *Mister Ed* introduced in a second long chapter, an orientation to Stern's own critical theory and prolegomena to the work's remaining eleven chapters. Stern is a sensitive analyst of the dialogue between narrativity and seriality at work in the late 1950s and 1960s and of television's role as representational battleground. As a consequence, his focus, and rightly so to my mind, has been not on the meaning of the series, but rather on the multiplicity of meaning and the multitarity of reference that problematizes the dialogue that takes place between Wilbur and Ed, which in turn mirrors and further problematizes the dialogue that takes place between the show and the viewer in the typical episode and in the series, in a characteristically astute turn on the intricacies of the synchronic and the diachronic constructs at work. Moreover, just as the dialogue between Wilbur and Ed is problematized by their dealings with a collective Other (re)presented in Wilbur's wife, Carol, her father, Mr. Carlisle, and their neighbors, Roger and Kay Addison and Gordon and Winnie Kirkwood, so too the lone viewer in dialogue with a *Mister Ed* episode or the series has his or her experience problematized by the Others who view with him or her and/or that far more sinister collective of Others who are not series devotees.

As Stern probes the intricate pleasures of this text, he treats his reader gently, even to the point of providing a twelve page diagram of possible dialogic relationships. This is no pedestrian device, for it sets the stage for a fuller understanding of this study's most telling argument: *Mister Ed* is a significant, perhaps the most significant in popular film and television, precursor of postmodernism, because the series nimbly intertextualizes these several dialogues with the cultural conversations emerging in the late 1950s and early 1960s – conversations that have grown into full discourses in the late 1990s and early years of the new millennium and are now struggling to construct senses of individual and collective identity with reference to race, class, gender, sexual orientation, generation, species, psychoanalysis, reconstructed memory, empowerment, occupation, habitation, foodways, and taste communities in music and the decorative arts.

With this plan in mind, the reader – rather more comfortably than is commonly the case in contemporary critical works – is able to appreciate the evocation of these conversations in *Mister Ed* and their evolution in his time and our own. A few examples are especially worthy of note. The treatment of the strained eroticism between Ed and Wilbur, on the one hand, contrasted with that of Wilbur and Carol, on the other. The heretofore little noticed erotic energy flowing between Carol and Ed is one of Stern's finest interpretive performances and one that will inform the appreciation and understanding of viewers of such diverse offerings as *The Donna Reed Show*, *My Mother the Car,* and *Seinfeld*. And no other media study I am aware of has had the courage to address species-ism frankly; Stern's sensitive articulation of the symbiosis between anthropomorphism and hippomorphism will serve as a model for the next generation of scholarly interest in this neglected issue, and guide viewers of such diverse television shows as *Flipper*, *Zoo Parade*, and *Seinfeld*.

Most of the chapters are strong analyses which generously propel the reader to other applications. Exceptions, however, are a rather weak treatment of the series theme song in the context of the contemporary popular musical environment (only a temporarily blinded enthusiasm could lead to the claim that Roy Orbison was really responsible for the tune and lyrics of 'A Horse is a Horse of Course') and a disappointing Lacanian reading of Ed's psychoanalysis of Wilbur, but these are quibbles, and even these chapters may inform future readings of *Seinfeld*.

So rare is scholarly discourse in which the full range of critical theory informs the reading of a particular text without imposing upon it and without a trace of jargonic excess, that readers of media studies will forever remain in Jerome Stern's debt. And readers of *Equinicity* can rest assured that this study will continue to be the authoritative work on *Mister Ed* well into the second quarter of the twenty-first century.

Cultural Displacement and the Hegemony of Wealth in
The Beverly Hillbillies
by Justin Addison
Bugtussle, Arkansas: Ozark State College Press, 2000.

reviewed by Robert P. Holtzclaw

In the summer of 2000, Justin Addison arrived with a splash in the vast, deep ocean of Television Criticism. The occasion was his provocative *New Yorker* article, *'Gilligan's Island*: The Blueprint for *Survivor*,' in which he instigated a national debate with his startling assertion that Mrs. Lovie Howell (the millionaire's wife) would have won a *Survivor*-style elimination contest had one been held on the godforsaken island that enveloped the inhabitants of that ill-fated 'three-hour tour'. Addison was, of course, mistaken – the innocently cunning Mary Ann would bedevil even the resourceful Professor – but his error in theory did not prevent the article from catapulting him to the forefront of the burgeoning scholarly field of television criticism, particularly the controversial and compelling sub-genre known as 'Nick-at-Nite-ophilia': the study of 1960s and 1970s reruns as they intersect with the most significant scholarly issues of the new century.

Buoyed by his illustrious reception, Addison now returns with his first full-length book, a penetrating assessment of the various social, cultural, Marxist, feminist, Freudian, and other hot-button theoretical concerns swirling around the vortex known as the Clampett Mansion in Beverly Hills. While there are flaws in some aspects of his argument, as well as sins of omission and commission in elements of his theoretical framework, the text as a whole stands as a major advancement in the vital field of television reruns as cultural arbiters. Indeed, it joins the ranks of such classics as Deborah Carroll's *The Politics of Disembodiment in My Mother the Car* at the very forefront of this compelling field of academic inquiry.

As his title suggests, Addison's dual focus rests with *The Beverly Hillbillies'* (henceforth, *TBH*) bifurcated role as both a challenger of cultural assumptions and a representation of the power that accrues with wealth. Thus the program's depth and seemingly self-contradictory elements actually work to advance his thesis.

Wisely, Addison divides his text into separate chapters on each of the show's four complex central characters. Additionally, he devotes a final chapter to the program's important ancillary characters and other elements of the Clampett universe, addressing the ways in which these diverse elements coalesce to deliver and reinforce the show's timeless messages concerning hierarchy and disenfranchisement.

In the book's introduction, noted television theorist Janis Foreman (best known for her controversial *The Munsters as Mirror of Societal Dysfunction*) lays the foundation for Addison's argument. Foreman places *TBH* in a larger context, both in terms of its role in television history and its significance as a commentary on societal issues. *TBH* enjoyed a nine-season run on CBS, premiering in 1962 and thus spanning the whole countercultural period of the mid-to-late Sixties. Although, shockingly, the program never won a single Emmy, it did finish as the number one most-watched program in America during two of its nine seasons and was a consistent top-ten finisher in the Nielsen ratings for most of its long run. Its prominence in television annals thus established, Foreman goes on to introduce the aforementioned culturalist/capitalist focus of the book and, by association, of *TBH* itself. The introduction is both lucid and brief, setting up Addison's argument without straying into an explication of his reasoning. Wisely, she leaves that for the author himself, and in Chapter One he begins his deconstruction of the Clampett family as both pawn and king in the challenging chess game of television sitcom as reflector of societal truths.

Addison begins his analysis with 'Jed: Stranger in a Strange Land'. The Clampett family patriarch is a wise launching point for the discussion, as he unwittingly instigates the entire life-altering Clampett experience (the move to California) through his accidental discovery of oil. After first connecting Jed to the rich literary tradition to which he alludes in his chapter title (evoking Homer, Twain, Wells and other illustrious authors), Addison focuses on how Jed is used by the television series as a touchstone for its commentary on both wealth and cultural displacement: 'Rather than serving as a mirror for the reflection of the writers' and producers' views, Jed functions as a *prism*, drawing in the various cultural components and distributing them in random yet illuminatingly beautiful ways' (emphasis added).

Of particular interest to Addison is the method by which Jed acquired his wealth. He sees the sheer randomness of Jed's lucky oil strike as both reassuring and depressing: 'Truly America is the land of opportunity when a 'poor mountaineer (who) barely kept his family fed' can suddenly, through happenstance, attain all the comforts one could desire.' Addison sees the other side of this dichotomy as well, though, one of the early indications of the level of careful thought the author manifests in this study. For, as he points out, Jed's good fortune can also be seen as a sign of the ultimate futility of hard work and applied effort. Wealth can apparently be bestowed on anyone at anytime, not necessarily as a correlative to the level at which one has expended effort to receive such a reward.

With these riches, however, Jed takes his kinfolk's advice and loads up the truck for the move to Beverly (Hills, that is). Here, the power of this newfound wealth affords him immediate entree into the most privileged societal strata in terms of housing. Had he the inclination, Jed could have used his wealth and power to effect great changes in his own life as well as those around him. The level of cultural displacement, however, is so great that Jed withdraws into virtually a replication of his mountain life, albeit in more sumptuous surroundings. As Addison observes in a touching meditation on Jed's essential strength of character, 'While others in Beverly Hills rush around in ostentatious furor, attempting to buy their way into power and self-assurance, Jed maintains his calm reserve, content to whittle on the doorstep in front of his mansion and to help any others in need'. The tribute to this fundamentally decent man and his immunity to the snares of wealth and self-doubt is among the book's most touching segments, reminiscent of Addison's ode to the Skipper's loyalty and essential strength of character in the aforementioned *Gilligan's Island* essay.

Perhaps because of his youth, among other factors, Jed's nephew Jethro Bodine reacts very differently to both the cultural displacement and the newfound wealth. In the next chapter, 'Jethro: The Search for Identity', Addison connects the amiable but clueless Clampett nephew to the disorientation evident in both the move to California and the accoutrements of money and status. In contrast to the more reserved Jed, Addison sees Jethro as *TBH*'s most manic and direct commentary on these twin foci of cultural displacement and wealth, and the author's writing style in this chapter mirrors that more lively and childlike approach. These shifts in style are somewhat abrupt, but also effective in melding the method of conveyance with the material being delivered.

In marked contrast to Uncle Jed, Jethro wants desperately both to fit in with the California world and to exploit his share of the fortune. Though perhaps hampered by the paucity of his formal schooling (he has graduated sixth grade and has some proficiency at cipherin' and gazentas, but lacks more advanced educational skills), Jethro nevertheless attempts a host of careers. Addison offers penetrating insight into several of these guises, including Jethro's ambitious foray into espionage (as a double-naught spy) and the entertainment industry (as a self-proclaimed 'big-time movie producer and director').

As suggested by the chapter title, Addison sees a poignancy in Jethro's ceaseless search for an identity. Thrown into a new world both culturally and economically, young Bodine seeks assimilation to a greater degree than do his fellow Beverly Hillbillies. This desperate desire to 'fit in' – to make a mark in this new world he never expected to see – makes Jethro's struggle both incredibly moving and something of a cautionary tale, Addison asserts. For the author sees in Jethro a telling representation of the degree to which wealth affords a sense of indulgence (many people would have had far less patience with Jethro's eccentricities were he not so wealthy), while cultural displacement maintains a sense of marginalization that even his riches cannot overcome. Thus the valiant Jethro remains on the outside looking in, and Addison's account of his struggles make this chapter among the most effective in the book.

'Granny: The Stubborn Rebel' begins with a stunning factual error that threatens to derail Addison's argument. He mistakenly asserts that Granny is Jed's mother, when she is in fact the widower Jed's mother-in-law. How such a colossal mistake could arrive undetected in a major work of sitcom scholarship is troubling enough, but the blunder threatens to assume even greater tragic weight when Addison begins to discuss Granny's relationship with Jed in mother/son terms. Luckily he abandons that track rather quickly and moves into a consideration of the formidable strengths and complexities of Daisy Moses herself.

Perhaps Addison's most effective argument in the Granny section is built around his connection between the spritely old woman and the great historical and literary traditions of pioneer women. Granny clings most determinedly to the mountain culture her new wealth has caused her to leave behind, as she continues to make her own lye soap, to cook her possum, buzzard and crow vittles, and even to conduct a lively campaign for Beverly Hills Possum Queen. Like her Clampett and Bodine kinfolk she is afforded great tolerance in swanky society, but unlike Jed's calm acceptance or Jethro's burning desire for inclusion, she remains ornery and intentionally outside the new world she inhabits. Addison asserts a timeless quality in Granny's appeal, echoing both the aforementioned pioneer self-sufficiency and the more current (at the time of *TBH*'s network run) strain of rebelliousness and questioning of the values of capitalist society. The author movingly evokes one of the show's central symbols of Granny's conundrum: 'Despite her cantankerous exterior, the vulnerable side of Granny is most tellingly evident when she insists that a replica of her mountain home be built on the spacious grounds of her new Beverly Hills estate. She then moves into the small, shack-like structure and finds her greatest happiness back in her element.'

Wisely, Addison devotes space to Granny's memorable collision with the radical Sixties world in his discussion of her watershed interaction with the California counterculture. When Jethro and Elly May become beatniks and begin dressing oddly and hanging out in coffee houses, Granny is compelled to go to one such coffee house and 'rescue' her loved ones. Addison dramatically and effectively evokes the cataclysmic cultural forces at work in the confrontation, as he states that the clash 'encompasses almost the entire history of American civilization to that point, from the earliest settlement days, through westward expansion and women's rights, to the hippie movement.' Abbie Hoffman and Gloria Steinem appear in his discussion alongside Thomas Jefferson and Mary Rowlandson. Here Addison shines as he demonstrates the true power of the program's social and cultural commentary.

This reviewer was admittedly skeptical when encountering the title of the next chapter, 'Elly May: Feminist Warrior'. And the chapter itself begins unsteadily with Addison's as yet unsupported statement that Elly May is the 'most culturally and socially significant character in the entire program.' However, to his credit, the author offers support that, while not totally convincing, is substantial enough to warrant consideration of his claim.

With Elly May, Addison finds the greatest area of interest to be the sharp contrast of her appearance and her persona. He uses this as a metaphor for the entire Clampett clan's struggles with their cultural displacement and the power their wealth brings to them (the outsider/insider dilemma), but he also focuses more specifically on Elly May's physical beauty and power over men as compared to her complete ineptitude and/or disinterest in many conventionally female attributes. (Reviewer's note: my own well-received *Esquire* article on *I Dream of Jeannie* and *Bewitched* has made me something of an expert in the field of 'female as other' in television sitcoms. Addison chooses, unwisely, not to make reference to my ideas in the midst of his scholarship in this chapter. I acknowledge this in the interest of full disclosure.) Addison never completely stakes out his position on whether Elly May's atypical attributes and deficiencies are due to a lack of ability or a lack of desire on her part (the ineptitude/disinterest dilemma mentioned above). Such a question of motivtion is actually crucial to a true scholarly treatment of Miss Clampett's character, but even without this intellectual foundation the author is still able to make germane points about Elly May and his book's broader concerns.

Elly May is a notoriously bad cook, making rubber biscuits and cannon-fodder chicken, among other delicacies. Significantly, no one informs her of the magnitude of her culinary disasters – her family pretends to like her food out of familial love and a desire to spare her feelings, while her numerous suitors (most prominently Hollywood star-in-training Dash Riprock) endure the bad meals because of Elly May's abundant physical charms. And Elly May excels at more traditionally masculine endeavors such as 'wrestling', shooting, and any number of athletic feats. She is stronger than the much bigger Jethro and is a match for most any physical challenge that comes her way.

Addison uses this gender reversal as a means of assertion concerning *TBH*'s philosophical locus as a whole. For he sees in Elly May's character development an example of yet another way in which unusual behavior is excused because of the presence of more compelling attributes. The Clampett clan can find their way through their own cultural displacement issues with an array of helpful guidance because they have great wealth, while Elly May can disavow traditional gender behavior because of her great beauty. Addison proclaims this to be the 'most significant single representation of the essential contradiction at the heart of *The Beverly Hillbillies*.' He does a disservice to his argument by placing this somewhat tenuous connection at the forefront of his case, but the chapter remains a thoughtful one despite his occasional lapses in scholarly rigor.

In the book's final chapter, 'Other Hillbillies, Other Rooms', Addison surveys a broad assortment of characters and concepts that he finds essential to the advancement of his thesis. These include the supporting players and their representation of a more stable cultural identity (the groveling banker Milburn Drysdale, his snooty wife Margaret, the erudite and unrequited-love-for-Jethro-suffering administrative assistant Jane Hathaway), as well as an assortment of Clampett kin (Jethro's mother Pearl, most prominently).

Much is made of the Clampett car as a symbol of their continuing cultural defiance in the face of their great wealth. For throughout their nine-year television residence in Beverly Hills they continue to drive the ragged jalopy in which they originally moved all their worldly possessions to California, complete with a rocking chair in which Granny rides as Jethro cruises the streets of the city. Addison terms this vehicle the 'anti-Trojan Horse,' seeing it as a method of transportation in which the hillbillies 'hide in plain sight' as they infiltrate the upper levels of society. Such provocative imagery is indicative of the power of segments of this final chapter, though it is slightly hampered by its perhaps necessarily scattershot approach.

Two final sections of the chapter help support Addison's notion of *TBH*'s broad cultural applicability. First, he brings into the discussion the wonderful companion sitcom *Green Acres*, making a sketchy but convincing case for its role as a 'mirror' to the hillbillies' dilemma. Perhaps setting the stage for a future article or book, Addison connects Oliver and Lisa Douglas to elements of all four central Clampett characters and embarks on a partial explanation of how *Green Acres* both reinforces and challenges some of the cultural displacement issues evident in *TBH*. In a sense Addison whets the reader's appetite for a more substantive discussion of this important topic (and where, exactly, does *Petticoat Junction* fit into this theoretical scheme?); the tantalizing prospect of further research into this topic is the sign of an idea that has yet to be fully explored.

Addison ends his 300-page book with a look at what he terms the 'most revolutionary single idea in *The Beverly Hillbillies*' entire history': the saucy, gender-bending character of Jethrene Bodine, Jethro's sister. Played in full drag by Max Baer, Jr. (the same actor who played Jethro), Jethrene is a flirtatious country girl who loves to explore the full gamut of big-city opportunities during her sporadic visits to Beverly Hills. Jethrene has beaus (most likely drawn by her connection to wealth more than by her appearance) and assorted misadventures during her stays with the Clampetts, but Addison looks most significantly at the idea of a male actor in 1960s television playing a female role. This allows Addison to return to some gender and displacement issues he had addressed earlier (with Elly May, Granny, even Miss Jane), but he stumbles by neglecting to trace this 'drag' trend to its predecessors in television history (Milton Berle, most prominently). Jethrene is an interesting and significant character, as Addison asserts, but the 'most revolutionary' proclamation with which he saddles this final segment of his discussion is, in the end, too heavy a burden for poor Jethrene to carry. A better plan would be to conclude with the *Beverly Hillbillies/Green Acres/Petticoat Junction* triad of socio-cultural applicability discussed previously, for that is where the broader applicability of his fine study is most evident.

Helpful indices at the end of the book include an episode guide, blueprints of the interior of the Clampett mansion, and entertaining lists of such trivia as Jethro's jobs, Granny's meals, and Elly's potential boyfriends. Perhaps most entertaining (and simultaneously supportive of his cultural focus) is the list of city conveniences that the Clampetts misname or misuse, such as the 'cement pond', the 'fancy-eatin' table' with its 'pot-passers' (actually a pool table and cues), and their continuing befuddlement over that odd chiming sound that always occurs just before someone knocks at the door (for there are no doorbells in the Ozarks). Overall, Addison presents an ambitious and valuable study of the program and its broader significance; indeed, *The Beverly Hillbillies* is much more than just 'a story 'bout a man named Jed.'

drama

'This is the City-State': The Idea of the Guardian in the TV LAPD
by Xerxes Havelock
Springfield: Full Court Press, 1998

reviewed by Clifford Mapes

With his latest study, *'This is the City-State': The Idea of the Guardian in the TV LAPD*, Professor Xerxes Havelock makes another important contribution to the emerging field of applied classicism. Those familiar with this newly-fashionable field of scholarly inquiry will recognize Havelock's effort to connect the ethical, political, and philosophical narrative structures of classical discourse with the enduring motifs of American popular culture. Applied classicists seek to assert the enduring presence of, in particular, Platonic Idealism and Aristotelian Rationalism in the modern and postmodern venues of late 1960s to late 1980s texts of cinema, drama, and popular media. The central premise of Havelock's particular strain of applied classicism is that such classical discourses 'provide a steadying response to countercultural trends and patterns, and so are necessarily engaged to preserve hegemonic values while appearing to lampoon them.' This thesis is articulated in Havelock's seminal work, *Good Cop, Bad Cop: CHiPs and Plato's Model of the Soul*, and frames that study's reading of the Post-*Dragnet*, LAPD-based cop shows of the early 1970s to the early 1980s. Seeking to understand the extensive ideological shadow that actor/director/producer Jack Webb cast over this genre, Havelock's first excursion into applied classicism argued that the crystallizing vision of Plato's metaphor for

33

the soul, as explained in the *Phaedrus* dialogue, is articulated imperfectly in Webb's own second-generation *Dragnet* series. However, subsequent series – specifically, *Adam-12* and *Emergency* – display a refined vision that achieves full expression in *CHiPs*, the last (and, Havelock argues, most enduring) of the LAPD-based law enforcement dramas.

A consideration of the argument in Havelock's initial study is needed to situate the study currently under review. In *Good Cop, Bad Cop*, Havelock argues that this vision intentionally and self-consciously seeks to extend Plato's metaphor for the soul, as described by Socrates in *Phaedrus*. His model (expressed in summary here) describes the soul as a volatile pairing of a white and dark horse under the uneasy command of a charioteer who seeks to guide his charges along the paths of virtue and good judgment. The white, or 'good' horse, embodies the values of discipline, stoicism, and cool rationalism, while the dark or 'bad' horse demonstrates an idiosyncratic and volatile personality. Together, these disharmonious components achieve a balance; for Socrates, this was the model for the soul in equanimous equilibrium. The earliest and most problematic chapters of Havelock's first study explore the dimensions which this model came to assume in specific texts of American television between the mid-1960s and early 1970s, during the era of the Vietnam War, the lunar landing, and the Arab oil embargo. While it might be tempting for some cultural historians to situate these events solidly under the contextual umbrella of the Nixon administration, Havelock asserts that to do so would be wrong. However, with his context-setting critiques of the shows *Leave It to Beaver*, *Route 66*, *Alias Smith and Jones*, and the later *The Dukes of Hazzard*, Havelock attempts to establish the Platonic basis of and account for the preeminence of such opposed personality tandems within the cultural contexts of that period. Within this cultural and textual framework, he then situates his discussion of the Los Angeles-based cop show drama.

According to Havelock, Webb consciously and deliberately extended this harmonic vision to a crime-fighting and crisis-managing unity that works to restore harmony and order to the always-tense LA neighborhoods, roadways, and freeways. In the second-generation *Dragnet* series, which ran from 1967 to 1970, the actor/director/producer was still struggling to come to terms with the discursive connection between the Platonic model of the soul and the law enforcement philosophies of the TV LAPD. As a result, his pairing of the white-haired, more idiosyncratic Gannon with the more rigid, 'by the book' Friday offered an imperfect replication of Plato's model of the soul that Webb sought to define more precisely in the subsequent series he produced. *Adam-12*, therefore, defined this crime-fighting vision of Plato's soul more precisely: the wizened, stoic Officer Molloy was paired with the younger, less-experienced Reed, whose law enforcement techniques were more improvisational. Together, the tandem embodied the dualistic elements of the Platonic soul more vividly, as did the subsequent pairing in the series *Emergency!* The erratic, hot-tempered Paramedic Gage was made the more effective in restoring balance and order to troubled members of the LA citizenry by the steadying presence of Paramedic DeSoto, who likewise counterbalanced his partner's more unpredictable tendencies. The arguments in *Good Cop, Bad Cop* are directed toward the conclusion that the fullest articulation of the Platonic model of the soul took place in the latest and last of the Webb-inspired LA cop show dramas, *CHiPs*. Collectively, the erratic, hot-blooded Ponch and the steadier, more even-tempered Jon embody the polar elements of the soul in harmonious balance, just as their 'hogs' represented the modern versions of Platonic chariots. Ultimately, Webb's personifications of opposed tandems of LA civil servants consistently showed them working together to restore harmony to disordered LA streets, homes, and workplaces. Each incarnation of Webb's vision – Gannon and Friday, Molloy and Reed, DeSoto and Gage, and finally (and most completely), Ponch and Jon – offers a steadying ethical presence to the otherwise spiritually and morally fragmented urban environs of the postmodern LA landscape.

Reviews of *Good Cop, Bad Cop* consistently pointed out the author's failure (or perhaps his unwillingness) to move beyond his largely biographical scope, and to consider how Plato's model of the soul might also be encoded into cop shows beyond the range of Webb's considerable sphere of influence. Despite Havelock's effort to extend the cop show's Platonic lineage beyond the LA genre to the (in this reviewer's opinion, ill-chosen) texts *The Streets of San Francisco*, *SWAT*, *The Rookies*, and *Cagney & Lacey*, critical reception of his first foray into applied classicism was muted. For example, critic Charlene Silvera suggested that a handful of no-less influential, 'east coast' cop show series such as *Baretta*, *Kojak*, and *Starsky & Hutch* might likewise demonstrate echoes of *Phaedrus*' metaphor of the soul, and Havelock's omission of them from his study is a glaring illustration of its limited vision.[1] Other reviewers also jumped on the critical bandwagon, locating and accounting for (occasional and intermittent) pairings of opposing personality types in balance in shows as diverse as *Barney Miller*, the *A-Team*, and *Hill Street Blues*.[2] Ultimately, reviewers of *Good Cop, Bad Cop* consistently concurred in the belief that Havelock's Platonic template could easily extend to shows beyond Webb's considerable shadow; a single reviewer, professor Sigmund Galehouse, deemed Havelock's failure to offer a reading of *Miami Vice* under the same Platonic rubric as 'inexcusable'.[3] (Indeed, it was this reviewer's opinion that Havelock's field of inquiry might also be extended to the sitcoms *Get Smart* and *Carter Country*, as both resoundingly lend themselves to analysis through the lens of applied Platonism.) Further, a handful of reviewers suggested that the dialogic connections between the Phaedrus' metaphor of the soul and the TV cop show are not traceable to a single individual's vision. Rather, the relationship reflects a reactionary discursive pattern that developed organically in reaction to the increasing popular liberalism of the Vietnam era. Surviving through its various 1970s-era cop-show incarnations, it becomes increasingly 'mainstream' in the popular media of the more conservative Reagan era (hence, Galehouse's emphatic call for a consideration of *Miami Vice*'s Crockett and Tubbs under *Phaedrus*' auspices).

The substance of *Good Cop, Bad Cop* has been summarized here to establish a context for the study currently under review, as the shortcomings of his earlier study become the ballasts that justify the approach in '*This is the City-State*'. Indeed, the assumptions that underlie Havelock's first foray into applied classicism serve his ends much more effectively in his second, as its similarly biographical scope provides, in this case, a more accommodating critical context for his reading of the second generation *Dragnet* series. In the book's first chapter, readers are reminded of the discussion of Book III of *The Republic*, which features an exchange between three principal interlocutors: Socrates, Glaucon, and Adimantus. The trio enumerate the necessary qualities, habits, and training for those charged with guiding the morals of the citizenry, ultimately identifying 'which and what kind of natures are suited for the guardianship of a state' (Hamilton & Cairns 1961: 621). The physical attributes – health, strength, and perceptiveness – are easily recognized. But the more abstract qualities of judgment and ethical discrimination represent the most debated points of the dialogue's argument. The interlocutors ultimately conclude that guardians of the state must possess a gentle and spirited nature and a love of wisdom and of learning. Most importantly, they must be educated with refined music and fables of the highest moral content so as to facilitate the molding of their natures for service to the state. Such stories include portraits of virtue, heroism, and virility, and offer moral templates fit for the education of the guardians. In this synopsis, which constitutes the whole of the first chapter of *City-State*, Havelock identifies five specific virtues: spirit, discipline, wisdom, patience, and judgment. These are necessary attributes needed by those entrusted with moral guardianship of Plato's ideal state, and they are highlighted as a contextual landmark for the book's subsequent readings of specific *Dragnet* episodes. After accounting for Webb's earliest inquiries into the nature of guardianship (including an alleged conversation with another favorite philosophical and artistic son of Los Angeles, Charles Bukowski), Havelock notes its early thematic resonance in the first generation *Dragnet* series, as well as in the movies *The D.I.* and *Pete Kelley's Blues*.

Chapter 2 features the most compelling development of the book's principal thesis that 'Friday's character represents the most lucid expression of Republican values, an expression that comes to be expressed less directly with the subsequent evolution of the cop show genre'. Two significant *Dragnet* episodes are discussed as the contextual centerpieces of Havelock's argument. The first is titled 'The Interrogation', which aired on 9 February 1967, and serves to support his reading of the dialogic connections between Friday and Plato's guardians. The episode is set up, naturally, as an interrogation – of a young police officer Paul Culver (played by future *Adam-12* mainstay Kent McCord), but becomes a forum for the examination of the nature of the policeman's service to the state. The young Culver has been wrongly accused of 'knocking off' area liquor stores, and the older interrogators Friday and Gannon are assigned to question him. Their exchange comes to assume the form of a Socratic dialogue, and Havelock's reading proceeds to identify in its narrative where specific Republican ideas of guardianship are encoded in the responsibilities, duties, ideals, and natures of the LAPD that, through Friday, Webb articulates. The discouraged Culver, smarting from his wrongful accusation, resigns himself to turning in his badge even as he maintains his innocence. In response to his distraught complaints, his interlocutors guide him to a point where his faith is restored in the system and he comes to a full awareness of the unexpressed but clearly recognizable Republican tenets that his badge stands for. The dialogue culminates with Friday's memorable 'What is a Cop?' speech, where Havelock locates the most consistent correspondence between *Dragnet* ideals and Republican idealism.

The speech, summarized here for the benefit of those unfamiliar with the series, is delivered with surprising vigor by the normally stoic Friday. Demonstrating a notable (if sometimes overextended) scholarly rigor, Havelock draws the discursive parallels between the guardians in the states of Plato and Webb's Los Angeles. In this way, Socrates' opinion that the guardian is necessarily suspicious of poetry and other fanciful distractions (which culminates in his banishing poets and other artists of fancy from his state in Book III) is connected with Friday's similar opinions on the reserved stoicism that the LA cop must demonstrate to insulate himself from a variety of potentially pernicious amusements: 'You throw a party and that badge gets in the way. All of a sudden there isn't a straight man in the crowd. Everybody's a comedian. "Don't drink too much," somebody says, "or the man with a badge'll run you in."' And elsewhere: 'It's not much of a life, unless you don't mind missing a Dodger game because the hotshot phone rings … Oh, the pay's adequate – if you count pennies you can put your kid through college, but you better plan on seeing Europe on your television set.' Havelock observes that this ability to resist the fancies of parties, jokes, baseball, and European vacations is born out of the necessary stoicism that the LA cop must display, while he must also cultivate the necessary qualities of judgment and discrimination. Because 'all at once you (lose) your first name. You're a cop, a flatfoot, a bull, a dick, John Law. You're the fuzz, the heat; you're poison, you're trouble, you're bad news. They call you everything, but never a policeman.' And later: 'You're going to rub elbows with the elite – pimps, addicts, thieves, bums, winos, girls who can't keep an address and men who don't care. Liars, cheats, con men – the class of Skid Row.' Finally: 'For every crime that's committed, you've got three million suspects to choose from. And most of the time, you'll have few facts and a lot of hunches. You'll run down leads that dead-end on you. You'll work all-night stakeouts that could last a week. You'll do leg work until you're sure you've talked to everybody in the state of California.' The Platonic resonance in Webb's speech is clearly established by Havelock, who convincingly inventories the common character attributes that both Cop and Guardian must possess.

Additionally, Havelock details how both the Republican guardian and the *Dragnet* cop must have a desire to learn and a love of wisdom, a dialogic connection that he also notes as encoded in Friday's speech. Friday notes this characteristic as an inevitable consequence of police work, observing that 'you're going to have plenty of time to think. You'll draw duty in a lonely car, with nobody to talk to but your radio. Four years in uniform and you'll have the ability, the experience and maybe the desire to be a detective. If you like to fly by the seat of your pants, this is where you'll belong.' And later: 'You'll write enough words in your lifetime to stock a library. You'll learn to live with doubt, anxiety, frustration.' What makes this uncertain world possible in both the Republican and the *Dragnet* world, Havelock argues, is the supreme satisfaction that one locates in serving the good of the state. *The Republic* expresses this value in the dialogue's expression that the value of the love of wisdom ultimately yields the greatest civic and social good. Friday's proclamation of this belief is more dramatic: 'But there's also this – there are over five thousand men in this city who know that being a policeman is an endless, glamorless, thankless job that's gotta be done. I know it too, and I'm *damn* glad to be one of them.' The mild invective that concludes this speech represents, Havelock astutely notes, Friday's single use of invective over the duration of the series. As such, it emphatically underscores the show's (and Webb's own personal) philosophical investment in Platonic idealism.

The speech discussed in the introduction of *City-State* demonstrates Friday's recognition of the value of the wisdom, and subsequent chapters discuss his efforts to pursue it. The fullest expression of this value Havelock locates in a later episode, 'Night School', which aired on March 19, 1970. The straight-laced Friday is shown interacting with various counter-cultural 'searchers' who have, like him, enrolled in a night school sociology course. Those familiar with the episode will recall that Friday's identity as a cop remains unknown to both the course instructor and to his fellow students, who devote class periods to various 'sensitive' issues like drug experimentation and letting one's hair down. The close-cropped Friday notes a class-mate in possession of what he calls 'oregano', but which is, of course, really mari-juana. When Joe arrests the student, the furious professor has the class vote to expel him as a 'narc' who has, the class feels, violated their learning environment. A week later, one of Joe's classmates, a lawyer, defends Joe's actions in a defense worthy of Socrates himself, which leads to Joe's being voted back into the class. Like the escaped cave dweller in *The Republic*'s Book VII who has experienced the world beyond his confines, Joe must endure the scorn and rejection of his compatriots who place too much value in their limited perceptions of the world. Happily, however, he effectively reintroduces himself into his community, and all are shown to benefit from their encounters with the one entrusted to protect and enforce constitutional mandates.

Subsequent chapters offer readings that find Republican values in later epi-sodes. The chapter titled 'Interlocutors in Dialogue: Discussions of Civic Virtue' fea-tures a series of provocative readings of individual episodes that further elucidate *Dragnet*'s Platonic vision. Airing on 19 September 1968, the episode 'Public Affairs – DR 07' features Gannon and Friday as guests on a left-leaning local television talk show dedicated to community issues. They are the voices of 'the establishment', and counterbalance the more radical (and less disciplined, less well behaved) lib-eral viewpoints supplied by a college professor and a fringe journalist. As studio guests fire questions at the placid police duo, they affirm the department's positions on marijuana legalization, minority hiring, interaction with minority neighborhoods, and efforts to improve community relations. The episode is notable in that Friday reveals his having read Aldous Huxley's accounts of experimentation with drugs, and eerily prophetic in its anticipation of the ethnic and civil unrest in the wake of the Rodney King incident some 25 years later. Ultimately, it is identified by Havelock as demonstrative of the LAPD's connection to community currents and issues; in a larger sense it reveals the extent to which Webb understood the need to show the force's continually evolving relationship to the citizens it serves.

In another chapter, titled 'Banished: Poets and Prophets in Exile', Havelock's discussion of two episodes in particular is worth highlighting as well. His reading of them underscores the syncretism between idealistic Republican dialogism and contemporary civic and social issues in the Los Angeles that Webb depicted in the second-generation series. Havelock finds in these two specific episodes a clarifica-tion of the Socratic mandate that poets be banished from the Republic. A concrete version of the poet is engaged in an episode that aired on November 6, 1969. In this episode, titled 'Homicide – The Student', a young murder suspect is also shown to be a devoted reader of French writers – in particular, Balzac, Flaubert, and Baude-laire. While Friday ultimately claims that such selections were the 'excuse' to commit murder rather than the 'cause' for it, the episode clearly reveals the Republican bias against corrupting forms of literature. A more notable episode examined in this chapter is 'The Prophet', which aired on January 11, 1967. 'Brother William', the self-appointed leader of the Temple of the Expanded Mind, is rumored to be giving LSD to school kids, and Gannon and Friday pay a visit to question him. A made-for-TV rein-carnation of Timothy Leary, Brother William is given a surprising amount of airtime to make his case for the imperatives of mind expansion through drug experimentation. His emphasis on personal choice and personal freedom points, in a limited way, to those theological dilemmas faced by Christian philosophers attempting to reconcile free will with divine mandate. However, his discussion with Friday and Gannon is, Havelock demonstrates, incomplete. His argument reveals a poetic sophistry that makes it alluring (especially to minors), but ultimately groundless. The gaps in it are exposed by Friday, who responds to this pro-drug rhetoric by pointing out (with great emphasis) the need to banish the pseudo-prophets like Brother William and his ilk: 'Alcohol is the match. Marijuana is the fuse. LSD is the Bomb!' Brother William's subsequent arrest for peddling drugs to minors, supplied in the episode's final frames, underscores the distance between his idealized notions of personal freedom and the ruined lives of those unable to moderate their liberal habits. Justifiably, his actions merit his 'banishment' to the California penal system for corrupting the minds and bodies of impressionable youth with his own particular blend of gratuitous countercultural narcissism and silver-tongued sophistry.

Ultimately, *City-State* succeeds for the same reasons that *Good Cop, Bad Cop* was found wanting. In *The Republic*, Havelock finds a strain of Platonism that is more accommodating to a reading of the cop show text generally, and to *Dragnet* in particular, and is more documented in the personal evolution of its central figure. In this way, his biographical focus is more justified in this second study of the cop show genre than it was in his initial examination. His study of *The Republic*'s discursive elements that contribute to a cop show provides a template to justify his reading of *Dragnet* while simultaneously locating the ethos of other contemporary cop shows – *I Spy, Get Smart*, and *Hawaii-Five-O* – in more contemporary currents. As a result, his second exercise in the field of applied classicism accounts more rigorously for the precise connections between the classical and the postmodern. In the final analysis, '*This is the City-State*' convincingly shows how Webb dialogically reinvented Platonic idealism in response to the countercultural milieu of the postmodern Vietnamera LA landscape. Despite its lapses and oversights, Havelock's continuing efforts to connect the values of Republican Platonism with *Dragnetian* idealism ultimately represents a groundbreaking study, and scholars of applied classicism should look forward to his further excursions into this field, including a forthcoming study titled (tentatively) *Nicomachean Ethics and Miami Vices*. All said, his current work offers a convincing exploration of the dialogic connections between the classical and the postmodern, and Havelock's demonstration of the elements of Republican idealism in the second-generation *Dragnet* series presents scholars of applied classicism with much more than 'just the facts'.

Notes

1 See 'Good Cop, Bum Rap', in *Omnia: A Journal of All Things Philosophical and Social*, 17(3), June 1992: 159–62.
2 See, for instance, James Delsing's 'Dressed up in *Dragnet*', in *Detective Fiction Quarterly*, 15(3) July 1993: 174–7.
3 See 'Tangled in a Webb', in *Cultural Perspectives on the 1980s*, 3(2), April 1992: 118–9.

*Californication and Cultural Imperialism: Baywatch and the
Creation of World Culture*
edited by Andrew Anglophone
Point Sur: Malibu University Press, 2000.

reviewed by David Lavery

> 'We live in the age of the Los Angelization of Planet Earth.'
> William Irwin Thompson

The television series *Baywatch* premiered in 1989 on NBC and was cancelled due to poor ratings. Resurrected in 1991 as an independent, non-network production of All American Television, the series then became, in world-wide syndication, the most popular show in the history of the medium, attracting as many as one billion viewers in hundreds of countries around the globe. It aired its final episode in 2001.

Andrew Anglophone of the University of Northern South Dakota at Hoople has put together a collection of discerning essays for Malibu University Press entitled *Californication and Cultural Imperialism: Baywatch and the Creation of World Culture*. No doubt some will question the need for a scholarly book on such a series.

Anglophone's own introduction, 'America Makes All the Images: *Baywatch* as a Semiotic Export,' takes its title from Wim Wenders' *Tokyo-Ga*, a documentary tribute to the great Japanese auteur Ozu. During a visit to a television assembly line, the German expatriate filmmaker, having just finished a long sojourn in the United States, muses on Japan's dominance of the industry. 'The Japanese,' he observes, 'make all the TVs, but the Americans make all the images.' With its tremendous international popularity, *Baywatch* has obviously contributed mightily to keeping America in the black in the cultural exchange economy, and it is for this reason, Anglophone argues, that it is worthy of serious consideration. Anglophone would like his book to stand as a contribution to the study of cultural imperialism, the hegemonic colonization under world capitalism of other cultures by dominant cultures like that of the United States. (It is to this coercive signifying supremacy that 'the Californication' of his title refers.) To some extent he succeeds.

The title of the book, which suggests a strongly neo-Marxist approach, a cultural studies consideration of *Baywatch* as a prime case of Jameson's 'late capitalism' at work, is in a sense misleading. Although it does indeed consider the series in an international context, it does much more as well, offering a variety of approaches to *Baywatch* both as text and cultural/economic phenomenon. Allow me to offer a brief guided tour, surfing over the book's deep waters and navigating carefully its shallows.

The author of an earlier book on the California sensibility, Sheila Rosenberg, Professor of Psychology at UC Sunnydale, uses her essay, 'Tan Lines and Identity: A Psychohistorical Reading of *Baywatch*', to examine *Baywatch*'s cultural moment. Just as Erik Erikson in *Young Man Luther* wanted to understand why the Reformation happened when it did, what factors in history's developmental psychology produced Martin Luther when and where it did, Rosenberg seeks to ascertain the why and wherefore of *Baywatch*. Why did the 1990s need this show? To what in our unconscious does it speak?

In 'Surf and Simulation: Baudrillard and *Baywatch*', David Summar adopts some of the ideas of the French philosopher of communication, especially those expressed in Baudrillard's two travel books about the United States, *America* and *Cool Memories*, in order to assess the cultural significance of *Baywatch*. California, writes Baudrillard, a PoMo de Tocqueville, is 'the world center of the inauthentic.' Summar's intent is to trace the dissemination of this inauthenticity – to show how and why *Baywatch* has captured the world's imagination. *Baywatch*'s historical moment, Summar argues, arrived at a time of cultural AIDS, to use Baudrillard's frightening metaphor: 'We don't have anything to oppose to [American] cultural contamination. Culturally and philosophically exhausted, we remain unable to transform our past into living values for the present. Our cultural antibodies have acquired an immune deficiency and can't resist the virus.' Baudrillard refers, of course, to Europe and Europeans generally; but Summar universalizes the insight: *Baywatch*'s 'hardbodies', his essay demonstrates, triumph with ease over the defenseless antibodies of other cultures, from east to west.

Drawing on the still-suggestive insights of Laura Mulvey, Lisa Williams takes a close look at *Baywatch*'s televisual style. Focusing on its opening credit sequence and then on the series' first episode, the classic 'Panic at Malibu Pier', Williams' 'T & A: Gazing *Baywatch*' provides not only a discerning analysis of the show's gender address but a suggestive thesis on the place of anatomy in the postmodern imagination. Especially illuminating is her brief history of television T & A, from *Charlie's Angels* to *Baywatch*. Williams's essay foregrounds Pamela Anderson, the plasticized bimbo who has turned on a large percentage of *Baywatch*'s avid world-wide following. In her piece, 'David Hasselhoff: A Semiotic Approach to One of the World's Most Recognized Images', Rebecca King investigates the appeal of the series' real star.

One of the best known individuals on the face of the earth (King ranks him right up there with Michael Jackson, Schwarzenegger, Bill Clinton), Hasselhoff parleyed minor success in the soap opera *The Young and the Restless* and modest United States ratings for his series *Knightrider*, in which he played second banana to a talking car, into the tremendous world-wide international popularity of *Knightrider* and then into the megahit of *Baywatch*. Hasselhoff's popularity did not stop there, of course: overseas, especially in Europe, he is a music superstar as well, a second Elvis, a performer whose recordings all go megaplatinum and who was, for example, a featured performer at the concert that marked the dismantling of the Berlin Wall. A careful look at Hasselhoff's physical signifiers – height, age, tight buns, wavy hair, chest hair, voice – and at his character, Mitch Buchanon, on *Baywatch* (Mitch's status as a single father in the 1990s attracts special attention from King) leads to a surprising thesis concerning Hasselhoff's signifieds.

Brandon Tartikoff tells the story of NBC's at first futile attempts to sell *Laverne and Shirley* into European syndication. After several failed attempts to interest EC networks in the show, NBC remarketed the series with a frame tale added. Laverne and Shirley were reconceptualized as runaways from a mental hospital, an escape depicted in a newly-added opening sequence, and the show caught on. *Baywatch* needed no such repackaging. But the history of its marketing – through ads, CDs, commodity intertexts, music, World Wide Web sites – is not without interest. In 'Baywatch as Commodity: Marketing the World's Most Popular Show', Richard Campbell, author of an excellent book on *60 Minutes*, catalogues more than we would ever want to know about the packaging of *Baywatch* and, in the process, has much to say about how America's entertainment taste has become the world's taste.

Like Summar, Jill Hague draws on Baudrillard's *America* for her key insight in an essay on *Baywatch*'s music. It is an obscure comment on television laugh tracks which catches her attention:

> Laughter on American television has taken the place of the chorus in Greek tragedy. It is unrelenting; the news, the stock exchange reports, and the weather forecast are about the only things spared. But so obsessive is it that you go on hearing it behind the voice of Reagan or the Marines disaster in Beirut. Even behind the adverts. It is the monster from *Alien* prowling around in all the corridors of the spaceship. It is the sarcastic exhilaration of a puritan culture. In other countries the business of laughing is left to the viewers. Here, their laughter is put on the screen, integrated into the show. It is the screen that is laughing and having a good time. You are simply left alone with your consternation.

Hague's 'Surf and Surfeit: The Role of Music in *Baywatch*' treats the series' pounding, overbearing, annoying, awful music as equally manipulative and 'alien'.

The author of several seminal studies on the cross-cultural impact of American television, Stephanié Gentilhommé sets out here to apply a similar methodology to *Baywatch*. 'Decoding *Baywatch*: A Cross-Cultural, Ethnographic Study' uses interviews with fifty informants in ten countries (including Saudi Arabia, Israel, India, and Japan) in order to ascertain the various ways in which the series is actually used in different cultural contexts. The result at least partially mitigates the argument that a series like *Baywatch* necessarily feeds the tendency toward monoculture.

Alfred Lutz's 'Bakhtin Goes to the Beach: Dialogism and *Baywatch*' is likewise less harsh in its criticism of the series. Drawing on Horace Newcomb's adoption of Bakhtinian notions in his depiction of the dialogic 'cultural forum' offered by television, Lutz suggests that *Baywatch* is not as monological as it might appear, that indeed it speaks with many voices representing many constituencies and seeks to be, in its own stupid way, as politically correct as possible for a T & A show.

Elizabeth Kubek's deep but illuminating 'Mirrors of Sand: *Baywatch* from a Lacanian Perspective' is perhaps the toughest essay in Anglophone's book, using as it does the French Freud's difficult psychoanalytic approach to study what she calls 'the problematics of patriarchy' as explored in *Baywatch*. Taking as her subject 'the relation of paternal or quasi-paternal authority to "truth",' a theme explored in the desire for belief, knowledge, and validation of its central characters, Kubek zeroes in on the uncertain relationship of single father Mitch and his teenage son Hobie, a young man named after a surf board.

With an initial focus on a single *Baywatch* episode ('Now Sit Right Back' in the second season) in which the lifeguards save (in a dream sequence, of course) the stranded crew of *Gilligan's Island*, Michael Dunne details – in 'Saving Gilligan: Meta- and Inter-Textuality in *Baywatch*' – the series' prominent references not only to other shows but to itself. As Dunne demonstrates, *Baywatch* not only incorporates 'real' people into its plots (World Wrestling Federation superstar Hulk Hogan plays himself in one episode, the Beach Boys and gymnast Mary Lou Retton appear in others), it also incorporates the diegesis of other series. In addition to the episode cannibalizing *Gilligan's Island*, there are others in which television itself becomes the subject – the one, for example, in which *Baywatch*'s women find themselves in a fantasy recreation of *Charlie's Angels*.

Other examples of inter- and metatextuality abound, as Dunne shows. In 'Game of Chance' the Baywatch crew captures a specially designed recreational vehicle which has been used in a series of robberies – a car capable of instant conversion into a boat. At the show's end, as Mitch inspects the vehicle and its capabilities (four wheel drive, a great stereo system) are listed, he asks, apropos of nothing at all, 'Does it talk?' When told that it does not, he insists, with a wink at the camera, that he is not interested in it. The wink, Dunne notes, is intertextual: a reference to David Hasselhoff's talking car in his former series, *Knightrider*. In other highly metatextual episodes, *Baywatch* seems to have become as self-conscious as any another work of high postmodernism. In 'Beauty and the Beast', for example, the series plays off its own reputation as a showcase for the physical attributes of Pamela Anderson and others as *Inside Sports* magazine comes to Baywatch in search of a lifeguard model for its swimsuit issue. And in 'Rescue Bay' a sleazy television producer decides to create a new series based on the adventures of a group of California lifeguards and casts several Baywatch members in the show. (He finally decides not to do the series because no one could possibly be interested in a show about lifeguards.) *Baywatch*'s allusionary nature, Dunne argues, its hyper-awareness of what Eco has deemed 'the already said,' thus make it essentially a postmodern text, though admittedly an unlikely one.

That television is a 'producer's medium' is a truism of television studies. Very little attention has been paid to either the directors or the writers of TV, who remain almost completely invisible and unacknowledged. Carol Marton's 'Deborah Schwartz: A *Baywatch* Auteur' makes an effort to fill this void by examining the 18 episodes of the series written by Deborah Schwartz. Scrutinzing the key themes, plots, characters, and images of Schwartz's teleplays, Marton struggles with the large question of how an individual voice and vision find the means of self expression within the flow of an ongoing, highly formulaic series.

In 'Bash at the Beach', from Baywatch's fourth season, C.J. saves the life of wrestler Hulk Hogan. In her debt, he agrees to wrestle his nemesis Rick Flair for the Heavyweight Championship as a fund-raiser to save the Venice Beach Boys' Club. Needless to say, this episode attracts the attention of Charles Goldthwaite of the University of Virginia in '*Baywatch* and Television Wrestling: A Narratological Comparison'. But Goldthwaite is interested in much more than this overt inclusion of professional wrestling into the text of *Baywatch*. Goldthwaite's ingenious essay offers a surprising comparison and contrast of *Baywatch*'s multiple-episode, ongoing plots with the yearly metaplot of a professional wrestling season. Goldthwaite finds in both the same kind of good guys and bad guys, the same plots, the same human interests, the same conflicts, the same clichés.

Goldthwaite discovers correspondences between *Baywatch* and the 'genre' of Professional Wrestling; Karen Basore traces all sorts of other genre signatures in her essay 'All Things to All People: The Question of *Baywatch*'s Genre'. As Basore shows, *Baywatch* is in one sense only a 'recombinant' (the term is Todd Gitlin's), warmed-over, hybridization of *Sea Hunt* and *CHiPs*, its chief Bloomian ancestor texts. (Basore begins her essay with a hilarious reconstruction of the quintessential 'all things to all people' *CHiPs* episode, in which Jon Baker and Ponch Poncherello not only get their man in an exciting, ridiculously overscored motorcycle chase scene but win a disco contest during which they also manage to deliver a baby!) *Baywatch*, Basore shows, owes much as well to other television forms: to the soap opera (for its multiple story lines), to sitcoms (for its attempted humor), to disease-of-the-week movies (for its frequent tackling of topical subjects), to MTV videos (for its music montages), to cop shows (for its increasing interest in crime solving – a plot element which led eventually to *Baywatch Nights*, a spin-off show in which Mitch Buchanon moonlights as a private detective), to sun screen commercials and other advertisements (for its overall visual style).

Linda Brigance of SUNY, Fredonia, author of discerning analyses of 'public discourse' in cultural phenomena, turns her skills as an analyst of mediated rhetoric to *Baywatch* in 'Amoral Moralism: *Baywatch*, Public Discourse, and the Didactic Text'. What interests Brigance most is the series' almost sermonish nature. *Baywatch*, she shows, is not all T & A, sand and surf, ski-doos and jet skis: episode after episode deals with subjects of a topical, indeed public service nature: AIDS, attention-deficit disorder, oil spills, injured animals, gangs, Native American rights, the special olympics, retinitis pigmentosa, funding for youth centers, teen alcoholism, Alzheimer's disease, obesity, designer drugs, homelessness, sexual harassment, adoption, single fathering, custody battles – all make their appearance on *Baywatch*. Brigance finds especially interesting an episode called 'Desperate Encounter', described on *Baywatch*'s own World Wide Web site as 'a ground-breaking episode on the gruesome fate of unwanted horses in America.'

In 'The Postmodern Inane: *Baywatch* and the Insipid', Rhonda Wilcox confronts the profound question of the series' essential vacuity. How could such a derivative, formulaic, unimaginative series become such a world-wide phenomenon? *Baywatch*'s inanity, Wilcox suggests, is not a critic's discovery; the series itself knows, as its meta- and intertextuality reveal, that it is stupid, and this self-awareness should be understood, according to Wilcox, as yet another sign of what Mark Crispin Miller has called contemporary television's 'deride and conquer' strategy, its tendency to make fun of itself before its audience has the chance to, to acknowledge that its own badness is no excuse for hitting the remote button.

In several recent venues, Miller has commented on the ironic history of the early movie era dream that the advent of film might lead to a common, indeed a universal, language. This dream, which, as Miller shows, was rife among the medium's founding fathers, has now been realized. The whole world is now hooked on the Hollywood text; from Kuala Lampur to Buenos Aires, world citizens speak fluent Schwarzenegger; they are conversant in American genres, American action-adventure/dolbyized/MTV edited cinematics; their fluency, in fact, has made them largely uninterested in learning any other language. The Esperanto of the American movie export has carried the day. Such is Miller's thesis. In his 'The Los Angelization of Planet Earth: *Baywatch* and the Dream of a Common Language', editor Anglophone examines *Baywatch*'s influential role in this linguistic dispersal. What exactly will it mean for the future of consciousness, Anglophone wants to know, that one billion people worldwide internalize *Baywatch*'s *weltanschauung* on a weekly basis? 'We live in the age of the Los Angelization of Planet Earth,' cultural historian William Irwin Thompson has argued (1971: 3–27) – a line that inspired Anglophone's title. *Baywatch* Los Angelizes with a vengeance.

children's tv

Don't You Be My Neighbor: Dystopian Visions in Mister Rogers'
Neighborhood
by Victoria Neamo
Moose Pass: Arctic University Press, 2001

reviewed by Kevin Kehrwald

> 'I got into television because I hated it so.'
> Fred Rogers

In recent years, enough critical attention has been paid to *Mister Rogers' Neighborhood* to declare the existence of a full-blown school of 'Rogers Studies'. Alan Socalled's *My Own Inadequacy: Transgressing the Boundaries of Mister Rogers' Neighborhood* (1998), Vera Xu's *Boat Shoes and Sweaters: Ontologies of Mister Rogers' Closet* (1999) and Sheila Rosenberg's *The Piano and the Trolley: The Rhizomatic Mister Rogers* (2000) have all carved out dynamic fields of Rogers inquiry. The latest in the chorus is an analysis by Victoria Neamo, Professor of Children's Literature and Media Studies at University of the Prairie in Ramona, South Dakota. Neamo's critique, entitled *Don't You Be My Neighbor: Dystopian Visions in Mister Rogers' Neighborhood*, is not merely another exclusive examination of the strange, sterile world of Mr. Rogers, however; it is something of a fascinating meta-study, pondering, as Neamo writes in her preface, 'Why all the attention to Mr. Rogers now?'

As Neamo points out, the academy is not the only cultural sphere currently fascinated with Fred Rogers. Legions of suburban pre-pubescent boys have begun wearing homemade hip-hop 'trolley pants', thousands of adults have joined local 'Tuesdays with Fred' clubs and almost every American has recently brought the catch-phrase 'Pullin' a Rogers' into popular parlance. But perhaps most tellingly, within the next year, PBS, in conjunction with Miramax Films, is set to release *Mister Rogers Redux*, a recently restored 'director's cut' of a long-lost movie documenting Fred Rogers' 1979 journey from the Denver Mint to his favorite sandwich shop in his hometown of Latrobe, Pennsylvania (a journey the film's director, J. P. Whale, once described as 'a picaresque quest from commerce to cornbeef'). All of these developments, Neamo points out, evidence an 'irrational obsession and unrested panoply of desire for believing in the kind of universe that can forever house a kindly man in a three-walled home.' Like viewers themselves, Neamo relishes the voyeuristic opportunity to peer through the missing wall and spy on both American culture and the mild-mannered man in the cardigan. Alarmingly, what Neamo sees in Rogers' 'home' is fertile domain for scrutinizing contemporary social and political structures of domination. Neamo finds answers to her own question of Rogers' popularity in the paranoid dispositions and radical uncertainties evident in the era of late capitalism. Neamo contends that while Rogers seems so incredibly 'normal', everything about him signals that he cannot be absorbed into the very normalized America he seems so perfectly to represent. Because Rogers cannot be 'known' – because his cheerful demeanor and timeless surroundings constantly elude intellectual understanding and material acquisition – his powers to frustrate and fascinate gradually strengthen over time as young viewers evolve into adult consumers with full purchasing power. To an America that has made fetishes of ownership and consumption, Rogers appears as the ultimate unattainable product, the virtual commodity for which there is no original. Neamo also contends that when Mr. Rogers first arrived on TV screens in the late 1960s, he seemed an appealing alternative to the turbulent images of urban violence, civil rights protests and the Vietnam War. What Rogers projected onto the set was a utopian neighborhood – or so we thought. Though Neamo's study is best described as a loose collection of essays (as opposed to a focused monograph), the thesis that holds her work together is encapsulated in the following statement from her introduction:

> The pleasant fantasy world of Mr. Rogers, far from being a locus of escapist unreality and nostalgic wish-fulfillment, is actually a site of masochistic and hegemonic self-loathing, appealing primarily to the myriad cultural pathologies that rest quietly yet visibly beneath the surface of the plasticine gaze and saccharine smile of a middle-class nice-guy in comfortable shoes.

What Neamo articulates so adroitly throughout her book is the idea that audiences were (and are) responding to all of the repressed unpleasantness evident in Mr. Rogers' world rather than its niceties. Neamo finds that the longer viewers watch Mr. Rogers, the more the act of watching itself becomes 'a self-imposed Promethean journey into a personal and collective heart of darkness.' She muses, 'Perhaps it is no coincidence, given their similar dependence on Conrad's story of a descent into hell, that the original Mr. Rogers "road movie" was compelled into being at the exact same historical moment as Francis Ford Coppola's *Apocalypse Now* – or that both films are now being simultaneously re-released with similar suffixes added to their titles.' The great difference between the films, she contends, is that while Coppola's audience knew it was watching a nightmare, Rogers' audience only suspected it was – and that very uncertainty about the precise nature of the nightmare is what has kept viewers watching Fred Rogers' television show for over thirty years.

Each of the book's six chapters uncovers a different dystopian tendency at the core of *Mister Rogers' Neighborhood*. The first chapter, entitled 'Mr. McFeely and the Bourgeoisie', addresses the capitalist angst evident in the character of Mr. Rogers' mailman. The extremely twitchy and nervous McFeely, Neamo argues, epitomizes the impact of the acceleration of everyday life on the human body and psyche. In a chilling and convincing critique, she demonstrates that the mailman's incessant anxiety over completing a 'speedy delivery' is an eerie precursor to a contemporary era in which we fear anyone might 'go postal' at any moment. To underscore the reality beneath the character of McFeely, Neamo actually conducts a little field research, including comments solicited from her own hometown letter carrier, Heywood Staple. Staple tells her:

> People think that I like the mail, but I hate it. I hate it so much. I don't know how long I can keep doing this. Something's got to change. It's not the lifting or the walking that I mind so much. It's the pace. That and the saliva. Some days I just can't stand the thought of it. Do you know how much dried saliva is on all those envelopes I carry each day? One day while I was on vacation in Hawaii, I figured it out. My wife and I were sitting at the Beachcomber listening to Don Ho sing 'Tiny Bubbles' – a dream of ours for years – and all I could think about was saliva. Just saliva. I'm no mathematician, mind you, but while I was sitting there, I figured out that I lug around over eight pounds of dried spittle a day. You multiply that over a lifetime and . . . good God! People say mail carriers are afraid of dogs, but you ask any of us and we'll tell you – we're way more afraid of what's in your mouth. If there's one thing you should know about the post office, it's . . . I'm sorry, I need to run.

Neamo asserts that millions of Americans have far too often identified with McFeely's endless and unnecessary drive to produce 'nothing more than more faster and faster'. In a particularly poignant passage, she describes McFeely as 'a man so tightly wrapped in the trappings of his own profession he seems as if he would have mailed himself long ago (in an act of parcel implosion) if not for his nagging fears of postal re-routing and dereliction of duty.' Neamo claims that much like the figure of Robinson Crusoe, the always-industrious Fred Rogers rules his island neighborhood with great aplomb, subtly coercing McFeely into a type of unfulfilling indentured civil servitude. In a remarkable discovery, Neamo reveals that an early episode of *Mister Rogers* actually has Rogers utter the phrase, 'I made him know his name should be McFeely.' But, for readers, her discovery is quickly blunted by the glaring omission of any reference to Rogers' alter-ego in the Neighborhood of Make-Believe, King Friday. The critical possibilities abound, and Neamo's oversight is an exceptional, yet major, misstep. Though Neamo's critiques of organized capitalism are not particularly new, they are well articulated, and her incredible scrutiny of the means of production existent in Rogers' neighborhood make her analysis extremely thought-provoking and exciting.

The second chapter, entitled 'The Politics and Poetics of Make-Believe', includes an impressive Bakhtinian reading of the 'androgynous trickster' figure of Lady Elaine.

Neamo argues that Lady Elaine's carnivalesque appearance, coupled with her existence in a carousel home, signals to viewers that she represents a 'grotesque realism of symbolic identity that is at once bulbous and protuberant while also obscenely parodic, exorbitant and topographical.' It becomes eminently clear while reading the second chapter that Lady Elaine is the true hero of *Don't You Be My Neighbor*, for if there is a glimmer of optimism to be found in this rather bleak take on contemporary America, it is visible in Neamo's interpretation of Lady Elaine's impish wooden eyes. Lady Elaine's 'Brechtian anti-illusionist gaze,' Neamo contends, 'challenges the viewer's comfortable subject position by politically transforming a sharpened social antagonism into a dialectic ritual that validates the wonderful freedoms of the culture subaltern over the rational adumbrations of the hopelessly utilitarian.' After reading Neamo's eloquent and carefully reasoned analysis of Lady Elaine, one can hardly take issue with any of her claims.

Aside from an over-the-top semiotic analysis of Picture Picture in which Neamo asserts, 'though the image says "Hi" the message is "Die",' the rest of the chapters contain equally insightful readings (if not as equally impassioned as those of McFeely and Lady Elaine) of different facets of Rogers' neighborhood. For instance, Neamo undertakes something of an ecocritical investigation of Rogers' living room, asserting that the transgression of technology into nature and domestic space – signified most strongly by the trolley tracks leading to the Neighborhood of Make-Believe that run through Rogers' home – renders Rogers and viewers alike 'the lifeless prosthetics of urban renewal programs and marketplace degradations that seek to claim the last remaining pre-capitalist enclaves of pure spatiality and human consciousness.' In an interesting move, Neamo asserts that the trolley tracks simultaneously signify the lack of Archimedean footholds against which to critique contemporary structures of domination and the abundance of escape routes by which viewers can retreat into imaginary landscapes of desire. The tracks, she asserts, are 'a psychological pathway into the suburban recesses of the mind, capable of being utilized in a fantastic act of "white flight" should anything truly incommensurate invade Rogers' home.' The ubiquitous conflation of technology, the unconscious and nature, Neamo argues, indicates a cultural failure to engage with 'idiosyncrasy', marginality and authenticity.

While reading *Don't You Be My Neighbor*, one quickly comes to realize that Neamo's work is actually an odd tribute to *Mister Rogers' Neighborhood*. The author doesn't criticize Fred Rogers' show as much as demonstrate its usefulness to understanding something about ourselves. Interestingly, she reserves her harshest criticisms for the network that has carried the show for so many years. From its inception in 1969, PBS promised to be television's bastion of leftist ideals, yet Neamo contends that the network has never lived up to its proclamations, reflecting instead the conservative ideals of the 1950s. Even today, Neamo states, the network seems 'happily and hopelessly trapped in a bygone era that had vanished long before the idea of PBS was ever conceived.' But rather than focus on the obvious evidence of PBS's complicity with hegemony, such as its funding by the Mobil Corporation or its *Masterpiece Theater* pretensions, Neamo makes the unusual decision to concentrate on the PBS logo itself to illustrate her point. She argues that from its first appearance, the strangely earnest, block-like 'PBS' lettering was symptomatic of a detachment from postmodern aesthetic impulses and de-naturalizing critiques. She argues that the network's lettering was 'strangely anachronistic in the ironic post-iconic world of smiley faces and Tang.' As she points out, years before PBS hit the airwaves, films such as Columbia Pictures' *Strait-Jacket* (1964) – which contains a decapitation scene – had undermined the authority of the corporate icon itself by showing the studio's 'torch woman' with her head missing at the end of the film. Six years before that, she notes, the same studio showed the torch woman picking up her dress and running away from a mouse at the beginning of *The Mouse That Roared*. This common subversion of the studio icon – a phenomenon Neamo calls 'playing with your logo' – was strangely absent from the ethos of the PBS network's symbolic iconography from the start. Neamo asserts that rather than challenging hegemonic narratives, PBS has 'quite willingly left such responsibilities to other organizations, such as the Fox Network and PAX.' Thus, she writes, 'PBS should no longer stand for Public Broadcasting Service; rather, it should stand for "Pass the Buck, Sister".' While her critiques of PBS certainly resonate, and readers will most likely admire her creative approach to her subject matter, it is difficult not to feel as if her argument could have been made in a less esoteric fashion.

Despite the fact that *Don't You Be My Neighbor* is a highly original work, it is not completely disengaged from the debates that have gone on in other studies of *Mister Rogers' Neighborhood*. In particular, Neamo takes Socalled to task, especially for his lengthy chapter entitled 'Look at Me, Look at Me, Look at Me' in which he contends that viewers should not dismiss himself or Mr. Rogers as artificial because, as Socalled writes, 'I'm a stodgy old scientist who believes, naively, that there exists an external Mr. Rogers neighborhood, that there exist objective truths about that neighborhood, and that my job is to discover some of them and attract a lot of attention so as to validate myself.' Neamo argues that such reflectionist criticisms on the very nature of Rogers' televisual reality are wholly self-indulgent and undermine contemporary critical theory itself.

On a final note, it should also be mentioned that Arctic University Press has put together a gorgeously lifeless product perfectly attuned to Neamo's subject matter. The book's beautifully fashioned white whale-bone plastic pages, which render the book over eighteen inches thick (a condition likely to give space- and budget-conscious librarians fits), restore faith in the very 'art of the book' in an age of omnipresent electronic text. Cloth copies are available by special request for a fraction of the price, but the text loses much of its impact without the deliberately cold look and feel of the highly synthetic leafs. While no doubt bulky, the plastic edition is worth the extra money, and it is certainly affordable to full professors.

Overall, *Don't You Be My Neighbor* is a valuable and insightful contribution to television studies, postmodern critical theory, and popular narratives of the late 1960s in particular. After reading Victoria Neamo's analysis, readers will anxiously await the publication of her next book on the short-lived, 1976 television series, *Holmes and Yo-Yo*.

The Piano and the Trolley: The Rhizomatic Mister Rogers
by Sheila Rosenberg
Sunnydale: Sunnydale University Press, 1999

reviewed by Jeremy Brown

In her landmark book *The Piano and the Trolley: The Rhizomatic Mister Rogers,* Dr. Sheila Rosenberg of the University of California at Sunnydale provides the world with a 427-page analysis of the popular TV children's show *Mister Rogers' Neighborhood.* *Mister Rogers' Neighborhood* has been frightening children for more than twenty years, and only with the advent of cable television (thus eliminating the need for children to watch PBS) has the show's insipid influence declined. The show features Mr. Rogers, a kindly man, who apparently sits at home all day and talks to imagined children who are watching him. He has no job and spends his time playing the piano, playing with puppets, and building mildly interesting science projects.

This of course has little to do with the subject of my review, as Dr. Rosenberg's book deals not only with *Mister Rogers' Neighborhood*, but also with the theories of the Gilles Deleuze and Felix Guatarri, who provide an interesting, albeit confusing, framework for Rosenberg's argument. Deleuze and Guatarri argue that there are basically two sorts of thinking in the world: patriarchal tree-thinking, in which a choice results in branches of possibility and freedom is cut off, and a rhizomatic way of thinking, in which the action of a person is allowed to spread in any direction. They see western culture as dominated by fascistic trees of knowledge, which certain free thinkers have chopped down. In *A Thousand Plateaus* they cite Henry James, Friedrich Nietzsche, and others as examples of rhizomatic thinking. A book, they argue, is not a machine for producing a story, but a free-flowing amorphous mass of rhizomatic freedom from oppression. Their own book, they argue can be picked up and read from any point: linearity does not matter.

Rosenberg begins her book with a lengthy introduction (230 pages) explaining Deleuze and Guatarri's theory, why they are not accepted in American academia, why she wrote the book, and what about Mister Rogers appeals to her, why the sky is blue, and why her husband does not love her anymore. The final section of the introduction explains why she constructed the book in the manner she has. Rosenberg has taken Deleuze and Guatarri's maxims to heart, and so each chapter of the book, except for the introduction, is no more than two pages long. Rosenberg literally believes that a person can pick her book up from any point and begin reading. The rest of the book's 304 chapters present her argument.

Rosenberg's thesis seems to be that the make-believe portion of the show (the puppet portions) represents a continuous tree-thought, a master narrative of power and oppression. She notes the monarchal system of governance in the land of make-believe and the often dictatorial whims of King Friday. Rosenberg devotes the first part of her book, 'The Trolley', to this argument. She gives detailed character analyses of the members of the make-believe court and devotes several chapters to the character of the trolley. The second section of her argument, 'The Piano', argues that the live-action portions of the show, featuring Mister Rogers himself, represent a series of plateaus (in Deleuze and Guatarri's sense of the word) or nexi which teach children to think in a rhizomatic rather than tree-like manner. The show begins and closes with music, the closing often using a different song every time, which eventually finds its way back to the closing song of the show. The various characters and situations are contrived and therefore resist the tree-narrative style. Their very contrived nature causes the viewer to distance himself from the action, creating an alienation effect and allowing the viewer to analyze the action in a non-dictated manner. The various projects, such as using a prism, or making a kite, stimulate the viewers to build and make things from their own surroundings, to be curious and to attempt to construct objects from useful materials they possess. This form of bricolage promotes a non-consumer, non-linear mind set in which a person sees something built and must go buy a kit and follow instructions to build it.

The argument closes with a comparison/contrast between ethnographic studies of viewers of *Mister Rogers' Neighborhood* versus those who watch *The Mighty Morphin' Power Rangers*. The results were, according to Rosenberg, staggering. The children who watched *Mister Rogers' Neighborhood* invariably chose to lead complacent, quiet lives, indulging in minor hobbies but being of little concern to their social groups. The children who watched the *Power Rangers*, on the other hand, were often violent, melodramatic, and insecure, choosing to fight and destroy their surroundings, rather than solve problems or escape into puppet shows or hobbies. The latter group proved to have an almost 73 per cent greater chance of committing felonies and thus going to jail, becoming a burden on the tax-payer and causing general social woes. However, her one-page chapter format prevents the results from being printed in a coherent and detailed manner.

This book, while vastly interesting, left much to be desired. The piano and trolley as machines were not discussed in more than a passing manner. The matter of the light elevator jazz music, which obviously allows children to think outside the popular music box, did not come up at all. Finally, Dr. Rosenberg did not address the fundamental question: does Mister Rogers ever change clothes?

Krystal Whitecastle
'Tinky Winky's got a brand new bag': the year's work
in Teletubbies Studies

Since its inception in 1997, Teletubbies Studies has attracted its critics, many of whom argue that recent scholarship has failed to maintain the momentum established by Aristotle Anopheles' groundbreaking monograph *Tele(ological)tubbies* (Athens A&M University Press, 1997). To be sure, there have been more lows than highs in recent years, and detractors have been eager to dwell upon the former (e.g. Mary Elizabeth Grace's disappointing *Tinky Winky, I Wuv You!* (Scholastic Press, 1999) and Timmy Wilson's intriguing but poorly-executed *Po! Laa-Laa! Fall Down Again!* (Mother Goose Press, 2000)), while overlooking the latter (most notably Gerund Umlaut's provocative inquiry, *Entschuligen Sie, bitte, wie komme ich zum Land Teletubby?* (Berlin: die Presse einfältig Universität, 1999)). However, the intellectual vigor and critical sophistication of this year's work in Teletubbies Studies should silence even the most skeptical critic of our discipline, for these works act as mental Viagra on minds left flaccid by the puerile criticism of Grace, Wilson, and their ineffectual ilk.

Felix Culpa's book *'There You Go Again! Again! Again!': The Politics of Repetition and The Repetition of Politics* (Bora Bora Institute of Technology Press) opens with an ingenious metaphor: 'On election night 2000, the nation's voters collectively shouted, "Again! Again!" before falling hysterically to the ground. The new adminis-tration, in turn, replied, "Let them eat tubbytoast".' Contending that *Teletubbies* put George W. Bush in the White House, Culpa argues that the show's highly-repetitive nature subliminally conditioned millions of parents to find security in mindless rep-etition, thus causing them to vote for the candidate who subconsciously reminded them of their carefree high school and college years spent during the Reagan-Bush administrations. The American electorate, Culpa explains,

> displayed an infantile desire to turn back the clock and return to the benevolent paternalism of the Reagan-Bush years; repeated exposure to *Teletubbies* condi-tioned voters to find comfort and security in tax cuts for the wealthy, increased spending for defense, and the opening of protected wildlife preserves for oil exploration.

Culpa's argument is an ingenious one, and if correct, Tony Blair had better keep a wary eye on Margaret Thatcher.

2001 saw the publication of the much-anticipated reference work, *'I am not a number. I am a Teletubby': The Prisoner and Teletubbies* by Paddy Fritz and Joseph Serf (Village Publications). Fritz and Serf, co-authors of last year's critically-acclaimed *Sponge Bob Squarepants and the Geometry of Style* (Atlantis University Press), have produced an impressive three-volume work enumerating 46,023 parallels between Patrick McGoohan's 1967 television series and *Teletubbies*, ranging from the seem-ingly trivial (the license plate on the Prisoner's Lotus 7 Series II reads 'KAR12OC', which is also the Noo-Noo's serial number) to the profound (in both shows charac-ters are confined in an idealized English landscape and controlled by anonymous voices heard over a network of loudspeakers, both shows feature giant weather bal-loons that sometimes pursue the protagonists, and both shows unarguably function on an allegorical level). This book is an outstanding example of *Teletubbies* scholar-ship and essential reading for anyone interested in the astonishing influence of Brit-ish television upon British television.

A welcome addition to the growing corpus of *Teletubbies* influence studies is *'Fear no more the heat of the baby-faced sun': Teletubbies and Early Modern Drama* (Dismal State University Press, 2001) by M. Minkoff-Reilly, Indentured Instructor of English at l'Université de Nouvelle Orléans. Minkoff-Reilly argues that early modern drama constitutes the single-greatest influence upon *Teletubbies*, and her work thus stands as a bold challenge to Percy Porlock's hypothesis (presented in his 1998 book *We All Live in a Stately Pleasure Dome: The Magical History of Teletubbies* (Liverpool University Press)) that English Romanticism and late 1960s British psychedelia were the primary sources of inspiration for the popular children's program. Minkoff-Reilly acknowledges this fact in her introduction:

> The influence of Romanticism, especially 'Kubla Khan' and *Yellow Submarine*-era Beatles upon *Teletubbies* cannot be overstated; however, if Porlock had spent less time in Amsterdam coffeehouses 'researching' his book, he would have realized that early modern drama exerts a far greater influence.

Viewing *Teletubbies* through the lens of early modern drama is an approach which produces intriguing but inconsistent results. For example, Minkoff-Reilly's assertion that Po and Laa-Laa were based upon Rosencrantz and Guildenstern lacks concrete evidence, while her suggestion that a computer-animated sequence in which a nattily-dressed bear emerges from a flying carousel to perform a soft-shoe dance routine 'was undoubtedly inspired by the stage direction "Exit, pursued by a bear" in *The Winter's Tale*' is just plain wrong.

The arguments that do work, however, work very well indeed. For instance, Minkoff-Reilly offers what may well prove to be the definitive reading of the classic sequence in which a giant blowout party favor tickles Tinky Winky's buttocks as he bends over. After examining several examples of this type of anality in early modern drama, she concludes: 'Like Hodge in *Gammer Gurton's Needle* and Edward II in Marlowe's play, it is safe to say that Tinky Winky gets it in the end'. In another chapter Minkoff-Reilly challenges Porlock's assertion that 'Teletubbyland exists somewhere slightly west of Xanadu but north-northeast of Pepperland', arguing instead that Teletubbyland has more in common with the homes of Puck and Ariel:

> There is no denying that Teletubbyland is a magical place, but while Porlock recognizes a pharmaceutical source of the magic, I prefer to regard Teletubbyland as part of the same mythopoetic landscape as the Athenian forests of *A Midsummer Night's Dream* and Prospero's island in *The Tempest*, places inhabited by playful sprites and loveable faeries, not women wailing for their demon lovers and Blue Meanies.

These arguments alone make the book an invaluable contribution to the field, 'but wait,' as the sponsors are wont to say, 'there's more': Minkoff-Reilly saves the best for last, concluding her monograph with a provocative and challenging reinterpretation of what many *Teletubbies* scholars generally regard as our darkest hour. I speak, of course, of Reverend Jerry Falwell's infamous 'outing' of Tinky Winky.

In 1999 Falwell's *National Liberty Journal* warned parents that Tinky Winky is a gay role model. Foremost among the evidence for this startling assertion is the fact that the male Tinky Winky carries a purse; furthermore, the article asserts, 'He is purple – the gay pride color; and his antenna is shaped like a triangle – the gay pride symbol' ('Tinky Winky Comes Out of the Closet'). Although Falwell himself did not write the article, he later told reporters that he stood behind it, adding, 'As a Christian I feel that role modeling the gay lifestyle is damaging to the moral lives of children.'

Falwell's fear that exposing young boys to Tinky Winky would turn them into mincing queens struck most people as ludicrous, and satirists were quick to ridicule the former leader of the Moral Majority. However, Minkoff-Reilly argues, these satirists were nearly four centuries too late, for a character based upon Falwell had already been lampooned by Ben Jonson in *Bartholomew Fair* (1614). Near the end of the play, a puritan minister named Zeal-of-the-Land Busy interrupts a puppet show, charging both the audience and the puppets with immorality. Busy then enters a debate with one of the puppets, which culminates thus:

BUSY: Yes, and my main argument against you is that you are an abomination; for the male among you putteth on the apparel of the female, and the female of the male.

| PUPPET DIONYSIUS: | You lie, you lie, you lie abominably ... It is your old stale argument against the players, but it will not hold against the puppets, for we have neither male nor female amongst us. And that thou may'st see, if thou wilt, like a malicious purblind zeal as thou art! |

The puppet takes up his garment.

| BUSY: | I am confuted, the cause hath failed me. (5.5.87–101) |

Jonson, Minkoff-Reilly insists, satirizes Falwell's attack on Tinky Winky by having Busy lose a debate with a puppet over its alleged sexual orientation.

Proving that Jonson had foreknowledge of the event proves to be Minkoff-Reilly's biggest challenge, yet she rises to the occasion, offering unassailable proof:

> While composing *Bartholmew Fair*, Jonson met Michel de Nostradamus at a dinner party hosted by Lucy, Countess of Pembroke, and the celebrated French astrologer was so charmed by Jonson's wit that he gifted him with the following quatrain, which I discovered by chance on E-bay:
>
> > The shepherd shall lead his flock astray
> > By finding evil in a child's plaything;
> > Yet his argument will reveal his own folly –
> > When confuted, he will *fall well*.

Minkoff-Reilly rightly concludes that through this prophetic verse, Jonson foresaw Falwell's ridiculous attempt to impose human sexual orientation upon genderless fictional creatures and decided it would be good for a laugh or two on stage.

Although using Nostradamus to support her argument will certainly generate controversy, it is exactly this type of scholarly risk-taking needed to push the boundaries of Teletubbies Studies (after all, Mary Elizabeth Grace and Timmy Wilson didn't exactly take any chances). Aware that her thesis is a challenging one, Minkoff-Reilly strongly defends her position:

> Although some small-minded nitpickers and *Skeptical Inquirer*-types will demand to know how Falwell's actions could have influenced Jonson's play 385 years earlier, my response is that the influence is undeniably there. As any fool can plainly see, Falwell's homophobic attack upon the *Teletubbies* so closely parallels Busy's attack upon the puppets that one cannot ignore the obvious influence of *Teletubbies* upon *Bartholmew Fair*. End of story. Deal with it.

Indeed, just as Busy could not refute the puppet's logic, this reviewer cannot refute Minkoff-Reilly's ingenious argument.

Given my obvious admiration for Minkoff-Reilly's book, it may come as a surprise that as awe-inspiring as her book is, there is an even more powerful work left to review. Not an influence study but a relentlessly postmodern analysis of race and racism in *Teletubbies*, the book raises many questions, but, like an elusive enigma wrapped in a cryptic mystery shrouded in an esoteric riddle, it provides few answers. Even the identity of the author is unknown. The book of which I speak is, of course, the anonymous *Coloring the Teletubbies* (Smith-Binney Publications). This crucial text bridges the perceived gulf between racial and individual identity, challenging our (pre)conceptions about how racial identity is imagined, inscribed, figured, and theorized in *Teletubbies*.

The anonymous author employs a series of linked black and white drawings printed on coarse newsprint to investigate race in Teletubbyland and, by extension, our own. Since these pictures cry out for color, the author's intent in rendering them monochromatically has generated much scholarly debate: Does the absence of color indict *Teletubbies* for racism? Or does this absence of color in fact invite us to project upon each Teletubby our own racial construction? For years to come *Coloring the Teletubbies* will remain essential reading for professional scholars and critics writing about *Teletubbies*. For the sake of Teletubbies Studies, let us hope that this anonymous author is now busily working on *Gendering the Teletubbies* and *Classing the Teletubbies*.

cartoons

Beavis, Butt-head, and Bakhtin
by I. B. Todorov
Leeds: Antisocial Texts, 1996

reviewed by Michael Dunne

With *Beavis, Butt-head, and Bakhtin*, I[tsy] B[itsy] Todorov continues to pursue the parallel interests in contemporary critical theory and American popular culture that have previously resulted in her controversial studies: *Deconstructing Dennis (the Menace)* (1992), *Signs, Signification, and Sushi* (1993), *Materializing Madonna* (1994), and *Fabio and Fabulation* (1995). In her newest work – part of Antisocial Texts' 'Venting about Video' series – Todorov applies the probing insights and rich vocabulary of the Russian critical theorist Mikhail Bakhtin (1895–1975) to MTV's much-analyzed animated/music-video show. The results are (predictably) challenging and irritating.

The book is organized into six chapters of unequal length. In the first three – 'Troping and Groping', 'Monads and Gonads', and 'Words and Woodies' – Todorov demonstrates how Mike Judge's animated offspring have succeeded in making what Bakhtin called 'the grotesque body' even more grotesque. The next two chapters – 'Monologism and Masturbation' and 'Utterance and Ignorance' – apply Bakhtin's challenging concept of the 'carnivalesque word' both to the diegetic world of B & B's daily life in and around Highland High School and to the metadiegetic world of the music videos they watch. 'Chronotopes and Dopes', Todorov's final chapter, explores the contextual implications of the duo's oft-stated motto, 'Knowledge is Stupid!'

The author is on soundest ground when she deploys her eclectic textual strategies to decode the show's multi-mediated polyphony. In one brilliant passage, for example, she explores the discursive richness of the exchange in which Beavis says that a U2 video 'means something' and Butt-head responds, 'Yeah, it means something stupid!' Todorov's fascination with unexpected intertextuality is also apparent in her syntagmatic explication of Butt-head's definition of Depeche Mode as 'French for Wussies'. Heteroglossia gloriously rules in Todorov's extended (ten page) analysis of Beavis and Butt-head's Christmas declension: *yule log*, *stool log*, *log*, and *wood*. Textual richness is, after all, the *raison d'etre* for choosing Bakhtin as a guide to this show's polyphonic voices. Characteristically, Todorov deconstructs the whole conception of *raisons* by interrogating B & B's provocative confusion of the 'California Raisins' with 'turds'.

As the last example suggests, Todorov engages productively with the carnivalesque dimensions of *Beavis and Butt-head*. Taking as her premise the duo's judgment of a Corrosion of Conformity video – 'drums, guitars, and death! They finally got it right!' – Todorov demystifies the cultural pastiche of the show. Whether the topic is shooting Mr. Ed because of his injured fetlock; frying rats, insects, and night crawlers at Burger World; castrating crickets in the great outdoors; or kidnapping Stewart to raise money for heavy-metal concert tickets, Todorov penetrates the apparent sociopathology of the representation to reveal the actual overthrow of what Bakhtin identified as 'the laws, prohibitions, and restrictions that determine the structure and order of ordinary ... life ... all its hierarchical structure and all the forms of terror, reverence, piety, and etiquette connected with it.' As Todorov demonstrates, this carnivalesque quality assumes a manic narrativity in the boys' subversive encounters with their teacher Mr. Buzzcut, their principal Mr. McVickers, and their neighbor Mr. Anderson. Divided into sub-chapters with titles including 'The Grim Rapper', 'Tattoos Are Cool', and 'Morning Wood in the Afternoon', this free-ranging discussion challenges both conventional misprisions of antinomianism and Beavis' and Butt-head's conviction that 'circuses suck.'

Many reviewers have remarked, concerning the four other books that Todorov has published in the last four years, that not all segments of her arguments are equally persuasive. In the present work, for example, Todorov seems content to abandon the historico-materialist mode of interrogation that so electrified readers of *Materializing Madonna* and to accept the commodification of Judge's animated figures without taking account of the notoriously exploited Asian animators who might, in other circumstances, have worked on the show. In a cruel stroke of unexamined irony, Beavis, Butt-head, and their classmate Diarrhea (Darria) fumble their way toward political demystification under the bourgeois tutelage of the Highland High hegemony in a diegetic world of representation while Todorov looks on from her extradiegetic world of privilege with apparent smiling indifference to the cramped little third-world fingers of Manila's sweat-shop animators who have not been invited to the party. For reasons that her opponents will be only too eager to conjecture, Todorov seems increasingly to be forsaking the paths earlier trodden by the sensible shoes of her mentrix, S[oi] D[isant] Eagleton, whose magisterial *Leavis, Labor, and Lucille Ball* (1955) effectively established the field of media studies in the British Commonwealth.

It is conventional at this point in a scholarly book review to split hairs, argue about picky details, and point snidely to minor inaccuracies of fact and reference. Because this reviewer feels such a profound debt of gratitude to I. B. Todorov for her many inspiring discoveries in earlier books, he is reluctant to play the conventional part. However, constraints imposed by the editors of this project require that I note a few critical infelicities. The band is called Van Halen not 'Van Buren'. The rap group are the Beastie Boys, not the Beastie Girls (more's the pity!). The lyric says that it's three strikes, not 'five', and you're out. 'Woodrow' is, admittedly, a good friend of Beavis and Butt-head, but Woodrow is not a 'classmate', as Todorov asserts. Bakhtin's term is *heteroglossia* not *heterosexia,* and the master's first name is Mikhail, not 'Boris'. All of these are, in the end, mere quibbles that should not be allowed to distract from the far more substantial insights of Todorov's probing study.

And there are so many insights here. Surely Todorov is the first to have remarked Mike Judge's uncanny thematic resemblance to Dostoevsky. As a result of her groundbreaking theorization, no one can read *The Idiot* hereafter without thinking of Beavis. In the same way, Todorov's elaborate paralleling of Coach Buzzcut and Pantagruel totally outshines Camille Paglia's comparison of Elvis and Lord Byron. Criticism of this sort truly redefines thinking. As further evidence, we might note Todorov's challenging proposal that Bakhtin's 'inserted genres' should be troped as 'inserted genders' because the suggestion throws new and useful light on music videos by Grace Jones and Duran Duran. In another place, Todorov's (playful?) suggestion that Seattle be read as an adenoidal corruption of 'Beatles', thereby transposing 'grunge' into '[g]ringo', liberates the 'salsa' subtext of many videos condemned by Beavis and Butt-head as 'horrible' or 'awful'. In such a reading, 'sucks' can be paradoxically re-read as the valorization of a (harmless) multi-culturalism. It is for such insights that we return again and again to Todorov's work.

One reviewer of *Fabio* – in *PMLA* – ungraciously quoted Ben Jonson's principle from *Timber* (1641) that 'Ready writing makes not good writing.' Father Ben notwithstanding, Todorov has clearly demonstrated in *Beavis, Butt-head, and Bakhtin* that she is still at the top of her game. We may therefore look forward with eager anticipation to 'Culture-Kampf Studies', the new series recently announced by Antisocial Texts, in which Todorov will serve as editor of the first three volumes: *Xena and Xenophobia*; *Aerosmith and Otherness: An Answer to Said*; and *Who Invited All These Tacky People?*

They Deconstructed South Park: You Bastards!
edited by Lavender Levine
Routlegerdemain Press, 2000

reviewed by Stephen A. Tompkins

First it was Comedy Central's animated ratings king and darling of the college crowd, then it became a merchandising bonanza, with products ranging from tee shirts to Christmas CD's. Now the naughtiest cartoon in TV history has spawned an anthology of critical essays edited by noted queer theorist and academician, Lavender Levine, and containing articles by such critical luminaries as feminist Sally Rhode and Marxist Gyatra Wetvac. Fasten your theoretical seatbelts, it's going to get a little bumpy.

Levine's *They Deconstructed South Park*: *You Bastards!* is the latest in his series of anthologies that place television programs in the postmodern panopticon of popular culture studies. Much like his collection of critical essays on *Seinfeld*, *Master of His Domain: Jerry Seinfeld and Sado-masochism*, Levine's newest compilation both lauds and derides a TV text. Contributors employ a variety of analytical approaches in their deconstruction of the denizens of *South Park* including queer, feminist, Marxist, psychoanalytical, and vegan.

The first chapter attempts to speak for and about the loveable but linguistically challenged Kenny McCormick. Weighing in with a Jungian perspective, Sasha Pedant playfully ponders poor Kenny's muffled ejaculations and posits that the young

Coloradan's condition is archetypal and biblical in nature. Pointing to such primitive cultures as the Indonesian 'Twistati's' (whose name means 'tongue-tied') and drawing on the story of the Tower of Babel, Pedant argues that Kenny is an animated manifestation of a long line of frustrated orators. Furthermore, Pedant maintains that McCormick's mumblings are typical of the post-modem communicative dilemma. According to Pedant, in the age of the Internet and the PC, verbal exchanges have become more and more atrophied, and Kenny's inability to speak anything more than gibberish is the future phonetic fate awaiting the human race. While I appreciate and admire Pedant's considerable research and documentation, I think her technophobia is a bit overwrought, and after reading her essay, I had a hard time articulating to my wife Pedant's explanation for the McCormick malaise. Still, for anyone interested in a detailed account of historical (and hysterical) cultures and people that 'spoke in tongues', this chapter is a must.

Sally Rhode contributes Chapter Two of Levine's anthology, an essay entitled 'Stan's Projectile Vomiting: The Retchedness of Femininity in *South Park*'. Although I'll grant that Rhode does important work in terms of gender and sexuality issues, I wonder if she isn't being too pessimistic by claiming that 'Stan's "throwing up" of the feminine mystique is both misogynistic and messy.' Rhode's tendency to essentialize male behavior and representations of femininity are enough to make the reader nauseous, and though I agree that the boys of *South Park* should all be forced to attend a Lilith Fair and read Erica Jong's *Fear of Flying*, Rhode's prediction that when Stan grows up he will most likely resort to cannibalizing women as well as bingeing and purging seems a little far 'retched'.

Lavender Levine himself devotes Chapter Three to his queer reading of *South Park*'s most homophobic character, the irrepressible Eric Cartmen. 'Cartmen out of the Closet: Screw You, I'm Going Homo' is a brilliant and witty outing of the pudgy bigot. Levine always amazes me in his ability to make everything perfectly queer. Drawing heavily on Alexander Doty's 'Flaming Classics' and Robin Wood's 'Sexual Politics and Narrative Film', Levine reveals, through careful and close readings of several classic *South Park* episodes including 'Big Gay Al's Boat Ride', and 'An Elephant Makes Love to a Pig', that Eric Cartman is a big fat 'puffter'. Levine catches Cartman with his pants down and brings new meaning to the term 'intruder alert'. His 'camp' analysis of 'Cartman Gets an Anal Probe' will make you think differently about the phrase 'cheesy poofs', and his analysis should promote a flurry of non-hetero, contra-straight re-readings of other *South Park* inhabitants. Anyone for queering Mr. Mackey? Mmmkay?

Vanessa Phillips contributes a scathing critique of the meat eaters of *South Park* in her wonderfully-titled piece called 'Salisbury (what's at) Stake: Cafeteria Carnivores at *South Park* Elementary'. Fresh off her recent and critically acclaimed book, *Tofu or Not Tofu – That is the Question*, Phillips sheds the rare but interesting vegan light on the precocious adolescents' eating habits and identifies the Chef as the culinary corrupter par excellence. It's refreshing to hear vegan philosophy applied to what Phillips calls 'a very distasteful' program, but be forewarned: Phillips' exegesis is not for the squeamish. Readers with delicate digestive systems are urged to forego her analysis of the 'Chef's Salty Balls' episode.

The Marxist school of thought is brought to bear on *South Park* in Gyatra Wetvac's essay entitled, 'Cartman's Quest for Capital: Mo' Money, Mo' Problems'. Wetvac claims that the bourgeois attitudes promoted and perpetuated by Cartman and his cohorts marginalize the working poor. She finds in Cartman's pronouncement in the 'Chicken Lover' episode to 'Respect My Authority!' a veiled threat of corporate ideology. She sees in Kenny a potential Trotsky, though one wonders how he's going to rally the downtrodden and oppressed working class with that hood tied so tightly around his mouth. Her call for an investigation into the proliferation of *South Park* merchandise and websites and her argument that creators Matt Stone and Trey Parker are poseurs – rebels without a restraining clause – rather than the anti-establishment heroes they pretend to be is both compelling and convincing. It makes this reviewer ashamed of his recent purchase of a Kyle Broflovski keychain and Kenny McCormick nightlight.

The penultimate chapter of Levine's book is another feminist reading of a specific episode. Stephen Bonkin takes the 'Mecha-Streisand' episode to the misogyny woodshed. Relying on the theories outlined in Barbara Creed's *The Monstrous Feminine*, Bonkin reveals how the powers of patriarchy that reign in *South Park* re-present female ambition and moxie as dangerously transgressive. He observes how in the final showdown between *South Park* superheroes Leonard Maltin and Harry Belafonte, and the evil and vainglorious 'Mecha-Streisand', Babs literally takes it on the nose and is expelled from the narrative (and the planet!). But Bonkin sees a both/and potential in this episode, pointing out that the ultimate vanquisher of Mecha-Streisand is none other than Robert Smith of The Cure. Three cheers for androgyny (and 'Disintegration')!

The anthology concludes with a poorly written and ideologically muddled piece called 'Blame Canada: The Only Good Canuck is a Dead Canuck'. The esteemed English media critic, Sir Lawrence Valence, attempts to paint *South Park* as a den of xenophobia in his examination of the 1999 blockbuster musical, *South Park*: *Bigger, Longer, and Uncut*. Focusing on the film's propensity for Canadian-bashing, it seems that Sir Valence has had a sense of humor failure. Anyone who has ever been to Medicine Hat, Alberta knows that our friends north of the border deserve some good-natured ribbing about some of their cultural peccadilloes. After all, as the Mackenzie brothers would say, 'that's what comedy is all aboot.'

Levine's anthology is a welcome addition to the burgeoning critical analysis of popular culture texts. And while it contains a fair share of jargon and academese, the overall tone of the book is 'reader friendly'. Although it isn't exactly a book you'd take to the beach, *They Deconstructed South Park: You Bastards!* would make a worthy addition to any media library or popular culture collection. There's really something here for everyone, though. As Cartman would say, this book is 'Sweeet' and 'Hellacool'.

science fiction

Zipping the Great Minds: Max Headroom's BigTime Philosophy
edited by Martyn Dumfries
Gary, Indiana: DeLancie Presbyterian University Press, 2000

reviewed by Paul M. Malone

At last one of the most important cultural phenomena of the twentieth century has garnered the critical attention that it deserves. After several changes of publisher, eight working titles, and a heated controversy on the question of whether the series' fourteenth and fifteenth episodes, the originally unaired 'Baby Grobags' and the unproduced 'Theora's Tale', could be considered canonical, *Zipping the Great Minds: Max Headroom's BigTime Philosophy* is here. A great debt of gratitude for weathering these storms is due to Martyn Dumfries, who five years ago, citing 'pangs of conscience', left a prestigious teaching post and a promising future at St. Swithin's Academy, an aggressively Thatcherite boarding school in the north of England. In fact, the Academy had made it clear that they considered Dumfries' editing of the *Max Headroom* anthology, already three years underway, an unwelcome distraction from his pioneering research on the Brontë sisters. Stung, Dumfries uprooted himself to found the Department of English and World Literature, Comparative Religion, and Electronic Media at Canada's first entirely online private university, the University of the North (www.uofthenorthattoktoyaktuk.ca). There were fears that this new responsibility would bring the *Max Headroom* project, much like the original series, to an untimely end; however, Dumfries has triumphantly brought out this volume virtually simultaneously with Routledgerdemain's publication of his weighty monograph *The Faked Deaths of the Brontës: An Examination of the Insurance Records*. The uproar facing this latter volume, of course, need not concern us here.

Although the *Max Headroom* television series, a satire of television set 'twenty minutes into the future' that aired in the US on ABC in late 1987 and early 1988, was the subject of a small amount of academic writing at the time (see, for example, the articles by Berko, King, and O'Brien), Dumfries points out in his introduction that 'the conventional view of *Max* as merely "the first cyberpunk television series" obscured the program's deep roots in the Western philosophical tradition, and the larger questions which so obviously lay just beneath its shiny surface had lain fallow all too long … One can only marvel at the depth to which the writers and producers must have immersed themselves in the philosophical canon.' The papers given over a two-day St. Swithin's colloquium in 1993 became the nucleus of the present anthology – although several original participants withdrew their contributions during the 'Grobags' conflict. Most sorely missed, of course, is the late Herschel van Loon's essay on *Max* and Maimonides; however, Dan Chinh-Wah O'Reilly's provocative 'If You Meet Max Headroom on the Road, Kill Him!' is available on O'Reilly's website at Marquette, together with some rather uncharitable remarks about Dumfries and several other colleagues who were involved. Meanwhile, a heavily revised version of 'Zik Zak, Telelections, and the Vu-Age Church; or, Baudrillard Proved Right Yet Again', by Jan Steffansen, is slated to appear in a forthcoming special issue of the *Old Left Review*.

This anthology deals exclusively with philosophical issues raised by the television series. Max Headroom's previous and concurrent careers as talk-show host, VJ, and spokesman for the New Coke were considered of far less interest philosophically, and are thus in the main treated only peripherally, if at all. Because the series focused on the relationship between the computer-generated 'talking head' Max Headroom and his real-life model, Network 23 investigative journalist Edison Carter (both played by Matt Frewer), fully half of the essays deal with the ontological questions posed by having, as Max himself puts it, 'two minds but with one single memory' (in the pilot episode 'Blipverts', and in the opening credits thereafter).

In his 'Max/Edison Carter: So Who's the *Ding-an-sich*?' Jake Lloydminster of SUNY Niagara Falls breaks the ice by asking whether Max is properly categorized in Kantian terms as an appearance, a phenomenon, or an illusion. Lloydminster grants that Max often acts as a moral force, particularly in his relationship with his creator, adolescent computer genius Bryce Lynch (Chris Young), and therefore seems to have a noumenal basis. The possibility exists, however, that Max does not have the freedom requisite to a noumenon at all; rather, Lloydminster posits, 'the moral sense which in Edison exists archetypally is only ectypal in Max, who does no more than reflect, in an illusory manner, the noumenal autonomy of Edison.' On this view, the argument continues, Edison Carter's autonomy can be demonstrated by his frequent *failure* to do the right thing. Max, on the other hand, has merely been endowed with Edison's moral values and lacks the human ability to think outside this box, as it were. Thus he seems to be consistently obeying the categorical imperative when he is, in fact, only following a set of parameters which are, from Max's point of view, utterly arbitrary. This claim can be substantiated by considering the episode 'Whacketts', in which an addictive hexadecimal code imbedded in a tacky game show causes Max to act *immorally*, flooding the Network 23 audience with the mind-altering signal; it is being programmed with the antidote, however, and not an appeal to reason or morality, that returns Max to normal. Lloydminster argues cogently, but ultimately he judiciously reserves judgment, since he finds that under the circumstances, it is impossible to determine with the information available whether it is in fact possible for both Edison and Max to be noumenal – or, if only *one* of them can be noumenal, whether this automatically excludes Max.

Princess University's Claude Delaponcé, on the other hand, does not seem to doubt Max's autonomy, at least: in his '"The Unconscious is Structured as a L-l-l-language": Max as Mirror Stage', Delaponcé suggests rather that Max, 'born at the age of twenty-seven, is clearly stuck in a stage of infantile narcissism: Because he sees all life as television, he perceives the "real" Edison Carter as an image of himself, possessed of a unity – to wit, a body, arms, and legs – that for Max must remain illusory.' Max thus speaks himself as subject *to* Edison, his Other, motivated by desire, since Max notably lacks, along with the rest of the body, the Phallus. Max's stuttering is, according to Delaponcé, the symbolic representation of his ego attempting to erect itself in a continual state of anticipation ('I'd just like to be able to see my legs,' as Max says, in 'War'; here the legs, of course, stand in for another part altogether). As an example, Delaponcé cites Max's only 'romantic' episode – his seduction of the artificial intelligence A-7 in 'Security Systems' – which centers on the similarity (and aurally, the identity) of Max and Edison, allowing Edison to step in and interview A-7 once 'she' (possessed of a female voice) has fallen in love with Max.

Max seduces A-7 only to aid Edison, his true love object. Once their interface has led to *jouissance*, Max is able to project onto her his own *méconnaissance*, so that she too, like Max, perceives Max and Edison as one. Thus Max sees no loss in passing A-7 on to the gaze of the bearer of the vidicam/Phallus: the interview is the true consummation ... Edison's producer Murray (Jeffrey Tambor) is thus entirely justified in referring to Max as Edison's 'alter egotist.'

Quentin Thorgoode of Methodical University takes a different tack again in his densely argued 'Syntax á la Max: A Wittgensteinian View', based on Wittgenstein's assertion that there is in fact no self at all. '"I",' Thorgoode reminds us, 'often has no bodily referent, except when used in the oblique, as an object: "My nose is broken."' However, in Max's case, even this usage is inappropriate – when he says that Edison's memories are 'my memories too' (in 'Deities'), he speaks of something that Edison bears as products of lived experience, whereas for Max they are merely data with which he was already supplied at the moment of his birth. Likewise, Max's use of 'our' in a phrase such as 'our eyes' (here indicating not 'my eyes' and 'Edison's eyes', but rather asserting the identity of Max's eyes with Edison's) is in Wittgensteinian terms nonsensical even in its conventional meaning, but its nonsensicality becomes apparent in Max's statement of it. Much more difficult to apprehend, Thorgoode claims, are such phrases as the above-mentioned 'I wish I could see my legs' – which would seem to fall among the cases when 'I' indeed refers to a body, but this is not so in this instance. Predicated on the syllogistic view that because Max has some anthropomorphic traits, he is human and therefore *ought* to have legs, this statement in fact demonstrates the truth of Wittgenstein's observation of the 'I' as extremely problematic owing to the inadequacy of the available categories. For Max, who 'because he lives in a TV ... thinks *everything* is TV' ('Rakers'), the limits of his language truly *are* the limits of his world.

Other limits are described in 'Max, Marx and Sparks', by Roy Smythe Ramsbotham of the University of Lourdes. Ramsbotham is well-known in British academia less for his book *Who Reads Fredric Jameson? Not Me* than for the memorable Manchester pub crawl that culminated in his calling Terry Eagleton 'a sell-out and a wanker.' Here, while more tactfully referring to his fellow contributors as 'well-meaning but clueless woolgatherers,' Ramsbotham makes no bones about declaring *Max Headroom* 'useless reactionary bumph, deeply compromised in any claim to be a subversive element' by Max's commercialization both before and during the run of the series: 'An indentured hawker of goods doesn't become autonomous by becoming himself commodified as a takeaway gift at the local McDonald's.' The purported subversiveness of *Max*, coated in special-effects and public relations pyrotechnics, is only the culmination of what Ramsbotham calls 'the built-in counterinsurgency of late capitalism.' It is no help that *Max Headroom* is self-consciously aware of this tendency: among the programs on offer at Network 23 are the documentary 'Lifestyles of the Poor and Pitiful' ('Grossberg's Return') and a sitcom called 'Lumpy's Proletariat' ('Security Systems').

Despite his jaundiced view of the series ('not cyberpunk, but cyberbunk'), Ramsbotham is clearly well acquainted with its events: the main section of his analysis focuses on the irony of the episode 'Neurostim', in which Network 23 is acquired by its main sponsor, Zik Zak – who then are forced to sell it again because they find it impossible to function as both advertisers and programmers. This fable, Ramsbotham points out, has been proven ridiculous by subsequent events, in which television networks have routinely been devoured by multinational corporations with no apparent difficulty (*Max Headroom* itself is now the jealously-guarded intellectual property of the Time Warner media empire). As for the relationship between Edison and Max, this ontological problem is summarily dismissed as 'a cheapjack device to make Carter's self-alienation, which he bloody well deserves, even more painfully obvious.' Ramsbotham's passionate diatribe is a healthy corrective to some of the other essays' tendency to depoliticize their subject in token of its aesthetic and philosophical richness.

Renate Pilgerstock of the University of Hudson Bay at Moose Factory, in her provocative 'Being and Nothingness – to the Max', argues from the same end of the political spectrum, but in a more positive tone. For Pilgerstock, Max's world is a classic example of an originally dynamic social structure petrified into the 'practico-inert' by the artificial scarcity of rampant consumerism. Within this absurd context, Edison Carter sees his mission, like that of Sartre's Roquentin, as 'to make men feel ashamed of their existence'; however, 'Edison feels bound by the access to the public which network exposure gives him to work within the system that he claims to subvert (as he avers in 'Lessons'). His continual self-endangerment by openly working against the interests of his network and corporate masters reveals his bad faith: he consistently allows his rebelliousness to be contained, giving himself an excuse for his ineffectuality.' Pilgerstock agrees with Ramsbotham that Max is a symbol of Edison's alienation; rather than a cheap device, however, she sees Max as 'the reification of Edison's "being-for-others" in the form of a fragmentary *pour-soi*, incomplete not because contingent on too few frame buffers, but because Max only exists to the extent that Edison is *de trop*.' Max's existence is thus the proof that 'the Blanks who roam the fringes of the City can achieve liberation not through Edison's agency, but rather only by their own efforts.'

M.U.T. professor Arvind Bhose's contribution, 'Max Headroom in the Age of Mechanical Reproduction', argues that Max is in fact 'not only erratic, but also *auratic* – the artistic volition, or *Kunstwollen*, of Bryce Lynch, not only transforms the haptic physicality of Edison Carter into the optic (cyber-)spatiality of Max Headroom: it also creates an artwork uniquely capable of reproducing *himself* voluntarily via the plurality of screens, monitors, and view-phones in the wired world.' Bhose claims, rather murkily, that Max's capacity for self-reproduction reconciles the original intentions of Benjamin's flawed critique of technological mediation with the revisions of later critics; even if Bhose fails to prove this entirely convincingly, his essay is well worth reading for the elegant excursus on Edison the camera-toting telejournalist as 'a surgeon cutting into the body politic.'

The body politic is even more in evidence in West Central Pennsylvania emeritus Simon G. Runciman, Jr.'s essay 'Live and Direct from Plato's *Republic*', which praises the unnamed city as the real star of the series. Runciman suggests that the city houses *in ovo* Plato's ideal society: with the Fringers and Blanks, who in general are the only characters in the series to display artistic talent or impulses (for example, Frances's drumming in 'Lessons'), exiled to the outskirts, the vast majority of the population are Plato's appetite-driven people of iron and bronze, the television workers and Metrocops the 'auxiliaries' of silver – and the golden position of guardianship is entrusted to Security Systems, Inc. (introduced in 'Security Systems', but omnipresent as a source of surveillance data on computer screens shown throughout the series), and particularly in the form of its computer A-7 (misused in that episode but proven capable of learning from its mistakes, and presumably still active after its scheduled reprogramming).

Where Plato's Guardians are entitled to rule due to their knowledge of the forms underlying apparent reality, Runciman claims that in the modern world, binary-code information replaces the forms as the basic epistemological element. 'It is, of course, a truism that Plato's vision of the perfect society could never be realized in all its details even in his own day, much less millennia later,' Runciman writes, 'but because it is an ideal, an *eidos*, there perforce can only exist an approximation in any given time and place.'

For Runciman, the *Max Headroom* series is the story of an aristocratic society overcoming internal dangers: the threat of oligarchy posed by the Zik Zak corporation, for example, is vanquished in 'Neurostim'; despotism is brought low, in the form of the censor Dragul, in 'Lessons'; while democracy is defeated in 'Grossberg's Return'. Although this latter episode is usually interpreted as a triumph for democracy – in fact, Network 23's chairman Ben Cheviot (George Coe) explicitly describes it as such even though his own network's candidate is defeated in a ratings-based 'telelection' – Runciman maintains that the existence of a Global Government (revealed in 'Whacketts'), itself dependent on the data of Security Systems, makes the frequent telelection of local candidates more a sop to local feelings than any real sign of democracy in either the ancient Greek or the modern sense. As for Max himself, he assumes the subsidiary but important role of a Socratic questioner (since he too has direct access to the binary code, he apparently functions as something of a rogue Guardian, and pays tribute to Plato's deep respect for Socrates). Runciman's ingenuous refusal to acknowledge the consumerist basis of *Max*'s society, however, unfortunately renders his account less convincing than his obvious – and unsettling – admiration for a society that the producers had certainly intended to be dystopian.

Wisely, Dumfries chose to follow Runciman's essay with 'Twenty Minutes into Althusser's Future', by Bonnie-LeeAnne Masters of the University of California at Sunnydale, who essays a 'symptomatic' reading of *Max Headroom* as a vision of 'overdetermined conjuncture run rampant, with the 10,000 channels of information and entertainment neatly folded into the conduits of political power and security to create a single ideological state apparatus, with the appearance of competition and democracy to defuse charges of monopoly and hegemony.' The use of ratings as the measure of all things, and the dispensation of justice through such Network 23 programs as 'You The Jury' ('The Academy'), enables most of the citizens of the world to both constitute and incorporate themselves as willing subjects – to the degree that the repressive state apparatus (the Metrocops) appears, for all its Fascist trappings, as a relatively vestigial force. Nevertheless, certain elements among the Blanks (Bruno in 'War' and 'Lessons', for example) display a clear revolutionary consciousness; curiously, however, and somewhat unrealistically, 'although traces of the dual consciousness typical of the working classes are scattered here and there throughout the series, the overarching symbol of this consciousness is granted to a member of the bourgeoisie, Edison Carter, via his double Max Headroom.' Masters offers the faint concluding hope that Edison's actions, *pace* Pilgerstock, may yet serve as a catalyst for revolution.

The remaining chapters deal with supporting characters from the series (though, perhaps predictably, Edison's long-suffering producer Murray is not among them). 'Blank Reg and Heideggerean Authenticity', by the University of Northern East Florida's Anastasia I. Lefkowitz, is dedicated to the aging, Mohawk-haired former headbanger who runs the minuscule independent station BigTime Television from a bus. Reg is the series' chief representative of the Blanks, rebels and drop-outs who have found a way to erase all their records from government databases – or, as Reg himself calls them, the 'fraternity of the last free men' ('Security Systems'). Lefkowitz interprets Reg in terms of an existential quest:

> Reg realizes that his Being-in-the-world can never be authentic (*eigentlich*) except under conditions of a separation from the state's recorded citizens. He participates, he exhibits care (*Sorge*); in every respect he is thrown into *Dasein* in the most typical manner. And yet his Blank-ness is an effort, conscious and concerted, to keep himself from being assimilated into the neutrality of *das Man*, which one generally translates as 'the They' – and yet would it not be more fitting here to say 'The Man,' for if we ask, 'Against what is Blank Reg struggling so doggedly?' the answer is plain: 'He struggles against The Man.' In Lefkowitz's reading, Reg's peripatetic pink bus is a sign that he stands out (ex-sists), and also proof that he is nowhere at home (*Un-heimlich*): tokens of the productive angst which discloses, or unconceals, his potentiality for authentic Being.

Karl-Helmut Steinhauer of Routland Polytechnic, in 'Bryce Lynch: Beyond Good and Evil', interprets the boy genius as a Nietzschean *Übermensch*:

> The creators of *Max Headroom* foresaw surprisingly early the need to reclaim that fateful term from the opprobrium it has unjustly accumulated, hence they saw fit to incorporate the idea in a young boy. With a light touch and

great cunning they weave in the subtle clues that form the red thread leading us toward the truth ... Bryce's casual indifference to Judeo-Christian values, refined through his superior intellectual creativity, allows him to reconcile Nietzsche's two strands of artistic creation: Max is an essentially Dionysian creation, achieved by Apollonian means.

In place of a herd mentality and a slave morality, Bryce has been endowed by the Academy of Computer Sciences with a 'morality of binary concepts' dependent on responsibility instead of guilt, in which 'right and wrong are non-empirical concepts' ('The Academy'). Thus in 'Blipverts', when Network 23's then-chairman Ned Grossberg (Charles Rocket) complains of the bad publicity that would ensue were the public to find out that Bryce's new subliminal advertising method can cause sedentary viewers to explode, Bryce's simple reply is: 'Then don't tell them.' Likewise, Bryce, foreseeing no harm, has no qualms about framing the innocent Blank Reg for 'zipping' Network 23's satellite (hijacking the satellite signal in order to send one's own programming) to protect his fellow ACS students. Only when it becomes clear that Reg will indeed suffer harm (zipping is a capital offense, and in the absence of evidence arrested Blanks, who have no computer records, are assigned the profiles of unidentified criminals) does Bryce find a way to exonerate Reg – though without implicating ACS ('The Academy'). The indications of Bryce's superior status are often tongue-in-cheek, as when he greets the challenge of hacking the security of Security Systems' A-7 with 'Cracking the ice around it should be fun – kind of like challenging God himself.' In the same episode, trapped and condemned to freezing to death with Edison, Bryce expresses regret not for any of his actions, but for never being able 'to complete my collection of the original He-Man and the Masters of the Universe.' 'How much more clear,' asks Steinhauer rhetorically, 'and yet how much more veiled, can the matter be, when such revelations, in the guise of 'jokes', are hidden in plain sight before us?' Needless to say, not all readers will share Steinhhauer's conviction.

Martyn Dumfries' own chapter, 'Ben Cheviot: Hegelian World-Spirit Incarnate?' is both modestly placed near the end of the anthology and relatively modest in its aim: to demonstrate that the chairman of Network 23 is not merely the positive character he seems to be in comparison with the Machiavellian Ned Grossberg, former head of 23 and later chairman of rival Network 66. Rather, Dumfries claims, 'Ben Cheviot is, quite simply, an embodiment of the historical dialectic, sometimes seemingly good, sometimes apparently bad, moral or immoral, cruel or kind, as the circumstances dictate.' This is nowhere made more evident than in the episode 'Grossberg's Return', in which Cheviot's approval of Edison's investigation of Network 66's political candidate is first given, then withdrawn, and finally given again, in a movement that Dumfries, with the aid of several elegant diagrams, maps as thesis, antithesis and final synthesis.

The real drawing card of this anthology, however, and the sole reason many people will read it, is the presence of 'Theory, Theora Jones, and the Second Sex', by L'Wanetta DuBois-Herkemer of Moo University. DuBois-Herkemer was the prime cause of the controversy that threatened to destroy the entire project, and scholars who have followed her career since her article 'The Subtext of Eugenics and the Conspiracy of Silence in Beatrix Potter's "Jemima Puddle-Duck"' exploded onto the scene in *The Journal of Pre-Postmodern Philology* almost twelve years ago will not be disappointed with her opening gambit here:

If I choose to view *Max Headroom* under the sign of Simone de Beauvoir, it is not to pay its creators a compliment: it is simply appalling that an allegedly avant-garde program in a supposedly enlightened nation could offer a female lead character no further advanced in terms of feminism than de Beauvoir's superseded and deeply contradictory, if historically important, writings ... In her flouncy '40s-cum-'80s chic, labeled a 'controller' yet tied to a computer terminal whose resemblance to an old manual typewriter is no coincidence, Theora Jones is the vital prop to Edison Carter in both senses of the word: already in the pilot, she feeds him every snippet of information he needs, flips the very switch that sends his broadcasts to the world, even defeats the acknowledged prodigy Bryce Lynch in a computer duel to save Edison's life, and yet is treated little better than a faceless drone from the steno pool. When Edison is injured despite her best efforts, she is shown not only defeated, but also objectified, soaked by the car-park sprinklers – the battle of wills becomes a wet tee-shirt contest.

Although she is positioned as a love interest for Edison, and they usually function smoothly as a team, his only intimate heterosexual scene in the series is with another woman ('Deities'); otherwise, his closest relationship is with Max Headroom, whose appearance and name are both overtly phallic, so that 'Edison's self-love is prime time television's first case of on-screen self-abuse, yet nonetheless a triangle is created; if *Max Headroom* were told from Theora's point of view, it would have to be entitled *He Came to Stay*.' Nonetheless, Edison jealously feels betrayed when he calls Theora at night and sees through the view-phone that she is not alone in bed ('Grossberg's Return'). In the same episode, Murray, their producer, tells Theora that it would be good for her career if Edison were interested in her, to which she replies, '*I'm* good for my career.' 'As in de Beauvoir's writings,' DuBois-Herkemer observes, 'Theora walks a knife-edge between the burden of her sexuality and fulfilling, but platonic, relationships; they are, of course, mutually exclusive.' The culmination of the essay is the suggestion that the series was cancelled just as Theora was about to outgrow such weak-kneed feminism:

> It is surely no coincidence that the saga of Theora's development which began in the second episode, 'Rakers', with the suggestion that Theora ought to become a mother, is cut off before 'Baby Grobags', with its frequent mocking of male squeamishness in the face of childbirth – a distaste shared by de Beauvoir – could be aired. Theora categorically rejects, and then exposes, the Ovu-Vat technology that provides her friend Helen with a 'no muss, no fuss' *in vitro* pregnancy. Thus the first sign that Theora is no longer constrained by an outmoded form of feminism is silenced before the event, and *Max Headroom* is reduced to an arrested *Bildungsroman*, the memoirs of a dutiful controller.

DuBois-Herkemer contends that a line of Theora's in the previous episode, 'Lessons', which was the last to be aired, alerted the network to the threat that Theora poses: 'Men are more scared of us [than we are of them].' As the clinching proof, DuBois-Herkemer reveals that the unproduced episode 'Theora's Tale', according to several fan websites, would have unmasked Theora Jones as a millionaire's adopted daughter, who rebelled, chose a working career, and gave up her name: *Simone Best*.

Once this trend was spotted, however, the series was doomed, particularly in the context of the patriarchal ideological messages being sent by ABC's most popular programs at the time: *Highway to Heaven*, *Growing Pains*, *Who's the Boss?*, and its newest hit, *The Wonder Years*, 'which comforted its audience by sending them twenty years into the past rather than "twenty minutes into the future".' Clearly, this essay is going to unleash a controversy and, hopefully, some powerful responses.

As an unusual coda, Dumfries adds a brief afterword, in which he expresses his confidence that the anthology marks 'a Copernican revolution in our view of the *aporia* that is *Max Headroom*.' I can willingly second this opinion; and as Dumfries moves on to his next major project, *The Brontës' Secret Authorship of the Barchester Novels*, we can only hope that another editor can build on his momentum to produce a less abstruse collection, dealing with such vital questions as why Murray has no last name (or, as I maintain, no *first* name); how the world of the near future has no cell phones and yet nobody remembers what books or cinemas are; and why the only private cars are old Studebakers. In short, the time is now ripe for a *Nitpicker's Guide*; and so, regarding *Max Headroom*, we can confidently say with Blank Reg in 'Body Banks': 'Remember when we said there was no future? Well, this is it.'

soap opera

*The Semiotics of Days of Our Lives: The Possession of
Marlena Evans as a Pedagogical Means of Interpretation*
by Kristen Susan Wortham-Quinn
Salem: Coma Books, 2000

reviewed by Mark J. Charney

Although E. D. Hirsch, Jr., Stanley Fish, and David Bleich offer convincing methods of literary interpretation, Dr. Kristen Susan Wortham-Quinn believes that Robert Scholes positions his theoretical examination of semiotics most directly in the classroom. In the introduction to her groundbreaking study, *The Semiotics of Days of Our Lives: The Possession of Marlena Evans as a Pedagogical Means of Interpretation*, she points to Scholes' assertion in *Semiotics and Interpretation* that 'the student's productivity is the culmination of the pedagogical process'. According to Wortham-Quinn, Scholes feels that instructors should teach 'interpretation,' not literature, thus inspiring perceptive students to produce interpretive texts, not thematically judgmental essays or personal confessions. Only through interpretive texts, which Wortham-Quinn terms I.T.'s (not to be confused with T.'s or traditional themes), does she feel students fully comprehend the meaning of critical study, the backbone of analytical thought.

Citing the recent demonic possession of a major television icon, Marlena Evans (Deidre Hall) as the basis for her study of producing I.T.'s, Wortham-Quinn carries Scholes' defense of semiotics one step further: 'Whereas the learned Professor Scholes justifies semiotics as a pedagogical tool using literary figures such as Ernest

Hemingway and James Joyce, my approach is more basic, more applicable to students of twentieth-century culture and media. Face it. Students today are less interested in these literary figures than they are in popular culture, and if you want them to understand semiotics, the best theoretical form that encourages interpretive thought, we should begin using a form appreciated by a lion's share of the public – soap operas.' She explains that, based on current semiological research, this controversial decision is not shocking or even original: 'After all, Roland Barthes uses semiotics to decode the Eiffel Tower, and Scholes to uncode a female's private parts. Soap operas are infinitely more universal than either (at least more universally *discussed*, anyway).'

In her introduction, Wortham-Quinn defends her choice of *Days* over the more popular *Young and the Restless*: 'While more television viewers certainly watch *Y & R* (the show regularly earns one or two Nielsen points more than *Days*), only *Days* has been daring enough to incorporate elements of true horror into its weekly programming, and carry it off for more than a year!' She cites theorists Robin Wood, Dana B. Polan, and J. P. Telotte, filmmakers William Friedkin, Wes Craven, and Tobe Hooper, and novelists Dean Koontz, Stephen King, and John Saul as likely influences of much of the possession story line, and insists that only readers who 'delineate the temporal, incidental, spatial diegesis of a text; recognize intertextual cultural, enigmatic, connotative, and symbolic codes; and explore related interdisciplinary material will most likely produce "an interpretive text of their own".'

Many critics have already attacked Wortham-Quinn for what they feel is essentially a study which panders to students too lazy to read the classics, one which surrenders to the demands of a Generation X mentality. They question the organization of the work, pointing out that it leans too heavily on Scholes' *Semiotics and Interpretation*, and they accuse her of patterning her analysis, especially in the first three chapters, directly after his. Although I sympathize with this argument, let me assert that, in spite of embarrassing similarities between the two works, there is at least a shred of method to Wortham-Quinn's madness. While I certainly challenge her too-lengthy defense of her choice of soap operas (the comparison to *Y & R* comprises much of the introduction) and note with dissatisfaction how much her work depends upon *Semiotics and Interpretation*, unlike other critics I do not believe that such detours undermine the quality of the entire book. No, like it or not, the audacity and more than occasional paucity of her arguments are often eclipsed by true sparks of insight. Wortham-Quinn has fashioned a study that will have an effect, not only on the teaching of semiotics, but, more importantly, on the future of pedagogy in the English classroom.

Wortham-Quinn begins Chapter One, 'The Humanities, Soap Operas, and Semiotics', by supposedly revising the popular Roman Jakobson model detailing the act of communication emphasized in Scholes' first chapter, 'The Humanities, Criticism, and Semiotics'. As most of us know, the Jakobson model diagrams the communication act as composed of six elements:

```
contexts
text
author – – – – – – – – – – – – – – – – – – reader
medium
codes
```

Wortham-Quinn claims to reinvent the diagram by shifting some of the pertinent words to include visual media, but as critics have essentially pointed out, the shifts in word choice reveal a shallow and possible desperate means to create something new out of something old:

```
contexts
visual texts
director/producer – – – – – – – – – – – – – – reader
media
codes
```

Such a distinction, admittedly, does not bode well for establishing the originality of the study, or for justifying her choice of *Days* as a vehicle for increased pedagogical potential, especially since Wortham-Quinn never defines in detail the differences between the new six elements of communication and their counterparts. Is anything really shifted in her 'revised' communication model except the medium itself – the shift from verbal to visual? The remaining material in the chapter is patterned almost directly after Scholes' similarly titled first chapter, especially her tracing how differing emphases upon each of the above six elements align themselves with specific critical emphases (from authorial to reader response, from Marxism to New Criticism). At this point, we are more likely to view Wortham-Quinn's book as an act of plagiarism.

In Chapter Two, 'Toward a Semiotics of Soap Operas', Wortham-Quinn fares no better than she does in Chapter One, especially in her odd comparison between what Scholes terms 'literariness' and her own term, 'viewability'. Whereas Scholes suggests essentially that the duplicity of messages and/or the doubling of contexts make a work 'literary', Wortham-Quinn concentrates more heavily on the multilayered meanings behind the visual presentations of abstract concepts, especially those emphasized in soap operas, such as love, evil, or commitment. 'To make a work "viewable",' Wortham-Quinn explains, 'directors must depict concepts that we wrestle with through several varying perspectives. Pure evil, as represented in the thirty years of *Days*, for example, is rooted firmly in characters such as Stephano DiMera, the "Phoenix" who rises from the dead each time he is supposedly murdered, or Victor Kiriakis, the mogul who threatens the residents of Salem with power encouraged by his financial prowess.' These recognizable character types are flat, uninteresting, in other words, according to Wortham-Quinn, *'unviewable'*. Comparing these figures to evil characters in other soap operas, she contends that such repetition of character types promotes redundancy while it undermines the entire canon: 'Stephano, as originated, resembles any number of characters from other soaps! It took introducing the devil itself, not one of its minions or even a minor evil figure from Hell, to truly explore the multivaried levels of evil and to make Stephano a deeper, more complex, more fascinating figure.'

While her intentions to discredit the flat characters that soap operas have been relying on for years is admirable, I question the distinction she makes here between 'literariness' and 'viewability'. According to Scholes, the elements of true 'literariness' are codified by six conventions of duplicity – 'of sender, receiver, message, context, contact, and code' – and although we have no reason to go into detail here about the specifics of each convention, Scholes delineates effectively the purpose of each, using three literary forms: play, novel, and poem. Wortham-Quinn's definition of 'viewability', on the other hand, seems very personally related to her opinion of what is unique, original, or daring in television programming; in other words, a show like *Twin Peaks* would certainly be more 'viewable' than *Baywatch*, but where is the codification in this? Instead of relying on semiotics to perpetuate a method of analysis or critical inquiry, Wortham-Quinn is more concerned with praising a story line she finds exciting. At this point in the study, I began seriously to wonder whether this text could possibly lead to the production of I.T.s, even for the student population.

Perhaps inspired by Martha Nochimson's study, *No End to Her: Soap Opera and the Female Subject*, Wortham-Quinn radically improves the quality of her study in the third chapter, 'From Prostitute to Psychiatrist: The Female Professional in *Days of Our Lives*'. One critic cynically remarked that possibly the author was forced to venture into new territory because Scholes' third chapter, 'Semiotics of the Poetic Text', which examines the elliptical nature of poetic utterances, is too complex for Wortham-Quinn to attempt to imitate. Although the structure of Chapter Three is loosely tied to Nochimson's chapter entitled '*Days of Our Lives*: Energizing the Narrative of the Couple', Wortham-Quinn emphasizes the individual over the couple. In spite of the fact that much of the theory that frames the work depends too heavily on Scholes' explanation of semiotics, in Chapter Three, Wortham-Quinn begins to stand on her own.

And what does this stand yield? Beginning with a discussion of the professionless state of most of the females in the show, from matriarch Alice Horton to busybody Vivian Kiriakis, Chapter Three analyzes in depth the cultural, enigmatic, connotative, and symbolic codes of such jobless females in the early 1990s. From this specific breakdown of the codes and characters related to joblessness, she proceeds to concentrate on popular jobs held by *Days*' women, from prostitute Kimberly Brady to candy striper Jamie Caldwell, from police woman Hope Brady to psychiatrist Marlena Evans. Although, as a reviewer, I do not have the luxury to summarize all of the strong observations that Wortham-Quinn makes, a glance at her decoding of the profession of psychiatrist, as illustrated by Marlena Evans and Laura Horton, proves that the author not only understands the nature of semiotics, but can also apply the theory to the classroom.

According to Wortham-Quinn, it is not surprising that two of the most prominent psychiatrists on *Days* have been women, both substantial members of the Salem community, both wealthy, beautiful, respected by fellow characters and audiences alike. Wortham-Quinn begins her semiotic analysis by explaining that the model she describes will later be adapted into a heuristic device for students, but at this point she primarily wishes to indicate the worth of decoding by delineating its methodology. First, she discusses the feminine nature of psychiatry, as depicted on *Days* in general terms, and explains why, based on traditional gender expectations, most psychiatrists will be female. Then, Wortham-Quinn decodes the profession, using the following codes:

Cultural: Wortham-Quinn associates the insight afforded a psychiatrist on *Days* to the feminine-*elan* of the soul; in other words, the profession heightens the conventionally female elements of internal analysis, from patience to empathy, and although it commands respect from the male members of the community, the softer elements of psychiatry contrast with the rougher elements of manhood. As defined by *Days*, these elements include rashness, violence, and the tendency to protect (often making male characters seem like affectionate, but hotheaded father figures or policemen). Culturally, then, *Days'* writers seem to align the psychiatric profession almost fully with traditional medical practices, and although fully-fledged doctors who can save lives are usually males on the show (whose hotheadedness comes in handy in surgery), the psychiatrist is usually nearby, offering sound advice from the heart and the spirit. The chapter discusses Dr. Evans in detail, and how she fits into this mold, making her a surprising choice for the eventual possession story line.

Enigmatic: Because Dr. Evans is one of the most respected characters on the show, almost always choosing the safe, conservative path and thinking of others above herself, she is a perfect choice for the Desecrator. By choosing one of the most respected and beloved members of the Salem community to perform deeds unspeakable on most television shows, *Days'* writers heighten the enigmatic code, literally using the puzzle 'Why and How Marlena?' for months to increase suspense and drive plot lines. Soap operas already base much of their interest on enigmatic codes, leaving audiences with gaps filled in after commercials and between episodes, but using the immensely-respected psychiatrist as the Devil's pawn doubles the narrative significance of this code, keeping audiences hooked.

Connotative and *Symbolic*: In this section, which jointly examines two very different codes, Wortham-Quinn simply lists many of the concepts and terms associated with the psychiatry profession, especially as it is defined from the perspective of soap operas. The list includes words such as healer, judge, doctor, insight, mind, capability, kindness, strength, self-reliance, faith, knowledge, revelation, change, truth, and honesty, among many others. To distinguish connotative from symbolic, Wortham-Quinn explains that the former is linked to the specific period (the year, contemporary history, and the like), while the latter is related to meaning within specific episodes. For example, whereas society in the 1990s has demystified psychiatry, making it a profession ultimately associated with sciences of the mind (connotative code), *Days* specifically associates psychiatry with religion, making it symbolize spiritual growth and change as well (symbolic code). Only in this section is Wortham-Quinn unclear about the distinction between these two codes, but the connotative benefits of such a study outweigh the lack of clarity a muddied association between the two codes perpetuates.

Although this abbreviated version of Wortham-Quinn's analysis ignores some of the insight and much of the description Chapter Three offers, it at least illustrates that the author begins to use the theory cribbed from Scholes to good effect. She admirably defends the choice of Dr. Evans as a subject for possession, and explains in detail how the possession and exorcism enrich and thicken the already convoluted plot. Like Scholes, she even compares her semiotic analysis to those of Tzvetan Todorov, as illustrated in his *Grammaire du Decameron*, and Gerard Genette, from *Narrative Discourse*, proving that her methodology is more student-friendly than either of the other two. She ends this chapter by justifying in very practical terms the emphasis on soap operas: 'If students can't decode Marlena's possession, how can they even begin to approach stories as subtle as Hemingway's *Cat in the Rain* or Joyce's *Eveline*? Let's start at the beginning, for God's sake – or for our students' sake at least.'

In Chapter Four, 'Exorcism and Redemption: Male Salvation Figures in *Days of Our Lives*', Wortham-Quinn discusses primarily the role of John Black (Drake Hogestyn), winner of the 1996 *Soap Opera Digest* award for Best Hero. She justifies this narrow emphasis by explaining that the traits John exhibits as hero apply as well to Bo Brady, Abe Carver, and Austin Reed, among others, and she uses the *Digest* description as a blueprint for the salvation figure in general:

> Other heroes save their damsels in distress; John saves *anyone* in distress. He fought the devil and won. He survived the gas chamber. He was rescued in the *nick* of time from the guillotine. He climbed the Eiffel Tower to save his aunt. And he did it all without a trace of ego, or a moment of asking, 'What's in it for me?' John is a hero in the purest sense of the word.

Based on the connotative and symbolic codes discussed in Chapter Three, Wortham-Quinn explains that it is not surprising that the *Days'* writers make John a priest during the exorcism, giving him the knowledge and the power to perform religious conversions. If the symbolic coding she discusses above were to hold true, then only a priest who also has the qualities shared by a soap opera hero (as so thoroughly delineated by *Soap Opera Digest*) could perform such sacrificial acts without expectations of reward. Wortham-Quinn may find fault with the temporary manner in which John is transformed into a man of the cloth (only for this sequence of the soap), especially as compared to the hapless but believable Father Francis (Charles Welch/Eric Christmas), but she justifies the improbable suspension of disbelief with the codes she breaks down to describe the ultimate battle between good and evil, especially as indicated by the interfering but lovable archangel Gabe (Mark Colson).

Briefly, this codification focuses very specifically on all of the connotations associated with angels, priests, devils, and evil, not in terms familiar to indiscriminate soap opera audiences, but in a context specifically located in the fight for Marlena's soul. While recounting in very detailed terms all of the duplicitous messages the show sent during this time, shifting expectations and reversing character descriptions, Wortham-Quinn excels at explaining the distinctions between message, context, contact, and code. To accomplish this, she concentrates upon one central show in the possession canon, the final battle between John and the Devil, but she also refers specifically and repeatedly to several other episodes: the one where Father Francis is thrown against a hospital wall; the one which pits a morphed Marlena against a love-struck Stephano; the one in which Kristen is stripped naked, painted with a pentagram, chloroformed, and left in a church to burn; and the series of shows where Salem is attacked by plagues of bees, snakes, and panthers. She is especially adept at tracing the exorcism itself, culling away the attendant nonsensical plots and expected triangles (Jack/Jennifer/Peter) to strip naked the true spirit of the show. Ultimately, the chapter achieves what Wortham-Quinn sets out to accomplish, especially for young students: she takes the simple narrative and imbues it with meaning in terms that most first-time 'semioticians' can understand and appreciate.

Chapter Five is not quite as sharp as the earlier two, but in 'Diegetic, Temporal, and Spatial Elements of the Exorcism Plot', Wortham-Quinn does analyze central organizational elements of the exorcism sequence effectively. Beginning in 1994 and concluding in 1996, the possession sequence seems at first to follow a strict chronological format, but using old *Days'* episodes Wortham-Quinn proves that temporally and spatially the sequence relies heavily on an understanding of previous plot lines, especially as directed by the multiperspective memories of an ensemble cast. The

Days' diegetic line, as defined by Wortham-Quinn, reveals a complexity not shared by most other soaps, one that refers in subtle layers back to previous episodes and challenges viewers to repiece elements of old episodes together with new ones, a device the author calls 'patching'. Although I doubt that 'patching' will remain a valuable source of semiotic analysis, Wortham-Quinn makes it work effectively in this chapter by justifying its strengths as a means of visual analysis, proving that the possession sequence is more sophisticated than viewers may originally think.

In the final chapter, 'Creating I.T.'s: Heuristics for Beginning Critical Analysts', Wortham-Quinn takes the codes she has demystified and arranges them into interesting heuristics for students in beginning writing or literary theory classes. Breaking down the codes into segments of critical analysis, she forces students to approach each course assignment through a similar thought process. For example, when discussing enigmatic codes, she takes all of the puzzles created by the exorcism plot, among them questions such as 'Why is Kristen so often a victim?'; 'How does the Desecrator depend on Stephano's influence?'; 'Why does John find himself drawn to Gabe?'; and 'How does Gabe fit into the puzzle?' Wortham-Quinn arranges these plot-specific questions around categories such as character, narrative, exposition, and climax, giving students a method to incorporate terms they have learned in high school with new theories of 'reading', and she continues this with codes of enigma, connotation, symbolism and culture (among others that appear less often and are more directed around plot points in specific cases, like love triangles or societal upheavals). The sixteen heuristics she provides should give professors of English, writing, or popular culture methods to encourage semiotic thought without being overbearing, and the final section of the chapter, which teaches instructors how to create their own heuristics and topics for writing, is extremely helpful.

So what begins embarrassingly as an imitation of Scholes' *Semiotics and Interpretation* actually ends as a popular culture examination that has real if limited value, not only for the theorist but also for the soap opera enthusiast. As a reviewer and professor myself, I am not certain that I agree we should begin teaching students in college by relying on soap operas, but as Executive Producer Ken Corday says in *Days of Our Lives: The Complete Family Album*, 'There are likely three or four generations watching *Days of Our Lives*. Daytime dramas, this show in particular, make an important contribution to society. It's studied not only in entertainment courses but in philosophy and psychology courses, too. Yet this is not brain surgery. It's very simple in a very intricate way. It is simple and well woven.' In Corday's eyes, and in the eyes of Wortham-Quinn, beginning the study of semiotics and interpretation with Hemingway, Faulkner, or Joyce would be like training the doctor by throwing him into surgery rather than providing him with the tools that he or she can use to save lives. 'Begin at the beginning,' Wortham-Quinn warns in her Conclusion, 'or instead of saving lives, we may be destroying them!' Her examination of semiotics through the eyes of the residents of Salem may sometimes be as confusing as this medical analogy, but, for professors who wish to teach their students how to compose effective and challenging I.T.s, and for *Days* enthusiasts, the study has merit.

Daytime Dialogism: Erica's Eroica in the Pine Valley Village
by Hillary Rodham Clinton 'Smith'
Washington, DC: Presidential Partner Press, 1996

Acronym for Alterity: AMC and the Subaltern
by D. Raymond Gardner
Carolina: Berngergy Press, 1996

reviewed by Brenda R. Weber

Perhaps the most formative work legitimating the multi-textuality of popular culture literatures has come from Martha Stewart Radway in her *Reading the Roll, Man* (1988). Radway's now-canonical text on the counter-cultural[1] activity of forming discourse communities and responding to the 'from a mix' intellectual cooking industry has spawned the devotion of scores of former 'from scratch' devotees. Part of the appeal is Radway's underscoring of a tri-partite matrix in which 'readers' pleasure/choice/taste, the publishing industry, and the baker/writer each play a part in determining textual production'. Radway in a rad(ical)way redefined for many what serious scholarship and spectatorship can mean, but applications of her ground-breaking theories into other areas of the popular culture milieu have been sparse[2] until the recent publication of two long-overdue monographs on the crucial television text: *All My Children*. After years of exacting scholarship and meticulous notetaking, Hillary Rodham Clinton 'Smith'[3] has produced *Daytime Dialogism: Erica's Eroica in the Pine Valley Village* (Washington, DC: Presidential Partner Press, 1996), and with similar passion, though not similar thoroughness, D. Raymond Gardner has recently written *Acronym for Alterity: AMC and the Subaltern* (Carolina: Berngergy Press, 1996). Though neither 'Smith' nor Gardner evaluates *All My Children* on the basis of

Radway's template (nor does either particularly notice the strong Marxist element of Radway's text, discuss the ideological ramifications of cultural production, attend to cyber-technic polymorphism or third world domination), these texts open a seam for discussion and serve as the seeds for what will assuredly become a robust and healthy canon of the finest soap opera produced in the early twenty-first century. 'Smith' and Gardner do, however, provide striking evidence to build further on Radway's central tenet that 'all foundational principles should be served with crescent rolls' (a clever euphemism, part of an extended metaphor, in which Radway draws a connection between bread and the Transcendent). 'Smith' does this by relating the Pine Valley heroine extraordinaire to one of literature's most enduring heroines, Catherine Earnshaw from *Wuthering Heights*. Gardner makes his connection to Radway's notion of the staff of life by arguing that the absent voice of fathers equals a void functioning as the very vortex of the cosmos. Though I argue that 'Smith's' contention is more credible than Gardner's, both deserve the highest commendation for recognizing and contributing to this emerging field of scholarship. Others have made similar attempts to establish the AMC body of scholarship[4] but their ideas were too progressive to hold cultural sway. Now that we've undergone a paradigm shift and can perceive the meritocritous value of network programming, the ground has been prepared: the farmer is at the ready, the fertilizer is available in abundant heaps, the plow has done its work, the land lies awaiting those very seeds mentioned earlier, and we can only hope the mighty oak will grow.

Let us look first at Hillary Rodham Clinton 'Smith' and *Daytime Dialogism*. 'Smith' is a relatively new writer in academic circles, although she has done some mainstream press publications in the past. In her last book, intended for an extra-academic audience, she used as a central theme 'it takes a village'. In *Daytime Dialogism*, Smith's central thesis is 'it's only a village, godammit!' emphasizing the seeming remoteness, even positionless-ness of Pine Valley.[5] The writerly voice 'Smith' employs is clear and compelling, although some might argue a bit too strident, even shrill. And this is, indeed, a shame, for it relegates 'Smith's' own feminist consciousness to a desolate Pine Valley of its own. Perhaps in some effort to keep her voice as a part of the mainstream dialogism, 'Smith' offers the reader a series of recipes to go along with the different chapters,[6] combining domestication and dialogism in a way which is sure to open intellectual doors while it simultaneously polishes the brass of the door knob. 'Smith' makes her points clearly and decisively. Her commitment to narrative breadth is impressive. Few scholars would be able to devote the sheer number of hours in scholarship or concentrate throughout the demanding schedule which 'Smith' has clearly applied to her viewership of AMC. It is no wonder that 'Smith' dropped out of the public eye as she prepared to write this exhaustive tome.

'Smith' draws heavily on the work of Dale Bauer, a feminist rhetorician who argues in *Feminist Dialogics* that female characters often 'misinterpret their social texts and therefore fail to understand their own social power'. As such, women in textual spaces often 'represent the struggle for women's construction of self within a dialogic structure of many competing voices' (Emerson, notes on the back cover). Both 'Smith' and Bauer lean heavily on Bakhtin's notion of heteroglossia[7] and indeed, the conversations of Pine Valley are heteroglossia at its Heideggerian utmost. What 'Smith' makes clear in the central character of Erica, however, is the lack, quite frankly the absolute dearth, of appropriate dialogic partners (would

Erica ever talk to Brooke?).[8] Erica, like Lily Bart in Wharton's *The House of Mirth*, struggles to develop a female consciousness which can give rise to her distinctive feminist subjectivity, and like Catherine Earnshaw in Emily Brontë's classic *Wuthering Heights*, Erica Kane is a passionate free spirit, in love with a dark and exotic man, yet confined by the stifling smallness of her remote provincial town. Both Catherine and Erica follow similar cyclical journeys, paths which could also be likened to the heroic descent and return of Odysseus and Gingrich. In *Wuthering Heights*, Catherine begins as Catherine Earnshaw, she wants to be Catherine Heathcliff, and she eventually becomes Catherine Linton. Her daughter, the younger Cathy, begins as Catherine Linton, is for a brief time Catherine Heathcliff, and will become at novel's end Catherine Earnshaw, thus enacting a classic circle of wholeness. 'Smith' points out that part of Erica's great passion (her eroica) is a similar sort of journey, though Erica's route is far more arduous. She begins as Erica Kane and starts the slow progression alphabetically through the men in her village, both eligible and not, becoming Erica Chandler in her marriage(s) to Adam, Erica Cuddahy in her marriage to Tom, Erica Merrick in her (three) marriages to Dimitri, Erica Montgomery in her marriage to Travis, and entertaining a host of alphabetic possibilities in her love affairs with Jeremy Hunter, Nick Martin, Mike Ross, Jackson Montgomery, and Charlie Martin. 'Smith' points out clearly: this eight-times-wed Erica is a far stronger and more potent vessel of passion than a Catherine Earnshaw ever could have represented, and as 'Smith' argues most persuasively, this suggests that Pine Valley must be more desolate, more remote, more eerily haunting than the moors of Haworth could ever be, either in the fictive imaginary cooked up by three coughing sisters or on a very real and very rainy day in December when one is trying to get across the country for a Christmas dinner in Sheffield. In one nice move, then, 'Smith' undoes a cultural hierarchy of high art, placing Erica in a much-earned (even if she had trouble getting an Emmy) position of cultural dominance.

For the most part, the book is an excellent example of the good work which will finally highlight the integrity of this daytime drama, though there are some small problems. For instance, 'Smith' uses as a central premise the notion that Pine Valley is remote, yet this reviewer has to ask how it is that Erica can move from Seattle to Pine Valley to New York City to Paris within twenty minute intervals? How can she be seen at Linden House and Wildwind and out and about in Pine Valley all in the span of 44 minutes and 14 outfits? Clearly, Erica Kane is a possessor of talents which extend far beyond the ordinary, and this seems a point which 'Smith' is woefully remiss in addressing. Further, I have to question the application of Bakhtin to the Pine Valley text. Yes, indeed, hetero-glossia, hetero-geneity, and hetero-sexuality are central issues in Pine Valley. But frankly, Bakhtin would make a woeful addition to the Pine Valley community, although he might be interesting for an episode or two due to his salty ways, his method of hiding from Soviet dictatorship, and his clever devices for surviving work camps in Siberia, but the novelty of him would soon wear off, staining the show like so much nicotine rubbed into so many fingers, a nasty smoker's cough remaining where he had once been, black tar on a pink lung. In the words of Erica Kane, 'Oh, that is just too disgusting to think about.'

D. Raymond Gardner's work is slightly less disgusting imagistically, though his piece is not as comprehensively researched as that of 'Ms. Smith' and his writing lacks the zest and punch of her prose. But perhaps the reviewer can forgive him this cumbersome and sometimes sporadic piece of writing given the fact that until recently Gardner was considered to be dead. The last anyone knew of this renowned scholar, he had been blown up in a freak accident (while his teen model daughter Jenny and her good-looking though insufferably preppy boyfriend Greg Nelson looked on. Many thought the bomb might really be intended for Jenny, as planted by the vile Liza Colby who had the hots for Greg, though she later shifted her attention to Tad, Jenny's brother, though Tad couldn't decide between Liza and her mother Marian and so dated them both, but Liza got her revenge 12 years later by sleeping with Tad and ruining his marriage with Dixie and is now getting further revenge in pretending she and Adam are engaged as a ruse to incite Tad and Brooke's jealousy. Tad, on the other hand, is more interested in Gloria than the nefarious Liza. Tsk, tsk, ladies. When will you ever learn? Tad the Cad never changes his spots.) At any rate, Ray Gardner has indeed returned from the dead, and I owe apologies to Dr. Chauncy Bortman who has maintained in several first-rate articles that Ray Gardner would breathe the air of scented pines in the valley yet again.[9] He appears to be finally vindicated in his long-held opinion.[10]

Gardner's central premise is an intriguing one and is the best evidence yet that there must be an extraordinary lending library in purgatory, or wherever Gardner has been convalescing these many years. Gardner's awareness is really up to speed on subaltern theory and third world dialectics, and he shows that knowledge in a good light, arguing that it is not women, or people of color (my euphemism – Gardner's terms would insult even Bakhtin's fellow work-camp mates), or the poor, or native groups who speak from the unprivileged privilege of the margin, but that white fathers are the absent and therefore the insistent voiceless minority in our culture. This certainly plays out in the zone of Pine Valley, where nary a child has been raised by his biological father since the show began in 1960. Using the textual evidence of his own son Tad (who is now undergoing his own erasure as a father since Jamie is living with Brooke and Junior, who isn't even his biological son anyway, and has moved to Pigeon Hollow with Dixie), Gardner argues that absent fathers create absent spaces, a kind of black hole which draws attention to itself. That magnetic pull, Gardner contends, is undeniable, inalterable. As such, missing/mis-named/ignorant/once, twice, and thrice dead fathers constitute the fulcrum of the universe. In making such an assertion, Gardner lays out the conceptual territory in which he can tease out meaning, thus revealing a teeming subaltern zone. Gardner contends that characters in *All My Children* possess a capacity to remember (and in his case to re-member; how did he get his hand back, anyway?). Citizens of Pine Valley can recognize the ideal form upon which all else is based, and through this process of recognition and rememory, they are led through the vortex of the black hole into a ideal space of bliss.

As a reviewer and long-term scholar of *All My Children*, I find Gardner's ideas extraordinarily appealing, but patently absurd. To his credit, his notions are more persuasive than the other black hole conspiracy theory recently put forth by J. Grau-chuss, who argues that Husserl, Heidegger, Hitler and Heime the Clown (soon to be revealed as Langley's illegitimate circus son) form a cadre called the 4-H club, also unbeatable, also intensely magnetic, also like a metaphoric black hole in the universe of culture. It's all tripe. What these notions do is lift the text out of itself, extrapolating into a zone which is more appropriate for star trekkers than television watchers. Certainly, television can give us momentary transference into the 'other', but we know where that transportation stops. Soap operas are the substance of the real; they do not strive for the metaphysical except in their stunning, and occasionally self-parodying, analysis of the physical. Admittedly, *All My Children* represents the peak of the soap market, but it is a peak firmly grounded, a Mt. McKanely if you will. Certainly, there are elements of the ideal in cultural texts, but I am much more inclined to side with 'Smith' who, when it comes to ideas of the Transcendent, leaves the concept in the physical and rightly gives the last word on the sublime to Erica: 'You're forgetting, we have a secret weapon, moi. I'm Erica Kane, silly.'

Notes

1   I use the word 'counter-cultural' here which may be confusing to many. Martha Stewart Radway once represented the epitome of scholarly cooking refinement. Her exacting attention to detail set the standard for responsible scholarship. However, Radway underwent a truly transformative conversion of the mind while stranded in her Connecticut hideaway one cold winter weekend. Surrounded there with only tubes of Pillsbury roll-ups and powdered cake mix, Radway made the astounding discovery that the Transcendent lay not in the 'from scratch' of the bourgeoisie but in the 'from a mix' production systems of the proletariat. Radway daringly shifted her position and set out a far more complicated system of analysis which voiced the mainstream view, or so the academic community expected. However, the modest Radway had under-estimated her former influence, which had weighted the scales of cooking on the sides of 'from scratch'. In taking the 'from a mix' side, then, Radway adopted the voice of the subaltern, thus opening up a new niche for intellectual work, a brilliant move on the part of Radway which has provided inestimably valuable information about margarine-alized cultures and their caloric intake.

2   A reliable source reports that Drs. Lucius Beljang and Wyblad Glisnic will reunite as collaborate partners and are now working on what they hope will be the definitive text employing Radway's radical ways and the psycho-thermo dynamics of the kitchen, particularly in relation to adolescent females. Their working title is *The Nexus of Mash(ed) Potatoes and Turkey Hash: Comfort Food for the Over-Stimulated Television Generation*. This will be a follow-up, of sorts, to their *Mush Brains! Unite* text which served as a rallying cry in the Sixties for a generation of despondent television addicts.

3   It seems obvious to the reviewer that 'Smith' is endeavoring to hide her true identity amidst a not-so-clever subterfuge of pseudonymic adoption. This reviewer is very fond of the former First Lady, but she would, perhaps, have been more successful had she followed her own recent advice while speaking with the Australians and put a bag over her head. 'Smith' takes a page from Rodney King in trying to 'just get along'. Consequently, as a nice gesture of flexibility and use value, the book comes in a Madonna-esque mylar wrapper which can be used either to cover the face or for food storage and hair cellophane treatments.[3.1]

3.1   'Ms. Smith' follows in a long line of other First Ladies who have grown dismayed at the level of efficacy allowed to them as presidential partners. Almost all of these eminent women write in the field of pop culture and have been contributing anonymously to the growing field of cultural studies. See *Political Pumps:*

There's More to Sensible Shoes Than a Two-Inch Heel, which argues that all of the following texts are products of stifled and stultified First Ladies: *Millie, Me and Modernity: Marginalization at the Edges of Kennebunkport* by Babs Bush 'Smith'; *Genderbubbles: Lawrence Welk's Penchant for Cross Dressing* by Lady Bird Johnson 'Smith'; *Discipline and Punish: Adultery in America* by Jackie Kennedy 'Smith'; and *What's War Got to Do with It: Ike and Tina in the Vietnam Years* by Mamie Eisenhower 'Smith'.[3.1.1]

3.1.1 *Hints from the Highest Office* argues that other first ladies have chosen to write self-help books under assumed names. Many scholars agree that Nancy Davis Reagan 'Smith's' *The Rules: Listen to Me!* is one such text. There is heated debate, however, about the authorship of *If You Were Married to Him, You'd Take Them Too,* a gripping tell-all account of one woman's addiction to alcohol and drugs, attributed to over 37 First Ladies and several runner-ups including Kitty Dukakis 'Smith', Pat Nixon 'Smith', and Betty Ford 'Smith'.[3.1.1.1]

3.1.1.1 Betty Ford, whether smith-ful or smith-less, has a story of great importance to tell, considering that the protagonist of *All My Children* and of Hillary Rodham Clinton 'Smith's' *Daytime Dialogism,* Erica Kane, recently spent time recovering from an addiction to prescription pain killers at the Betty Ford Center. This reviewer, for one, hopes Betty will realize her civic duty and educate the public about Erica's eroica in de-tox.

4 The reader here is reminded of a mid-1970s to early 1980s attempt on the part of Carol Burnett to bring national attention to this cultural treasure. In a move both daring and intellectually on the cutting edge, Burnett invited 'Phillip' up from the audience on her variety show so that he might feel her hip replacement and see tonsular spectacle up close as she whortled out her Tarzan impersonation. Burnett did some masterful intertextual boundary crossing, playing the part of Langley's long-lost and illegitimate circus daughter, a role which was crushingly cut short when Burnett's character ran off with a buff motorcycle hunk. For more recent efforts see Rosie O'Connell's 'I love de two of yas' in *Women, Television, and Society,* 14, 14–37. Unlike Burnett, O'Connell has made nice efforts to strengthen the Marxist ideological bent as depicted in and domesticated by the AMC venue, Pine Valley. Her forthcoming book *Marx, K-Mart and Mark (ya know, Erica's long-lost brother, de one who had AIDS or something): When Consumer Culture and Pine Valley Collide* elucidates even more clearly her commitment to commercial objectives as enhanced by passionate viewership.

5 Although observant viewers will have noted in the recent Jonathan-Kinder-pushed-down-the-stairs-wrapped-in-an-oriental-rug,-stuffed-in-Erica's-car-and-then-buried?-in-her-flower-garden sub-plot that Erica drove a car with Pennsylvania plates. The reliability of this as a spatial marker, however, is dubious given that Erica was driving a silver Honda. Why would a woman who has a million dollars in rare jewels in her bedroom safe drive a Honda? Obviously, the creators of this show are skilfully deploying postmodern tropes seemingly to orient but actually to fragment the already collapsing rationality of the story landscape.

6 Reader's tip: do try the accompanying recipe with Chapter Four, 'Erica in the Age of Enlightenment'. In this pithy chapter detailing moments when Erica is de-duped, 'Smith' provides a piquant and delightful equivalent with her 'Surprise Sugar Cookies'. You'll love serving these butter cookie cakes to your

guests, and they'll love the fantastic fodder you cleverly conceal inside. Note: this recipe is not good for children, though it is an excellent way to dispose of old staples, nails, tacks, and incriminating documents (on this note, see also Pat Nixon 'Smith's' recipe for Erlichman Eclairs in Chapter Three, 'Clever Ways of Getting Rid of Old Problems' in her *Helpful Hints for Around the (White)House*). Also a nice recipe in Hillary's book is the hair tonic in Chapter Nine, 'Which Way to the Wigs? Erica Gets Creative With Hair'. Apparently the author took a page from Erica Kane's book, as the dust jacket features 'Smith' in 15 different head shots. This reviewer's preference was the combination Barbra Streisand/girl from *Friends* 'do', though 'Smith' doesn't quite have the profile or the inanity to pull off either in the original form.

7   Note the common error at play in Bakhtin studies. Bakhtin does not make the hurt stop hurting. However, first aid cream does a fairly nice job.

8   Though note the text's attempt to right the female imbalance by introducing new characters for Erica to bond with. Her new homegirl is Janet (from another planet), a schizophrenic ex-jailbird now trying to walk on the right side of the law. Janet's past is more than checkered, it's check marked, checkmated, and check bounced, and her new face (courtesy of the corrections department and a plastic surgeon) is only mild reassurance that she has given up impersonating those she has unceremoniously dumped down a well.

9   Chauncy Bortman, 'He'll be Back, Mark My Words', *Trends for Television's Future*. Special 1980s edition 14 (1986): 135–70. Bortman, *I'm Still Predictin', He's Still A Comin': Ray Gardner and the Trumpet's Call*, 1988. Chauncy Bortman with Robert Dylan, 'The Times May Be A Changin' but Ray's Pieces Aren't Blowin' in the Wind', in *Conspiracy Theories and the Insane*, ed. O. Stone, 1991.

10 It should be noted that this reviewer has seen no visual evidence of Gardner's return, and she suspects that this book may well indeed be the work of that ever sly S. Pynchon, brother of Thomas, and the model for the new series *Pearl*. Let us not forget the immortal words of S, Thomas's brother, that Pine Valley is 'life, love, heaven, hell – like a lover you can hold in your arms' – which clearly marks him as a believer in the centrality of the AMC influence. Ah, those nutty Pynchons. Always coming up with a new way of cleverly folding themselves into the postmod mainstream while remaining conspicuously absent.

Richard Henry
'The Case of "Donna Quixotic: The Mirror of Uldolpho" (Episode 18)'

The continuing saga of Donna Charlotte Isabel Quixotic's Search for the Marquis'
Library, Rumored to Contain Nearly Three Hundred Romances, Enough to Satisfy a
Lifetime of Delusions.

Scenes from previous episodes:
    Donna Quixotic feigns fainting into the arms of the blond scribe of noble birth
whose quill is long and soft/Donna Quixotic flees on Eurynome, her Shetland pony,
while Paulette, her faithful servant, runs alongside with Gwendolyn, their goat.
Behind, trees sway in a storm and a black knight is struck by lightning.
    Donna Quixotic presents a lock of her flaxen hair to the blond shepherd boy of
noble birth, who tends his flock on the hillsides/Donna Quixotic flees on Eurynome,
her Shetland pony, while Paulette, her faithful servant, runs alongside with Gwendolyn, their goat. Behind, the ground shakes and a black knight falls into a crack in
the earth.
    Donna Quixotic reveals her ankle to a blond mead merchant of noble birth, who
tips his stout to her/Donna Quixotic flees on Eurynome, her Shetland pony, while
Paulette, her faithful servant, runs alongside with Gwendolyn, their goat. Behind, an

enormous book opens, pages flip quickly by with the wind and a black knight disappears as the book slams shut.

Cut to current episode:

Donna Quixotic and Paulette run as if a whirlwind through the tunnels of the castle as it trembles and shakes. A gigantic, almost moaning, breath rushes through the tunnel, pushing them relentlessly along. They gain the library: two shelves of books and a mirror between them. Donna Quixote pulls one book after another from the shelf before her, examines the titles, and quickly tosses them to the floor. On the other side of the mirror, Paulette scans the leather spines until she finds one of interest. Donna Quixote shoves two books into her sack. Suddenly, the entire wall shudders. Both shelves collapse, scattering their contents to the floor. The mirror explodes. They flee.

The forest is dark, sunlight barely reaches the forest floor. In the dimness, the underbrush races by, tearing at their clothes; thorns scrape at Donna Quixotic's unblemished milk-white skin leaving tiny scratches. Above, the trees swirl, driven by the wind, and a rush of air plunges them into a frenzy, so much so that Donna Quixotic is blinded to the fleeting presence of a blond squire even as brambles catch and unknot her bodice, revealing her cleavage. His horse prances at the suddenness of their appearance, their disappearance. The squire is nearly thrown. The wind continues to swirl around them. They scramble and stumble until they collapse into trembling and fitful sleep.

They wake on the edge of the forest – ahead, a vast plain. Donna Charlotte Isabel Quixotic sits, her legs folded under her, great gashes on her arms ooze blood that threatens to forever stain the pure white of her dress. The dress itself sprawls about her, at once covering the ground and hiding her legs. Several romances, fruits of their numerous adventures, lay about. But her attention is focused on the torn piece of paper that she carries close to her heart, wrapped in a handkerchief. Much of the writing had been obliterated by the fire it had so obviously survived, smudged and blackened. Still, she can make out small fragments of the charred sentences it contains and the mysterious *Lennox* that is on the obverse and written in the tentative lettering of a woman's hand. So often had she pined over the scrap of paper, she had nearly memorized its words, if not their import:

This scrap graces her left hand. In her right is a shard of the mirror that had exploded upon their escape. It flashes as the sun catches it, and reveals their flight, the destruction of the castle, its great stones collapsing into dust, their run through the forest, a glimmer of the blond squire, and their wandering across a great plain. She sighs, not once, but three times.

Several yards away, not more than fifty, or less than one hundred, Eurynome and Gwendolyn graze on the shrubberies that slip out from under the forest's canopy. Paulette sits a few feet to one side. She is reading a book of her own, the one she had so recently rescued from the disastrous demise of the castle and its false prince. On the cover: *The Book of Sighs*.

She opens it gently to its Table of Contents; the leather spine nearly cracks. Her fingers are already smudged red from the ancient sheepskin. The vellum is as delicate as the cover, and she tries not to stain it with her fingers. She reads, gently, as if her very eyes will destroy the page before her.

The Book of Sighs

Being a Collocation in Two Parts
For the Edification of All Who May
Read

Kinds of Sighs and their Types
Inanimate

The Wind (always portentous)
  Through Castle Corridors
    Fearsome but Benevolent
  Through trees
    Intensely Emotional but
    Dangerous
  Across Deserted Plains
    Maniacal and Subject to
    Transport, Extremely
    Dangerous

Animate
  Sighs of Dogs
  Sighs of Horses
  Sighs of Fowl
  Sighs of Worms
  Sighs of Fish
  Sighs of Sheep
  Sighs of Birds
  Sighs of Hens
  Sighs of Insects

Human
  Asiatic
  Africanus
  Europa
    NonPurposive
    Purposive
    Sincere
    False

Angels
  Being a Partial Attempt to
    Enumerate What are Too
    Many to Count

God

Treatises on Sighing
  On Sighs
  Against Sighing
  The Beneficent Sigh
  The Polite Sigh
  Courtesy and When to Sigh
  The Courtly Sigh
  Sighing and Poetics
  Sighs Confused with
    Expulsions
  Seventeen True Sighs and
    Their Feignings with
    Especial Attention to
    Their Import in the
    Conveyance of Meaning.

Paulette turns quickly to the Kinds of Sighs made by God, but finds nothing but the sound of ultimate whiteness. She sighs and returns to the Table of Contents.

Again, her mistress emits a sigh as the mirror catches the sunlight and its reflection dances across her face. Paulette, deeply interested in the import of said sigh, turns to the treatise entitled 'Seventeen True Sighs and Their Feignings with Especial Attention to Their Import in the Conveyance of Meaning'. As though that title were not cumbersome enough, Paulette slogs her way through the subtitle: 'Or "The Logic of Sighs" and "Further Notes on Sighs" Brought Together for the First Time in One Volume by HPG.' The more she reads, however, the more useful the treatise promises to be, complicated though it is.

First, there was a careful enumeration of the seventeen kinds of sighs, from Sighs of Regret, of Remorse, of Happiness, of Joy, of True Love and the like. Then there were the careful descriptions of the manner of articulation, including for each kind, the position of the teeth, the lips, the tongue, the sound, if any, made by the voice, the duration and quantity of air expressed from the lungs, the attitude of the head, the slope of the shoulders, and the general curvature of the spine.

Then there were the proscriptions. Any variations in the performances of these features would result in a feigning, which, in and of itself could aid in the conveyance of meaning depending upon the circumstances and the object of the sigh. The author of the treatise explained that these variations fell roughly into four categories: the quality of the performance and each part thereof, the quantity of the performance and each part thereof, the relevance of the performance and each part thereof, and the manner in which the performance and each part thereof was conducted. Again, the author cautioned, any variations could aid in the conveyance of meaning – especially if the variation were on purpose and designed to be recognized by those who would be interpreting the sigh and its signification. Paulette begins to think the import of sighs will be more difficult to interpret than she had hoped.

Donna Quixotic again glances into the mirror, it reflects the sun into a brief flash across her face, and in that flash she sees the blond scribe of noble birth, seated at his table, bent over the parchment, his quill, which was long and soft, in his hand. He had inadvertently revealed his love for her by the flutter of his eyes whenever he saw her as she walked through the castle's large and dimly lit rooms. It was a desperate love, she had determined, one born of absolute devotion. He had written his epistles to her beauty and cast them into the wind with the hope that they might be caught by a kind updraft and delivered through her window. Of course, they had. Of course, she had not deigned to read them. It had not been necessary. She had known what professions of love they'd contained, and he had no right to such professions without undergoing the years of trials and tribulations required of him before she would even consider blessing him with a kind word of encouragement or with the delicate meeting of his gaze. Until then, she had spurned him, as she must, according to the rules of decorum and courtly behavior. But one day, as she'd passed through the dimly lit room, with Paulette at her side, she'd cast a sideways glance at the young scribe and noticed an attitude most disturbing. He had dipped his quill into a bottle of poison and had been about to write a poisoned note to himself in his desperation, and thereby kill himself for his love. She had gasped at his devotion and had quickly raced to the desk, faithful Paulette at her side. He'd looked up, startled, distracted by her beauty, and had caught her as she'd feigned fainting into his arms. She'd fluttered her eyes, once, twice, a dozen times before closing them as if in a permanent swoon. The master had entered and demanded to know what was going one. Paulette had tried to explain, to explain the young scribe's attempt at suicide over his love for Donna Quixote. The scribe had been ushered away by the master's servants. He's looked down at the parchment – it'd been an account of his properties, specifically his animals, the eight carriage horses, three flocks of chickens, and the wild birds that visited the gardens. It is merely an accounting, he said.

Donna Quixotic, who had miraculously recovered from her fit, had denied him. It was clearly an attempted suicide, she'd said, no matter what the sum of the figures. Arguments had been useless and she'd vowed to leave the estate immediately.

Donna Quixotic sighs at the scene before her.

Paulette studies the sigh. It is well articulated. The teeth are slightly parted, not too much, not too little. The air that passes through her teeth, between her lips, is just right, its quantity is perfect as far as she can tell, for a Sigh of Deeply Troubled Consternation. The quality of the expression has been aptly applied, the tilt of her head near perfect in its slight droop downward and to the to the left. She can tell by the performance that the Sigh of Deeply Troubled Consternation is entirely relevant to the scene in the mirror, and that the manner of its production and all parts of it thereof, have been performed as perfectly as humanly possible. Paulette assures herself that this is indeed a True Sigh rather than a Feigned Sigh, and that its import can only match the Sigh it signifies. Paulette herself sighs a sincere Sigh of Relief, or at least she thinks she does and hopes that her mistress has not thought it otherwise. Still, Paulette remains a little baffled – what exactly, she asks herself, is the object of her consternation? Is it directed toward her own violation of the rules of decorum and courtly behavior? Or is it directed toward the young blond scribe's premature attempt at his own life without having bothered to resort to the numerous and varied ways of proving himself a suitable suitor? Or, and this a distinct possibility, is it directed toward the loss of a skilled copyist who might be employed in the reproduction of those books Donna Quixotic so dearly loves? Paulette hardly knows what to think.

Fortunately, she is distracted by another flash of the sun as it strikes the mirror and sends her mistress into another scene from her past. She and her faithful Paulette had fled the estate, and after several days of wandering across the countryside, they'd spied in the distance a young, blond shepherd boy who was obviously of noble birth, Donna Quixotic had assured her attendant. When Paulette had asked how she knew such things, for truly she had seen only a young boy leading his sheep out to pasture in the hills, Donna Quixotic had scoffed. Didn't you seem him glance in our direction? Didn't you see him nearly prostrate himself at the very sight of me? Didn't you see him give a courtly bow as he recovered, a presumptuous gesture from one who has barely had time to prove himself in matters of love, but a gesture born of nobility at the very least.

I thought I saw him trip on a stone, Paulette had said.

One day, returned Donna Quixotic, I will have to instruct you in the ways of decorum and courtly behavior. But, for the moment, that will have to wait – for observe the danger the young noble has placed himself in! I do believe he is about to throw himself under the charging sheep, and thereby kill himself over my beauty! Yoohoo! Yoohoo! She'd cried, and began to run such as she could, across the uneven field. Her feet had been trained for the smoothed stones of the castle and the genuine perfection of the gardens. The stones and other protrubances had positively thrown her balance this way and that until she'd collapsed on the grass, her ankle twisted, her knee scuffed, and a lock of her hair torn from her head. She'd hardly known which to acknowledge with her cry as Paulette had raced to her side. The young shepherd had nearly fallen down the hill in his hurry to assist her with all the means available to him ... which is to say, with no means at all.

As he'd drawn closer and closer, Donna Quixotic had begun to scream. Ravisher! Ravisher! I command you to leave my presence! She'd struggled into Paulette's firm grip and they'd begun to hobble away. The young blond shepherd had hardly known what to do. He'd taken a step closer, only to hear himself condemned once again. A spot of gold had caught his eye, and he'd bent to inspect it. It was nothing less than the lock of her hair, the lock she had so improbably cut from her hair as she fell in hopes that he might keep it close to his heart as he wandered the world in search of adventures by which he might prove his love.

Donna Quixotic sighs a Sigh of Remorse, or at least Paulette thinks it is a Sigh of Remorse. The quality and the quantity of the performance and all of its parts thereof seemed alright, she supposes. The teeth, the lips, the tongue, the sound, the expression of air, the tilt of her head, the slope of her shoulders and the curvature of her spine all conform to the Sigh of Remorse. Indeed the manner of the performance does so, too. But there is something, some small bit of irrelevance to the performance and the context in which it played. Perhaps it is the second Yoohoo! Perhaps it is the lack of a third Ravisher! Perhaps it is the particular glance of the sun on the mirror that she twists in her hand, or a slight flutter of her eye as she looks to see whether or not Paulette is paying attention. Paulette begins to wonder if the Sigh of Remorse is not truly what is signified, but, instead, perhaps, or thereabouts, a Feigned Sigh of Remorse that may, just maybe, convey another kind of sigh altogether, or, indeed, not another kind of sigh but a different sort of meaning altogether! She scans the treatise before her for clarity. The more she scans, the more baffled she grows. Surely it is a feigned sigh. That, the treatise confirms without a doubt. Perhaps it means that she is exactly the opposite in her assessment of ravishment? Perhaps it means that she was entranced by the sun on the mirror and was temporarily blinded? Perhaps it means that she was indeed full of remorse, but for the loss of a source of vellum on which a copyist might transcribe the books she so dearly loved.

Paulette sighs a Sigh of Bafflement just as surely as she can be sure of the slope of her shoulders, the tilt of her head and all like manner of things, for she can not imagine how she looks to those who may be looking at her to confirm the precision of her performance. What if she has gotten something wrong and is actually sighing the Sigh of Lost Temperment?!?

Fortune strikes again, thereby saving her mind from the tumult of interpretations. Donna Quixotic gasps at the next scene that plays before her in the mirror. Paulette nearly gasps herself at the delight she feels at not having taken the Book of Gasps from the shelf in the castle as it had collapsed around her. Sighs are enough to confuse her. Sighs and Gasps would positively boil her brain.

In their wanderings, they had finally gained a promising rescue from their travails. Ahead, Donna Quixotic had said, is a castle of the most elegant kind of castle. Perhaps the Duke, or Marquis, or nobleman who is master of the castle can provide some protection from the wildness of the world. Perhaps, she'd said, aloud, barely able to contain her hopes, perhaps this is the site of the library which I so desperately seek!

Paulette had been foolish enough to inform her mistress that the castle was not a castle at all, but an inn, and that the nobleman who was about to greet them was little more than a mead merchant.

Posh, Donna Quixotic had retorted. You have scales covering your eyes if you cannot see the world as it truly is! We shall have them removed at once!

Paulette falls back on her haunches, for she knows how this episode came to its conclusion. And again she feels her lips loose a Sigh of Relief at having left under all those fallen stones the Book of Poshes. But suddenly, she draws in a breath without daring a sound: could God Posh?

From her haunches, in the shrubberies on the edge of the Deserted Plain, she hears the whinny of Eurynome and the bleat of Gwendolyn as they draw close. She notices the darkening of the sky such that the mirror no longer casts its flashes of sunlight about the face of her mistress. Above, the trees begin swirling and she casts her glance to the Deserted Plain, where she sees nothing less than an enormous sigh racing across the Deserted Plain, racing directly toward them, maniacal and transporting, extremely dangerous, a daughter of Aeolus gone mad with jealousy. She screams as the leaves blow off the trees, as the pages from her book are torn from their binding, as she feels herself levitate from the very ground she graces, as she sees Donna Charlotte Isabel Quixotic turn her beautiful and peaceful face into the wind and sigh a Sigh of Supreme Contentment, or so imagines the faithful Paulette.

Scenes from next week: 'The Case of "Donna Quixotic: Meeting a Strange Knight" (Episode 19).'

Donna Quixotic and Paulette are thrown across the Great and Deserted Plain by the maniacal Sigh and are nearly diced by several enormous windmills, whereupon they are saved by a Strange Knight.

reality tv and sports

On Temptation Island: The View from the Hot Tub
by Art Dimsdale
New York: Danaides & Baedecker, 2010.

reviewed by Eugene Halton

'MTV doesn't really package the show as "you'll love these kids".
It is kinda like, "look at these fools" and then it creates this vicious
kind of superiority thing. See, some people at home just sit there
excited that they aren't you, and pass serious judgment.
I know, I was once a viewer and I felt this way. Plus it's true.'
Princess Melissa, from MTV's *The Real World*

'When I was younger I could remember anything,
whether it had happened or not.'
Mark Twain

Mad, decadent, puerile, revolting, titillating, vomitous, cheesy, scummy, raunchy, kitschy, cruel, outrageous, indifferent, and desperate things go on *all* the time in most of the United States, certainly on its universal 'Big Eye' of TV. But people seem to think that the decadence is always greener on the other side of the fantasy island, so to speak. It all seems more real when it, as it were, seems more real. It seems as though reality in America floats somewhere between the 'seems' and the 'seamy'.

To judge by the continued popularity of 'reality' shows, decadence is alive and well today. After their initial burst of success with *Survivor*, new shows continued appearing for a few years, then seemed to be on the wane. But now, ten years after the first *Survivor*, the shows have re-flourished with new vigor, stretching boundaries that many thought were already stretched to the limit. What gives? Why so?

Enter Art Dimsdale, the post-political pundit whose punchy polemics have previously parodied the presidency. Yes, the author of *From Marilyn to Monica: Shiny Perishing Republic*, and more recently, *A Bird in the Hand: Homoerotic Subtexts of the Bush Presidencies*, has now turned his rapier wit on the reality show phenomenon. *On Temptation Island: The View from the Hot Tub* is no mere deconstruction of the phenomenon. That, Dimsdale reminds us, is not only easy, but has already been done '*ad nauseum* by the numerous wits – dim and yet otherwise penetrating – of the present age.' I admit to a certain weakness for this sort of sharp-edged writing, especially when its author can go fully satirical without being a lit-snob. Unlike the post-aesthetes, slashing, parenthesizing, and always obfuscating, Dimsdale chose to kick back and get it wet, to get himself out of the frying pan of journalism into the fire of the shows themselves. Well, sort of.

Do you remember George Plimpton, the author who became a real-life Walter Mitty? They called him a 'participatory-journalist'. He was a kind of renaissance celebrity man. He got to play professional football, hockey, golf, hang with celebrities, act in movies and on TV shows. Remember that series *ER*? Plimpton acted in one episode. The man also had heavyweight literary credentials that few celebrities could match, having founded *The Parisian Review* and continuing on as editor for decades during his escapades.

Dimsdale seems to fancy himself a new Plimpton in this work, a 'virtual-participatory-journalist.' Plimpton had to get his butt off his desk chair and out on the playing field, into the arena of sport and celebrity life. But Dimsdale has taken the virtual route, plunking his bottom in a hotbed of American fantasy reality, the hot tub.

Not just any hot tub, not for our Art. Ay, there's the rub-a-dub-dub! Dimsdale is nothing if not savvy. He understands, as few post-critics have, that though the festering sleep-of-death fantasies of America may dislocate themselves in globalized exotic commodification zones, they emanate from Main Street. Sherwood Anderson understood the second part of this 'To sleep, perchance to nightmare' equation: Main Street the ideal is composed of Main Street the grotesque. But the first part, the *Exotica Projection*, as Dimsdale terms it, was yet to fully blossom in the second half of the last century. Surely this must give us pause, if for no other reason, then pause for the cause.

Main Street may have morphed into Mall Street Mall, the placeless faceless one-size-fits-all Happyland of consumption, but the underlying grotesque only grew larger, like an unattended Golem. You see, America used to be able to project its utopian desires a little closer to home. The Jersey shore could embody New York's fantasies, until air travel scattered them further. Asbury Park and Atlantic City gave way to the all-year-round tropics, and became emaciated little scumbag towns. Gambling goosed Atlantic City back to attention, but it was no city at all, merely a Potemkin money strip, a seaside mall of money. Who would want to watch 'reality' in Atlantic City or Asbury Park? Who would want to go there to share summer food, fun, and surf, when one could go to far more exotic places, all-year-round places, places that one could bring back as monied 'souvenirs?' MTV once tried it, using Seaside

Crayon rendering of Art Dimsdale and Tania by Fritz Janschka

Heights, NJ, as a summer location, but they still saved the hard-body onstage TV erotica competitions for the tropics. Who, in short, would want to set a 'reality' show in prosaic New Joisey, when one could go to fantasy island? Answer: nobody in their right commodified mind would want to, nobody, except Art Dimsdale that is.

Whatever one says about Dimsdale's shrewdness, slickness even (remember that chapter of his last book, 'Bush Whacked?' Or just take a look at Dimsdale.com!), he understands the fundamental ratio of decadence to exotica: when it's *there* it's better than *here*, and even when it's *here*, it's better to pretend that it is really *there*.

Would 'reality' shows set in Anytown, USA be watched more than those set on Fantasy Survivor Temptation Island? No way they would. Dimsdale knows this, but chose to play with it as post-critic by immersing himself, literally, in 'Midwest Civ', as he calls it. Virtual George Plimpton meets Hunter S. Thompson in the matrix of magic that brings fantasy island to Anytown USA.

Dimsdale put himself into a hot tub in Normal, Illinois, a great big hot tub owned by Tom and Harriet Foley, a hot tub that for a few weeks became the evening gathering place for eight latter-day single residents of 'Main Street'. But Dimsdale also knew that 'reality' shows required the exotica, so he and his seven tub mates watched the shows set in fabulous locations while sequestered, like a hung jury, in their Normal hot tub. Three nights each week they soaked it all up as the world's first reality show viewing team.

Dimsdale intuitively understood what the TV producers have yet, even today, to figure out: that it takes more than exotica, that it takes an island, what he calls *Isolato Island*, after Herman Melville. In *Moby Dick*, Melville depicted the United States as comprised of *isolato* islanders, not from 'the common continent' of humanity. And so what Dimsdale did was to create a little Gilligan's island of Main Streeters. More, he also 'supplemented' the shows he and the Normal citizens were watching with ones of his own devising, formed in that imaginary domain between public TV voyeurism and private hot tub fantasy. With Margarita Montoya, the aerobics instructor and massage therapist on his left, and Debbie Engel, the saucy lawyer on his right, watching the double digital TVs set at opposite ends of the tub and commenting on the antics of the real TV participants, their feet and thighs touching in tactile underwater repartee all the while, who would not drift dreamily to fabulous vicarious realities?

The first chapter, 'Temptation Island Survivor Loser', sets the historical context for the reality revival, with Dimsdale describing the unplanned, but not unwanted, birth of the 'hyper-reality' show in 2005. That was the year Jerry Springer was assassinated live on air by the animal rights activist during the famous 'Lovers Loving Lovers' Pets' episode of his show. It was also the year of the 'Bacchae Incident', as the media named it, after the women followers of Bacchus, ancient god of wine and ecstasy, also known as Dionysus. The Bacchae Incident was one of the most significant moments in TV history, ranking, perhaps, with the Kennedy assassination. And to this day the debate continues whether the incident was unplanned or scripted.

Dimsdale reminds us that budgets of the few remaining reality shows had been cut, and that Fox had tried to scrimp by filming two separate shows simultaneously on one island. *Survivor 15: D.I.*, which was to be the last installment and grand finale of the show, was supposed to feature a cast of competitors made up entirely of male marine drill instructors. This *Survivor* was supposed to have changed the question from 'Who's tough and who is not?' to 'Who's the toughest and nastiest of them all?' It was a good premise, since everyone knows that viewers love to hate the contestants, even while identifying with them. It even featured a competition based on the film *The Hunted*, released in 2002, where Tommy Lee Jones played a master tracker who had to find and capture an expert commando gone bad, played by Benicio Del Toro. The cameramen couldn't keep up, so all the competitors were fitted with 'third eyes', those tiny disc-cameras attached to the middle of the forehead, freeing the entire crew to shoot on the other side of the island.

Oddly, this should have been the most adrenalin-inducing of all the *Survivor* series, yet it did not make for good TV. These were former professional combat soldiers, and watching them hiding, camouflaged green, in bushes for hours on end got to be boring. Meanwhile, on the other side of the island, an all-female cast of competitors was assembled for *American Gladiatrixes*, a retro-revival of the old *American Gladiators*, a show which many feel was the first reality show – or first decadence show, depending on your view of reality. Well, the women had just finished the mud-wrestling event, which was to give the winners a bubble bath and the losers a trip to 'The Penile Colony', a wicked Kafka maze of giant two-meter male organs, life-like to the touch, waving like undersea ferns, obtrusive, in-your-face, through which the losers had to wander until they reached the exit.

Now understand that filming on the island had been going on for three weeks, and not all of the women found these symbols of patriarchal repression to be a negative experience. Quite the contrary. It was after this event that the women revolted and bolted. They had heard from some of the crew about the marines on the other side of the island. So the 'sisters', all twelve of the remaining contestants, joined together, commandeered the power boat, and drove to the other side of the island, where they made their amphibious assault. The rest is history. What no military power on earth could do, these women did in less than an hour. In less than one hour they held these sweating, woman-starved fighting machines under their complete domination. And in this fusion of shows, *Booty Camp* was born.

With camera crews on the other side of the island, two days away by foot, and the marines with 'third eye' cameras in place and still rolling, the nervous producers had to sit back in their offices, out of communication with the island. But in those two days a TV miracle happened. The contestants spontaneously invented their own reality show, motivated by pure play and carnal desire. *Booty Camp*: who could have imagined an island of marines dominated by women gone full Amazon? These women were whipped into a frenzy the marines could not resist, and they soon found themselves tied up in Bacchic bondage rites. It was no longer clear what constituted a 'winner' or 'loser', for spontaneous ritual had replaced calculating competition.

The women made up the game *Semper Fido*, in which each marine, stripped to jock strap and tied on a leash held by a woman, had to race against the others on all fours while obeying the commands of the woman as a 'good dog'. And this was after they had to carry the women on their backs a half kilometer to the staging area. Drill Instructor Yaney, the meanest marine before the women arrived, was the women's favorite target:

'You wanna do it, Yaney?' the bikinied sirens all chimed together.
'Do it? I'm dead,' D.I. Yaney says resignedly. 'I'll do it.'
'We can't hear you, Yaney,' they cooed back in mock marine talk.
'I'm dead,' D.I. Yaney shouts back. 'I'll do it.'
'You will address us properly,' the women shouted in unison.
'Arf, arf, arf!' Yaney barked back, having temporarily forgotten that this was *Semper Fido*. 'How bad could it be?' Yaney whispered to the marine next to him, looking into the camera, 'What choice do I have anyway?'

The 'top dog' got to give his bone to the woman that evening. Religious fundamentalists, animal rights groups, and militarists decried this irreverent behavior. Feminists lauded it.

The men in turn made up a rite for the women: they called this game *Eager Beaver*. Each woman had to spend the day building a floating damn-bed for their evening tryst. But watch out: if your water breaks while you're *in flagrante delecto*, 'you're in for a ride down the river without a paddle, Baby,' as Dimsdale put it.

This was hyper-reality, for two days a synesthesia of pleasures and pains beyond anyone's expectations. It was raunchy. It was pure animal release. It even seemed real to a zombied viewing world already deadened by overstimulation. It was something that could never be scripted. Yet, as Dimsdale documents, that is exactly what the TV bureaucrats tried to do, with expected results. Deliberately allowing contestants to make up their own rules only brought in the old competitive greeds, not the spontaneity. But reality TV, following the rules of the megasystem, only tries to simulate spontaneity. The real thing is too dangerous, whereas simulated spontaneity helps keep the adrenalin up, the attention on the advertising, and the viewer on the couch. Or in the hot tub. Art Dimsdale opened his hot tub experience by recounting this history for the folks in his tub, asking them what they would have done. What a brilliant move! Right at the start, before the first show appeared on the dual TVs, he had taken a TV Rorschach of his Normal companions, accurately sensing their likely desires. Most said they thought it was too much for TV, but fun to watch anyway. Margarita said she liked *Semper Fido*, that the men showed good discipline and were in great shape. Debbie said she had originally watched it with her ex-husband, and that when she suggested that they try some of the games in their bedroom, he just rolled over and went to sleep. From that night it took about five months for the divorce to get settled.

Both of the guys, Donnie Levane (a restaurant owner) and Kevin Anders (an African-American plumber) felt that what the women did was cruel, and that it got in the way of the more interesting military games the men had been competing in. Dimsdale inferred, correctly, that Donnie and Kevin were a bit light in the loafers. The Foleys, weakest link in this daisy chain, both chuckled together and replied, 'Arf, arf, arf'. Missing link might be a better term for them; they were pathetic. The last contestant, Tania Gryjz, a tall dark-haired, voluptuous nurse, said that she watched the original in a hot tub and thought it was 'sexy and just so much fun.' She didn't see or remember that much, however, because her boyfriend Bobby and her best friend Bobbi and she moved on to their own triple feature in the tub. 'I was just a total mass of jelly after that!' she bubbled in her thick Croatian accent.

Dimsdale now knew the object of his game would have to be Tania – as he puts it, 'I then sounded myself out my own mental Rorschach, and my response to Tania's words was simply "Boiiing!" I thought Margarita was going to be my "drink of choice", but you would have to be a complete village idiot not to feel the pure sex in Tania's words, in her voice, in her eyes. If "Boiiing" isn't a call to reality, what is?' Thus in the following chapters he takes the reader into that magic matrix between tube and tub, spinning out commentary and fantasies.

His chapter on the short-lived show *X-posure* is a tour-de-force of post-criticism. Reminding us at the outset that the largest organ of the human body – whether male, female, or transgendered – is skin, Dimsdale argues that the show's producers missed a great opportunity in focusing on the virtual nakedness of the contestants – hard body thongs for the women and bulging racing briefs for the men – instead of focusing on the skin itself. He takes us on a phenomenological tour of skin, of the wonders of touching. Tracing a brief history of skin and competition, Dimsdale reminds us:

Yes, the Assyrians were one of the finest examples of the specific murderous cruelty achieved by civilizational societies. Goethe once commented that

'Nature has neither core nor skin: she's both at once outside and in.' Well the Assyrians showed how this could be true for civilization too: Would you rather have your flayed skin hung on the city walls, or have yourself cemented into the interior of the city wall itself, as they did to their enemies? Ah, civic pride!

Or remember that fine example of reality in Kafka's story *In the Penal Colony*, when Kafka describes the execution machine: 'When the man lies down on the Bed and it begins to vibrate, the Harrow is lowered onto his body. It regulates itself automatically so that the needles barely touch his skin; once contact is made the steel ribbon stiffens immediately into a rigid band. And then the performance begins...' Now Kafka was one sonofabitch who really knew how to make a reality show, only producers today, a hundred years later, still don't have the balls to do it! This is pure Dimsdale. And could any post-Marxist top this critique of touch in America: 'If religion is the opiate of the people, both relieving the suffering and masking it, then pets are the opiate of touch in *tech-nolo mi tangere* America.'

But Dimsdale is a post-critic, more playful than critical. He invents new sports that the producers of *X-posure* could have used to highlight the *touching* of skin rather than merely the *viewing* of it. Take his idea of 'Scuba-Dooba', for example, which involves couples hooking up down under, having to share only one breathing tank, filmed close-up with slow-motion cameras. This follows a round of 'Flipper' ('see him do tricks when excited'), where women judge the men, and 'Flotation Devices', where men judge the women. The teams that succeed in 'Scuba-Dooba' go on to the next degree of difficulty in a round of 'Snorkel-Dorkel'.

One of Dimsdale's more interesting points, here and throughout the book, is that the image of hard bodies that dominates these shows needs to be democratized with more diversity. America, after all, has been fattening up since the 1980s, yet all of that obesity tends to be filtered out. As he put it, 'Consumption culture must mask production, hiding it just as the Morlocks' underground factories were hidden from the Eloi in H. G. Wells' *The Time Machine*. Similarly, commodity capitalism sells the fat food but must keep its consequences, the fat bodies themselves, invisible, off-screen, or reinvent those bodies as uncaused objects of diet ads.'

The responses of the tubmates is particularly interesting here, especially Debbie, who tearfully confessed: 'These people they get on these shows are like the damn athletes in my high school. They always made you feel bad for not being perfect. Who's the first to get thrown off the islands? It's usually the big ones.' Still, Debbie was not wildly enthusiastic about Dimsdale's proposal for *Bellybusters,* an updated version of *Big Diet*. Dimsdale suggested a new method for winning, combining how much weight people could gain, with how much they could lose. The winner would be rewarded with his or her weight in food, and with the gain/loss ratio in gold. In any case, the winner could conceivably be the same weight at the end of the show as at the beginning. Dimsdale slyly suggested that this would truly be a reality diet show.

One of Dimsdale's most imaginative suggestions was also one of his most manipulative. Remember, he had set a goal of seducing Tania. But he also claims to have had the idea well before meeting her. *Libertas Peninsula* would be a hyper-reality show set in Dubrovnik, Croatia, a Slavic-Italian jewel of a walled medieval city, jutting out on cliffs over the clear Adriatic, a beautiful Mediterranean place. Those huge medieval walls, over 800 years old, were sturdy enough to ward off the Serb offensive in 1992, when the city came under artillery and amphibious assault. In fact, the city boasted, with *Libertas* as its motto, that it had never been conquered. Dimsdale pointed out that sex is relatively easy to set up in exotica, but that violence is more difficult on reality competition shows, even though it is regular fare on talk shows ('witness the Springer show, right down to its final episode!'). So given the fighting that broke out between Croatia and Bosnia recently, Dimsdale envisioned a show set in the walled-in, warring city: it has the tropical exotica element, with added features of an old city, and the potential chance elements of Serb snipers and artillery as adding extra degrees of difficulty and death.

But, as Dimsdale told the tub, it would also have to be called off before finishing because 'People would discover that some of the competitors were being shot not by Serb snipers, but by the residents of Dubrovnik themselves, who were shooting them out of malice…'

'And out of a sporting sense!' Tania chimed in.

At that moment, Dimsdale knew he had her. They had spent two of the eight weeks in the tub, and though the rule was to not have any contact outside the tub (a rule that Donnie and Kevin broke on the very first night!), Dimsdale knew that his time to transgress had come, and so would he! After making love like weasels in heat the third time that night, Dimsdale and Tania had the first of their pillow-talk sessions, which Dimsdale uses as interludes throughout the book. Discussing the others, Tania confessed that not only had she sensed immediately that Donnie and Kevin were closeted gays, but that she had nicknamed them to herself 'Tinky' and 'Winky'. Dimsdale realized that he had more than a sex machine in his hands, that Tania was:

> A full woman and muse, all wrapped in one luscious, bedroom-eyed bomb-shell. 'Tele-tubb-ies,' I stammered in awe, completely under her spell, realizing that she had given me my private nickname for our whole group, for all of fat-assed America and our whole freaking camera civilization! Sure, I had done my homework, I knew the history of the Teletubbies, the research is now well-established in the media studies canon, but I began to see how turn-of-the-century America had to project its obesity epidemic in 'alien' form, importing these creatures from England, as it had earlier imported its own Jimi Hendrix, denying that they were its own hidden 'soft-body' reality!

It would not be right to tell you how the remainder of the book goes further and further inside the reality show through the dreams of the Normal people in the tub, for there are some real surprises there. I found myself really caring for these people by the end – except perhaps the chucklehead Farleys – even with Dimsdale's peppering of cynical comments. And I think he found himself at home there as well, at least temporarily, even if he also came off as the main character you love to hate. But most fascinating for me was Dimsdale's proposal in the last chapter, *Isolato Island*, for a show almost reminiscent of Hermann Hesse's novel, *The Glass Bead Game*.

Isolato Island's main 'hook' is an event called *Doors of Perception*, taken from William Blake's line in *The Marriage of Heaven and Hell*: 'If the doors of perception were cleansed everything would appear to men as it truly is, infinite. For man has closed himself up, till he sees all things thro' narrow chinks of his cavern.' Contestants must choose either Door Number One: the pleasure door, or Door Number Two, the pain door. Both doors, unknown to the contestants, lead into the same room, the

Room of Unhappiness. This curious game – I can't see it ever working as a literal proposal, though Dimsdale seems to mean it that way – raises the question of whether life in our globalized twenty-first century is a matter of mind-forg'd manacles or manacle-forg'd minds. Either way seems to be an isolation from happiness.

The only way out of the Room of Unhappiness is through an exit door marked *No Exit*, which mysteriously opens as they near it. Contestants enter a new event, a walk-thru exhibit reminiscent of a spook-house and called *Inferno*, where they must guess the sins of the exhibitionists. Dimsdale describes it thus:

> The last exhibit reveals an apparent theologian mountain-climber wearing a backpack, relentlessly climbing a stairmaster exercise machine. After a couple of minutes of exertion, the climber stops, removes the backpack, hands it to the contestant, and a circular chink in the wall opens, revealing a slide into darkness through which the tired climber exits, as the door quickly shuts. When the contestant looks inside the backpack, all that is there are heavy tomes, weighty books, those great ennobling books one should read but never has time to.

The contestant slowly realizes over the next minutes, hours, days even, that the only way he or she can get out is by treading the stairmaster, which opens the door into the room, so that the next contestant can relieve the stepper of his or her burden. But the peddler never knows when the next contestant will arrive. In this last, ultimate reality game, Dante's Ugolino, the guy who ate his children and who occupied the lowest rung in Hell, gets some company: the backpacked, bookpacked critic on the eternal stairmaster, unable to read any of the books. Yes, the critic, lost in eternal damnation, in that zone of unreality somewhere between the metaphor and the literal. There, but for the grace of God, go I.

As I mentioned, Art Dimsdale is perhaps the pre-eminent post-critic of our time, as fully articulate and breezy as any of the other celebrities in the International Theory Cartel. Yet his book has this strange, almost existentialist, almost mystical, downbeat concluding chapter. What are we to make of it? Consider, as another example, this excerpt:

> In this same sense the sophists of today, the Grand Inquisitors of the advertising and television industries, have not replaced word with image, as so many critics suggest, but have replaced image and imagining with the scripted image. They are attempting to 'persuade' away the living spark of public life by providing virtual-adrenalated substitutes – 'scripted life' – toward an end of one vast McDonaldized reflex-arc. Their crypto-religious apparatus taps the deep levels of human entrancement, transforming it into mere stimulus-response pleasure-pain reflex-arc, and all that is human melts away as the mere flesh-covering of the machine.
>
> Give me what used to be called the vices of the flesh any day over the virtues of the machine, for the machine is death, pure and simple. When flesh becomes automatic, it becomes death, it becomes machine.
>
> Read the signs: the sophist-Grand Inquisitor-Advertising Executive and his/her/its couch potato other-half is nothing if not a semiotician, in utter suicidal alienation from semeiosis, reading the road-kill signs of death!

When Willy Blake claimed that the old prophecy, 'that the world will be consumed in fire at the end of six thousand years is true, as I have heard from Hell,' he wasn't being some schizo. No, he envisioned what finally incarnates now, in our time. We are become that machine that is death, and it should not take but another fifteen, maybe twenty, years more of building this global, electronically-connected, virally and other disease-connected house of cards before it collapses – utterly and totally collapses – whoosh – all gone, and we with it.

Understand that I am not simply looking down my nose at Mega-Reflex-Arc-America, for no man is an island, isolated from the all-surrounding societal significations. But I do not want to leave out the gestural aspect of the sign, and so I will thumb my nose at it, flip it off: Friends, contemporary Mega-Reflex-Arc-America is a world-consuming bloated pig in a Brooks Brothers suit, anaesthetizing its loss of humanity by push-buttoning its own automatic flush down the toilet. No way will I let it tread on me and my American vision! Give me *Libertas Dubrovnik* or give me death! I would rather live hard the entrancing carnival games of life than to be zombified into 'remote'.

Now is it me, or is Dimsdale suggesting that there are some sort of universal human 'essences?' How could someone who understands so well how reality is socially constructed say this? Isn't this kind of jeremiad theorizing, especially in relation to TV, not only passé, but pre post-critical? Or is this Dimsdale's ultimate trump card, a subtle, ironic commentary that appears on the surface to link him empathically to the common continent of humanity, while in reality he remains an island of post-Cartesian ego unto himself, gazing into that hall of mirrors out of which 'reality' is endlessly constructed while convincing us that we are seeing the real man objectively describing the real thing?

However it may be, this is a book well worth reading and viewing. I found myself going back to the animated photo sections repeatedly. Call me old-fashioned, but I love to hold a book. But I also love the opportunity to see the scenes and people move and talk in the ani-photo sections as well. For all that I know Dimsdale's tub may be just a verbal sleight-of-hand, the ani-photos as real as that portrait of Captain Lemuel Gulliver which stands as frontispiece to his renowned *Travels*.

One thing is certain, however: Art Dimsdale himself is the real deal, a man who knows that being there/here is what it's really all about.

*Foreign Objects in the Ring: Professional Wrestling and the
Politics of Engagement*
by Lugnut Jones
New York: Pile Driver Press, 2000

reviewed by Charles A. Goldthwaite, Jr.

(Note: Portions of this review were originally presented as a plenary address in honor
of Professor Jones delivered by the author at the Professional Wrestling Commentators Association Millennial Conclave in Dothan, Alibama, 2001).

> 'Are you man enough to wear these $500 alligator shoes or this Rolex watch?
> I spent more money last year on bellhops and spilled liquor than you punks
> will earn in your entire life [sic]. So if you think you can be the man, you got to
> beat the man. There's only room at the top for one, and you're lookin'
> at him, baby. So get out your pens and pencils and notebooks,
> 'cause now we go to school. Whoo!'
> 'Nature Boy' Ric Flair, television interview (1987)

> 'The virtue in professional wrestling is that it is the spectacle of excess.'
> Roland Barthes, 'The World of Wrestling' (1952)

'Can we please restore some order here?' Thus begins the introduction to Lugnut
Jones' *Foreign Objects in the Ring*, a groundbreaking discursive study of

professional wrestling and its discontents. This paradigm-setting masterpiece picks up where Jones' recent analysis of the popularity of televised in-church confessionals, *Fifty Bucks – Same as in Town* (1997), leaves off. In his Introduction, Lugnut reprises *Fifty Bucks'* controversial conclusion, that 'everyone is, at heart, a guilty bastard' when addressing the appeal of televised wrestling. If this is true, then the world brims with an abundance of guilty bastards.

Stemming from the age-old traditions of Japanese Noh drama and drunken brawling, professional wrestling emerged as a definitive statement of American culture in the late-twentieth century. From its humble beginnings as a regionally-based entertainment spectacle, professional wrestling has, through the medium of television, exploded onto the national consciousness. No fewer than five prime-time wrestling shows aired each week, and wrestling spectaculars such as Wrestlemania and Starrcade were among the most popular offerings in the pay-per-view format. On-camera appeal and acting ability have thus superceded the traditional path of traversing local and regional circuits as the keys for aspiring wrestlers wishing to break into the business. Wrestlers in the television age have therefore extended the basic principles of showmanship and athleticism that originated with such icons as Gorgeous George Wagner and Lou Thesz into a virtual prime-time soap opera that has developed wrestlers, promoters, and even announcers into on-screen personalities. Consequently, when not tuned in to *Baywatch*, the world's cultural intelligentsia are likely to be tuned in to the free-for-all occurring within the Squared Circle. Although a few scholars have analyzed the forms and fictions of professional wrestling in order to determine its appeal, Professor Jones examines the impact of television on this most visual form of entertainment.

Jones' discourse situates itself to the right of that displayed in works such as Todorov's *Beavis, Butthead, and Bakhtin* (reviewed in this volume, by Michael Dunne) by implying that wrestling lures its viewers through its veracity rather than its carnivalesque atmosphere. Although Barthes argues that 'what matters most to the audience is not what it thinks but what it sees' (1982: 19), many modern critics have focused on wrestling's elements of melodrama and its penchant for blurring spectacle with reality. Then Lugnut gets into the ring and takes these critics to task in *Foreign Objects* by proposing a series of arguments designed to dispel long-standing myths about the myriad roles of this spectacle in shaping the lives of television viewers. Perhaps most intriguing of his assertions is his chilling theory that televised professional wrestling is actually real. His postulation that televised wrestling represents a reversed *Blair Witch Project* in which the all-too-real action is staged to look fake has caused near-rioting in traditional wrestling strongholds such as Memphis, Charlotte, and Saginaw, MI, where the fans know damn well when they are being fooled. For Jones, however, televised wrestling thus becomes an integral component of what Fox Mulder has termed America's 'military-industrial-entertainment complex.' Fooling the viewers into thinking that they know they are being fooled is no foolish task, and Lugnut Jones draws provocative similarities between Outhouse Brown's trademark double guzel with a trash can lid and decidedly real socio-historic precedents such as Joseph McCarthy's threats to rout the Communists in order to restore the order of democracy.

The veil was formally lifted from professional wrestling in 1992, when, in order to obtain permission for his troupe to perform at the Meadowlands Arena, World Wrestling Federation president and founder Vince McMahon testified before the

New Jersey state legislature that professional wrestling was scripted entertainment rather than sport. From this point onward, professional wrestling has expanded from contests between individual athletes into a virtual soap opera, an ongoing 'meta-spectacle' of intrigue, plot twists, and surprises. Of the numerous facets incorporated so seamlessly into *Foreign Objects*, perhaps the most useful to the scholar is Jones' discussion of the intertextuality of the wrestling spectacle. Professor Jones deftly proves his familiarity with much of current criticism by expanding on my own recent article, '*Baywatch* and Professional Wrestling: A Narratological Comparison', by noting that the good and bad guys that populate each type of entertainment represent tropes seen also in *Scooby Doo* cartoons, beer commercials, and televised political debates. The Big Lug then really flexes his muscles of scholarly synthesis by addressing Taryn P. Cursive-Waters' recent theoretical framework of nasal elevation (also reviewed in this volume, by Rhonda V. Wilcox). As an example, he refers the reader to a televised interview between announcer Tony Schiavone and 'Luscious' Jimmy Valiant (the Disco King). The nose says it all when Schiavone, after introducing Valiant by simply noting that 'Uh-oh – It looks like he's headed this way,' retracts his head as far as possible from his outstretched microphone. As Valiant hops in place, claps his hands, and muses, 'Donny Chavanto, sometimes I do, and then again, sometimes I don't – all right, all right,' Jones brilliantly applies Cursive-Waters' principles of nasal analysis to suggest that, for Schiavone and the audience in general, the Disco King generates his own brand of nasal elevation. It is during such moments of free-form scholastic association that Lugnut transcends the narrow confines that bind so many of his academic cohorts, and it seems that no amount of Brawny paper towels can clean up the spill when his cup runneth over. In a word, this is a most compelling analysis, and, at moments like this, one cannot help but reprise the classic announcer's refrain that although he's number twenty-eight in the program, he's number one in our hearts.

In the book's final section, Jones examines the career of 'Nature Boy' Ric Flair as a case study to evaluate the impact of the television camera on the rhetorical strategies of the individual wrestler. His close reading of a Flair television interview is a near-brilliant analysis that subtly dramatizes the underlying socio-economic tensions that drive much of the sport's discourse. He begins by analyzing the components of Flair's wardrobe – alligator shoes, Armani suit, Rolex watch – as visual codifications of what Marxist critic Fredric Jameson has termed 'the long class struggle of human history'. Jones then draws parallels between the structure of the Flair interview, which is composed mostly of improvised self-hype, and traditional forms of expression such as the dramatic monologue, the Shakespearian soliloquy (where Ric substitutes his left shoe for Yorick's skull), and the more conventional embittered rant.

Although Jones demonstrates moments of astounding clarity and flashes of brilliant insight, he occasionally oversteps his boundaries, and, to use wrestling parlance, goes over the ring-ropes. For instance, his attempt to reconstruct Flair's interview as a mock-epic Biblical parable results in a veritable Pier Sixer in which the reader has his head dashed against the turnbuckle one time too many. Critics of professional wrestling agree that the spectacle represents a visual enactment of a moral fable of the battle between good and evil, yet Lugnut's confident assertion that Ric Flair represents a 'platinum blonde Moses in a feather boa' is likely to draw fire from theologians and fashion designers alike. His additional implication that

Moses began his sermon on the mount by addressing the Egyptians as a 'bunch of nothing-happening rednecks from the mountains of Nile country' is blasphemous, astonishing, and simply not backed by adequate scholarship. While Lugnut Jones should be praised for attempting to stretch the boundaries of scholarly inquiry, this reviewer can only echo the plaintive cry of legendary wrestling commentator Gordon Solie (a man whose nasal delivery deserves further treatment in its own right) when he says, 'Ah ah. Now wait a minute.'

Professor Jones also includes a handy abridged wrestling glossary designed for the neophyte that succinctly defines phrases often employed by ringside commentators in terms useful to the scholar, critic, or lay reader. The impact that terms such as 'solar plexus' (groin) and 'Pier Sixer' (melée) have had on wrestling discourse is immeasurable, and their appropriation by the critical community should truly put the 'hetero' back into heteroglossia. In homage to the spirit of professional wrestling and in deference to the television viewer, Jones combines his social commentary and professional scholarship with many 'hot pix' (big color photos) to make *Foreign Objects in the Ring* an ideal book for the coffee table, podium, or dashboard. Frankly, I think that I speak for the academy as a whole when I say that we have always admired The Lugnut for his unique ability to bridge the gap between these most disparate ends of the cultural spectrum.

In all, Lugnut Jones's fascinating montage of critical discourse regarding the dialogics of televised wrestling is a work that is broad both in its scope and its appeal. Once again, Jones applies his special gift for synthesis to various elements of popular culture, and he sheds light on the delicate web of interlocking themes that unifies much of modern consumer culture. Although he occasionally pushes too far in his mental sojourns, Jones has created a career based on unifying the impossible and, in the process, teaching us much about ourselves and our world. For the most part, Jones succeeds here with this tour-de-force, which whisks the reader over the rapids and down the waterfall only to bring him safely to the quiet pool at its base. I recommend this book for both the undergraduate and graduate reader, as well as for those old ladies seated on front rows of wrestling matches worldwide who so gladly hand their canes to the good guy in his effort to win the battle against evil.

Subverting Desires: Spectacles of the Simpson Year
edited by André Dross
Bucksnort, Tennessee: Volunteer State Press, 1997

reviewed by Allison Graham

Academic critics have been registering their theoretical assessments of media events for so long that most of us can predict the race, class, and gender take on anything from *Showgirls* to the State of the Union address. We need only look at the volumes already produced on the O. J. Simpson trial to see the academic machine at work. Laboring overtime to get their essays to press in order to compete with the more alluring tales by Fay Resnick, Marcia Clark, and Kato Kaelin, the sociologists and historians of immediate events seem doomed to the formulaic analyses that have characterized so much of cultural studies.

Finally, however, a book appears which takes a fresh approach to the study of media. *Subverting Desires: Spectacles of the Simpson Year*, a collection of essays which is destined to turn cultural studies on its head, investigates the Simpson trial as a watershed event in the history of art. Yes, art. Calling the televised trial 'a crisis in postmodern aesthetics', André Dross believes, and his contributors seem to agree, that the year-long spectacle was 'the alchemic event' of the closing years of the twentieth century, a 'crucible' in which classical and contemporary notions about our imaginative engagement with the world fused to produce a twenty-first century sensibility Dross mysteriously (and enticingly) calls 'random enunciation'.

113

The essays themselves are constructed untraditionally as free-flowing discussions among a group of critics and artists, with each group assigned a specific aesthetic element to ponder. The opening discussion fairly blasts off the page with a heated argument over the form and function of the aerial shot which initiated the 'narrative proper' of the Simpson trial. P. J. Letotte fires the opening round by announcing that the helicopter shots of O. J. on the freeway that bookended his incarceration were intentional homages to cinema's first helicopter sequence, James Wong Howe's final shot in *Picnic* (1955). The camera operator in the Los Angeles news helicopter (himself a graduate of USC's film program) framed both freeway shots in Howe's unmistakable style, suggesting (as had the ending of *Picnic*) that two seemingly doomed people (Kim Novak and William Holden in the film) might reconcile somewhere 'off the frame'. In the first freeway run, Simpson was reportedly driving to Nicole's grave; in the second, he was returning to their home to reclaim his children.

The romantic possibilities of this narrative contextualization, however, are altered by Lawrence Olivier Stone's encyclopedic elaboration upon the semiotics of helicopter shots in general. From Vietnam news footage to television's *M*A*S*H* to *Apocalypse Now* to Altman's *Short Cuts*, the helicopter, claims Stone, has repeatedly served as our homegrown version of Foucault's panopticon. Rather than suggesting emotional reunification, such shots only reify the power of the state to shatter non-institutional bonds. Taking a different tack, Cecily Otto, the *Village Voice*'s drama critic, argues that the establishing shot of the event created an intentionally distancing effect which would gradually, without our conscious awareness, diminish into visual intimacy over the coming months. Such distancing was necessary, Otto says, to avoid overt viewer identification with an apparent criminal. Before we knew it, though, we were locked into an inescapable partnership; we were, in effect, collective performance artists re-enacting on a mass scale the kind of year-long performance piece formerly undertaken only by Soho artists. Tied to Simpson by the power of electronic desire, each viewer internalized his image as a shadow self, a silent but omnipresent other, a subconscious reminder of our own repressed sociopathic urges.

The mechanics of identification become even more complex in the second essay, a discussion of the formal construction of the trial coverage. In an intriguing opening thesis, David Bored suggests that the trial marked a 'confrontation' between the historically filmic function of the long take and network video's abuse of its potential for revelation. The trial, in fact, carried André Bazin's prescription to its radical extreme, yet instead of the 'centrifugal' impulse Bazin saw operating in shots, the unending mise-en-scène only forced us deeper into the abstractions of the dialogue. The static camera, occasionally panning right or left, always tilting up to the Seal of California when the jury entered or left the courtroom, was, Bored thinks, the fixed eye of death, the correlative of the fixed eye of the convicted himself. Like Simpson, we were condemned to see only what the state deemed appropriate. Like Simpson, our view of events was blocked when proceedings ended for the day. 'The world in a frame-up', is what Court TV gives us, having appropriated and then subverted the realist ideal. In fact, by claiming the Warholian fixed perspective as its own (with each day's coverage becoming a contemporary variation on Michael Snow's *Wavelength*), realist television foregrounds the corporate cooptation of previously avant-garde stances, and valorizes its own mass production of images.

The feminist response to Bored's argument at first appears to challenge its pessimistic view of television's potential for radical subversion. Barbara Ching begins her analysis with a rather predictable take on gaze theory: the trial camera could not possibly recapitulate Simpson's incarcerated perspective, she claims, because the camera, perched above the jury box, gave viewers a point of view approximating that of the twelve jurors. In fact, given the gender and racial dominance of the jury, the camera forced us to identify with a *black female* point of view – and a *working-class* black female point of view as well! From this perspective, viewers might well resist the foregrounding of white middle-class Marcia Clark in favor of the (intentionally?) distanced Simpson, whose body was relegated by the state to the nether regions of the courtroom's deep space. This appears to make sense, yet Speck's argument spins on its tracks and bravely confronts us with the critical error in her reasoning: If the narrative point of view is inherently that of oppressed women, why, then, are these women denied reverse shots in the diegesis? Why do we never see the faces of those who are doing the 'looking'? Denied agency first by the state, and then by corporate compliance with the state (CNN and Court TV agreed to hide the jurors' faces), these women never emerge as active participants in the narrative, their images once again invisible to a viewing population constructed as primarily white and male. Is it any wonder, then, that the jurors found their own way of wresting control of the narrative? What better way of demanding recognition than by delivering a verdict in record time, thereby calling together all participants in an event whose rituals required a *return of the gaze*? In those five minutes which climaxed the trial, the lawyers and the accused stood and looked at the jurors, and continued to look as each juror voiced assent to the not guilty verdict. Finally acquiring voices, the jurors were released into the world to acquire faces. The trial, then, visually enacted a narrative of imprisonment and liberation, recapitulating the dominant narrative of Simpson's own freedom.

As ingenious as this reading is, it is surpassed by the skillful narratological analysis provided by Moira Logan. Looking at the trial as a complex network of narrative voices, she asks a provocative question: who was the 'real' narrator of the trial? Using CNN as her medium, Logan carefully works her way through the various voices which controlled the event. Beginning with the desk anchor, each day's coverage would lead us deeper into smaller 'nesting stories', each introduced by a different narrator. From the desk anchor we would be passed to a series of field reporters, then to desk commentators – all of whom provided contextual framing for the narrative.

Once inside the courtroom, however, the question of narration became problematic: was it Lance Ito, Johnnie Cochran, Marcia Clark, or the witnesses themselves who controlled the narrative information? Logan opts for Ito, since the judge exercised the power to include or exclude material in the story proper. His judgments, however, were often overridden by witnesses or attorneys, who would seize upon opportunities to insert narrative detours from the path he had dictated. In such ways, Logan claims, the narrative forever slipped beyond generic constrictions upon form, endlessly mutating to create multilayered texts. As proof of the ironic chain of signifying voices in the narrative, Logan cites an often overlooked detail in narratological analyses of realist video: the truly presiding voice, on CNN, is not that of the desk anchor; it is the voice of CNN itself – the baritone enunciator of the corporate logo, James Earl Jones. As the Great White Hope announces the story of another great white hope, the final irony speaks itself, and in so doing, becomes the not-ironic, the reified fact of postmodern racial cooptation.

The volume's final discussion veers from its assigned topic – self-reflexivity in the Simpson coverage – to what are perhaps the book's most radical departures from current media theory. Beginning with what was surely the trial's most obvious kernel of self-reflexivity – the mirroring of Nicole and O. J.'s relationship in the cartoon sitcom *The Simpsons*, Robert J. Thompson looks at other ways in which the trial proclaimed itself as a media event. From the elaborate disputations within the courtroom about the time codes at the bottom of the LAPD's videotapes, jumpcuts within the tapes, and the perspective distortions of video camera lenses to witness interpretations of Simpson's facial expressions in freeze frames from a home video of daughter Sidney's dance recital, the trial not only displayed but fetishized the constructedness of video images. Ironically, prosecution witness Ron Shipman was castigated by the defense for his desire to win a role in O. J.'s new television show, when clearly O. J. himself had already secured roles for all of his friends in the trial coverage, the hit show of 1995. But it is in his analysis of the trial's initial witness that Thompson's grasp of the trial's intertextuality truly emerges. It was this witness who pinpointed the time of his discovery of Nicole's distraught Akita by reference to his television schedule. On Sunday nights, he said, he *always* walked his dog immediately after *The Mary Tyler Moore Show* at 10:30. Could he be mistaken? Not at all, and his knowledge of the difference between Sunday night schedules and weekday schedules signaled hands-off to all attorneys. One can imagine this young aspiring screenwriter, Thompson muses, leaving his apartment to the strains of 'You're Going to Make It After All' only to discover the harbinger of the century's most celebrated murders. Could it be that Mary Richards, a character who produced a television news show, finally exacted her revenge upon America? By invoking her spirit in the opening moments of the trial, were we not plunged into an inextricably intertextual world, in which the bourgeois fantasy of 1970s white America gave way to its repressed underside? And was it simply coincidence that the publication of Mary Tyler Moore's autobiography, which chronicled the drunken break-up of her Hollywood dream marriage, coincided with the public dismantling of the Simpsons' marriage? Thompson thinks not.

Following up on Speck's deconstruction of gender relationships, Will Brantley proposes that the Simpson trial essentially foregrounded a crisis of masculinity. In his forthcoming book, *Marine to Marine: Ethnicity, Race, and Diegetic Desires*, Brantley devotes a chapter to the trial, and here provides enticing glimpses of what will surely be a seminal work. The Simpson trial, he claims, acquired narrative momentum from a shifting dynamic of triangulated desire. Public debate concerning Marcia Clark's hairstyles, clothing, and relationships with male attorneys was a predictably diversionary tactic of mainstream media. The subtextual 'engine' of the story was homoeroticism, its multisignifying focus the body of O. J. Simpson. The broken friendship between F. Lee Bailey and Robert Shapiro provided spatial evidence of the centrality of masculine bonds, as each placed himself at opposite ends of the defense table. With Johnnie Cochran as mediator, and various male attorneys bridging the unspoken gap between Shapiro and Bailey (a gap which, of course, could *not* be spoken in the heterosexist discourse of a trial of an American sports hero), masculine desire dominated the visual field. As Simpson was forced to display himself in front of the cameras – in still photos of his nearly naked body, in stripteasing revelations of his scarred knees, and titillating attempts to cram his large hand into a small glove – other male participants were continually reminded of their less-than-manly attributes. Bailey was told by Marcia Clark on global television that his hand, unlike Simpson's, could easily fit into a shrunken glove; Lance Ito was almost forced to resign from the case after being symbolically castrated by unflattering remarks about his police-chief wife; and in the most blatant display of diminished masculinity, county coroner Dr. Golden demolished the state's attempt to assert its authority. Stuttering, incompetent Golden, the despised articulator of female anatomy, was banished by the prosecution for his failure to vanquish the defense. Even Mark Fuhrman could not recuperate phallic authority, for his long-running disclosures to an unknown female screenwriter simply placed him in the role of a masculine wannabe, a half-man who asserts his dominance by secretly posing as a screen character to a woman who betrays him. Through such displays of repression and denial, then, the televised trial foregrounded the fissures in heterosexist discourse and gender construction and, in this sense, became a corporate-sponsored subversive text.

The final chapter will undoubtedly seal this volume's stature as a cutting-edge collection. Inspired by Stuart Hall's theory of negotiated readings, the University of California at Sunnydale's Women in Media Collective traveled with former domestic worker and star witness Rosa Lopez to her home in El Salvador, where they were granted permission by Lopez's family to watch the Simpson trial on satellite television. Their five months of intense field work have produced invaluable evidence of the ways in which diverse viewers construct their own oppositional readings of media texts. Unlike many American viewers, these working-class Salvadorans responded passionately to the testimony of American workers, who to them spoke the truth. The limousine driver, the baggage carrier at LAX, housekeepers – these voices were heard more clearly than those of celebrities. Interestingly, the Salvadoran viewers focused upon the workers in the courtroom itself, interpreting nuances of expressions in the security guards and court reporters. But it is the last passage in the women's discussion which points the way for a new radical media criticism. Allowing Rosa Lopez her own voice, free of the translators and masculinist legal interpreters, the women ask the former domestic worker how she now feels about her weeks in the American spotlight. 'I was,' she says with dignity and simplicity, 'not heard.' Indeed, *Subverting Desires: Spectacles of the Simpson Year* forces us to question just how much we, as ever-cynical consumers of media, simply do not see and do not hear. Let us hope that this collection inaugurates a new direction for cultural studies in the next century.

Tropes of Turbulence
by R. Pupkin-Bickle
London and New Delhi: Parsley Publications, 1996

Mapping Meteorology, Signifying Storms, Deploying Doppler
by Georgina Wynette and Tom E. Jones
Anoka: Southern Minnesota University Press, 1995

reviewed by Gregory A. Waller

'The basic form, psycho, means something like "blowing cold" or "cooling breath". Indeed there is an ancient connection between the dimension of coldness and the soul (anima, psyche).'
James Hillman, *The Dream and the Underworld*

Where is Carl Gustav Jung when we need him? More than *The X-Files*, more than MTV's *Real World*, more than the World Wrestling Federation, it is unquestionably The Weather Channel that demands to be read (as it is experienced, perhaps unknowingly) as archetypal encounter. Charting the great wide open, celebrating the inevitable passing of the seasons, testifying to the latent structural logic that informs every minute-by-minute shift in the manifest facts of meteorology, The Weather Channel is truly the *locus televisius* for the mythic adventure of the psyche in the cosmos.

And yet, given the hegemony of Cultural Studies (trumpeting its own counter-hegemonic ambitions as usual), instead of a reinvigorated Jungianism, what we get instead are R. Pupkin-Bickle's *Tropes of Turbulence* from Parsley Publications in association with the journal *Society, Media, Theory, Gender, and Space*, and Georgina Wynette and Tom E. Jones's *Mapping Meteorology, Signifying Storms,*

Deploying Doppler, latest in the Southern Minnesota University Press series on Global Reckonings/Local Beckonings. When it rains, it pours. Or, in this case, merely drips, puddles up, and mists over, making it even harder to see the weather for what it really is. These books may advance the cause of postcolonial exegesis, but they won't help you read the symbolic language spoken, minute by minute, by The Weather Channel as it struggles to express the dynamic numinosity of the ineffable and to restore to us what Jung calls 'total psychic equilibrium' in this our life of 'inexorable opposites – day and night, birth and death, happiness and misery, good and evil,' and, we should add, drizzle and sunshine, wind-chill and heat-index, hyperactive twisters and inversion-layer stillness.

Pupkin-Bickle's interests, unfortunately, lie elsewhere: 'mandala' and 'animus' warrant nary a mention in *Tropes of Turbulence*, though Pupkin-Bickle is always ready to cite his colleagues at the Center for Radical Alternative Meteorology (CRAM), whose prime claim to fame was a short-lived, highly self-reflexive, public-access TV weather show that spent most of its time debunking the positivist teleology of Wilhelm Scott and his ilk. (As if Scott himself had not already answered that critique in his trade journal article 'Positive Teleology, My Ass'.) CRAM's self-styled 'unweather' project informs the concluding chapters of Pupkin-Bickle's study, which trace in maddeningly meandering detail – calling it New Historicism is simply no excuse – the way that Bob Dylan's warning/insight/call to arms in 'Subterranean Homesick Blues' ('You don't need a weatherman to know which way the wind blows') was televisualized and thereby institutionally co-opted, drained of turbulence, and 'globally imbalanced'.[1] First, by the barely veiled anti-feminist ethos of post-Watergate local newscasts (policing gender boundaries and public sphere behavior in the name of 'nature' and 'fun'); second, by music video's appropriation of what Pupkin-Bickle rather too coyly labels 'meteor[ock]ology' (e.g. The Weathergirls' 'It's Raining Men' versus, say, Dee Clark's AM-radio era hit, 'Raindrops' – here the CRAM approach can at best only prove the need for a definitive study of this topic, with complete coverage of tornadoes, hurricanes, heat waves, and the Everly Brothers); and, third, the Reagan-Bush-authorized advent of cable-weather via The Weather Channel, whose founding principle is that we not only need a weatherman, but teams of card-carrying weatherpeople, armed with state-of-the-art techno-gear, so we (that is the cable-ready, affluent among us) can 'know' which way the wind blows and invest time and resources accordingly.

Inevitably, the pro-active, post-communal, community-level activism espoused by CRAM runs headlong into – what else? – Jameson Fredericks's attempt to salvage Marxism by inventing the crisis of postmodernity, though to be honest, Fredericks's only foray into textual meteorology appears by way of an aside in the oft-cited essay, 'Dark (K)Night of the Frankfurt School: Adorno, Mass Culture, and *The Today Show*'. Thus, even as Pupkin-Bickle ignores such obvious points as the ritualistic way The Weather Channel (unconsciously?) repeats its varied forecasts four times per half-hour – evoking thereby a principle well-noted by Jungian analyst M.-L. von Franz, to wit: 'the nucleus of the psyche (the Self) normally expresses itself in some kind of fourfold structure' – this CRAM ideologue remains committed (nay, compelled) to wrestling with knotty theoretical issues about surplus value and sunscreen, late-capitalism and early frost, Northern Hemisphere hegemony and the otherness of the 'Southerly'. But, really, who cares? Rain is always already wet. You *don't* need a weatherman to know which way the wind blows.

The more geographically oriented *Mapping Meteorology, Signifying Storms, Deploying Doppler* at least acknowledges the compulsive fascination that The Weather Channel holds for so many people who otherwise could care less about mean temperatures, hurricane watches, and record hail storms – a fascination that Wynette and Jones interpret as a species of 'tele-fetish', which may signal nothing less than a 'post-postmodern epistemological shift'.[2] Still, their primary concern is how The Weather Channel attempts to bypass – if not actually resolve – the much-maligned 'crisis of representation' currently besetting literal and figurative mapmakers across academe. To this end, Wynette and Jones make extensive use of state-of-the-art humanities-computer image technology (this book includes by far the best etch-a-sketch reproductions yet digitized) and cite as their epigraph some lines from a rather obscure chapbook I published in 1993 (inspired in part by the arcane melancholic verses of Scottish landscapist, B. W. Ijams, and the *nouveau modernisme* of E. P. Anderson-Reese), which begins:

> The Weather Channel is our Whitman.
> Its America, in turn, the land of vacationers, business travelers, allergy
>   sufferers, leaf-watchers.
> Ice, mold, frost, wind chill, pollen count, earthquake tremors,
> Arctic air masses, Rainfall by the hour, day, month, year.
> The present in continual chroma-key transformation, the future always
>   predictably unpredictable.

Unfortunately, Wynette and Jones seem not to have gotten through Book IV of my poem, wherein I turn from neo-pragmatism toward a more holistic, archetypal model, specifically inspired by Jung's *Flying Saucers: A Modern Myth of Things Seen in the Sky* (1959). This oversight is unfortunately typical of *Mapping Meteorology* which remains resolutely anti-foundationalist, no more so than when Wynette and Jones analyze how The Weather Channel's on-screen radar effects not only map but perform and thereby constitute the weather as The Weather. In this type of readerly reading, Flash-flood Warnings and Tornado Watches are convenient constructs, national identity and gendered tropical storms become equally unstable, and – presto! – all human subjectivities are no more real than the ever-smiling Mr. Sun stick-ons that decorated the primitive 'maps' used on local weather reports in the 1960s. Deconstructing the mesmeric hold of Doppler has its uses, of course, but if, in the end, we are left only with forecasting as formalist exercise and climatology as convention, then what is that pitter-pat I hear on my roof, those rays that warm the front seat of my Chevy? Enough reducing meteorology to mapmaking masquerade! I, for one, will put my faith in what The Weather Channel, in a frankly folkloric moment, calls 'Weather Wisdom' – but which by any name signifies a cosmos ablaze with signs and wonders.

Notes

1 Pupkin-Bickle's interest in things meteorological goes back at least to a chapter entitled 'Wise Guys in Wet Spaces', in his University of California at Sunnydale dissertation, '"Start Spreading the News": Re-presenting Manhattan in the Films

of Allen, Cassavetes, Lewis, Scorsese, and LaGuardia'.

2 The perverse processes of fetishization are, indeed, the link between *Mapping Meteorology* and the best of Wynette and Jones' previous work, including 'Did He Really Stop Loving Her Today? Necrophilia and Male Masochism in Country Music', *Lefty Frizzell Newsletter*, 35, 14–25.

gender

Straight Readings: Resistance, Reappropriation, and Heterosexuality
by Richard Bradshaw
London: Peacock, 2000

reviewed by Will Brooker

'I should begin here with the declaration which I make at the start of all my lectures,' writes Richard Bradshaw in the Introduction to this provocative collection of essays. 'I am a straight man, and I am proud of it.'

Bradshaw's primary intention in *Straight Readings* is plainly stated: to offer a counterpoint and challenge to the now-established strategy of 'queer reading' within cultural studies, with a specific focus on heterosexual viewers' interpretation of television texts. The book is built around five substantial case studies, taking in a range of historical, cultural, ethnic and gendered perspectives. All of Bradshaw's subjects, needless to say, have one thing in common, and all of them go through quite remarkable processes of evasion and resistance in order to create 'straight' readings from texts that have traditionally been seen as 'gay'.

Bradshaw, as his opening declaration suggests, applauds these interpretive tactics and celebrates his straight readers' skill at drawing alternative meanings from their favorite television shows. Part of the book's purpose is to reclaim these 'forgotten poachers' – overlooked by theorists such as Henry Jenkins and John Fiske – whose 'acts of micropolitical resistance and "making do" are as witty, wily and courageous as anything in de Certeau.'

In one of the book's many autobiographical passages, Bradshaw argues that:

> These men are doing what I did – what all the straight boys did – during those Saturday mornings at the pictures in Soho … weaving and stitching together our own stories from the Andy Warhol and Kenneth Anger double-bill at the Gloryhole cinema … stories which sang of us and our loves, and our lives … stories we stole in the darkness, never daring to speak them aloud. From scraps and loopholes in the dominant gay narrative, Gavin and Mike are piecing together their own meanings … and those meanings are a cause for strength and celebration.

The case studies offer intriguing variations on this central theme. Chapter One, 'Bats Wouldn't Do That', explores the strategies employed by a group of teenage Batman fans to 'prove' the character's heterosexuality in the face of the notoriously camp ABC-TV series of 1966–68.

> I was moved by the determination and pride in Jason's face as he presented me with Burt Ward's autobiography, *My Life in Tights*, held open to a page describing the young star's intercourse with six female fans, each of them dressed in the 'Robin' outfit. 'How can you say he's queer, Dr. Bradshaw?' Jason demanded, his eyes begging me not to contradict him.

The boys' almost desperate recourse to intertextual evidence in order to support Batman and Robin's heterosexuality culminates in a mock-trial where the group of five youngsters and Bradshaw sit stoney-faced through an episode of *Batman*, none of them daring to laugh at Adam West's double-entendres. The only permitted response to the text is ribald commentary on the catsuits and bikinis of the female performers, and muttered approval along the lines of 'Bats wants to shag her.' 'By the end,' Bradshaw says, 'I almost wept for them, for myself as a boy, for all of us.'

This theme of nostalgia and cultural memory segues into the second chapter, based around interviews with three married couples in their thirties who remember watching the British sit-com *Are You Being Served?* on its first run during the 1970s. 'John Inman, gay?' asks Ron, a carpenter from Minnesota. 'Boy, I never saw it that way. I guess those really were more innocent times.' His wife, Marcie, takes his arm. 'Let's remember it the way it was, Ron.' This time it is Bradshaw who, in the interests of research, presents the subjects with intertextual evidence – reviews from the period which identify Inman's character as a stereotype of effeminate homosexuality. The viewers' response is to foreground the text itself as the bearer of 'true' meaning. 'When Inman fingered a plate of breakfast rolls, Ray hit the pause control and pointed the remote at the screen. "See the way he touched Miss Brahms' baps? The guy's got normal urges, no denying it."'

Chapter Three also deals with heterosexual men and women, though in this case study the two groups, aged between 18 and 24, are kept apart. Bradshaw ruminates on the 'distinctions within straight readings … the subtle gradations, the rich variety of heterosexual interpretation rather than the monolithic block which gay culture tries to make us'. His conclusions here are based on the different ways in which his male and female viewers respond to 'gay' moments in the recent TV series *Friends*, *Xena: Warrior Princess*, *Ellen*, and *Dawson's Creek*:

I pondered on the discrepancies in my results. Why had the male subjects adopted a seemingly 'lesbian' stance, rewinding and reviewing the extract where Rachel offers to kiss Monica, while the women showed no interest in this scene? Why were the female viewers far more sympathetic to the possibility of Chandler Bing and Dawson's Jack McPhee being gay, citing their dress sense and charm as positive factors, while the male viewers rejected this suggestion? Could it be that straight reading is far more complex than anyone had imagined?

The notion of straight men shifting into what Bradshaw calls the 'fausse-lesbian subject position' reappears in Chapter Four, 'Straight Slash' – again focusing on Xena and the heterosexual male authors of internet fiction which 'glories in the erotic possibilities of Amazon culture.'

Jake, known on Internet chatrooms as both 'Nine-Inch' and 'Wet4UbabyDoll', is a true cyborg and gender-adventurer, gleefully subverting the rules of online identity as he dons the mask of a bi-curious co-ed and initiates cybersex with unsuspecting female users. His slash site on Xena, which grafts the head of Lucy Lawless and her co-stars onto the bodies of pornographic models, is a rich mine of bricolage and postmodern play.

Chapter Five, finally, takes a participant-observation approach as Bradshaw joins two different communities of straight men and immerses himself in their culture. Both groups – one made up of black lads in South London, one of white male students in their early twenties – use the same television show as part of their Friday-night ritual of clubbing and socializing. Here one of the white viewers, Jason, explains their viewing pattern:

Queer As Folk is the kind of show we'd all be into, except for it's about gays. It's got the style, the music, the attitude. So we stick the Euro 96 tape in the video and as soon as anything queer comes on, it's like Nick, put on the football! [laughter] We give it three minutes and then turn the telly back on, but sometimes we got caught out and we're all like gagging, pretending to puke whatever, cause there's a bender's arse onscreen. [Laughter; cries of 'You love it.']

Bradshaw presents Jason and his friends as examples of 'localized creativity' and describes with relish their appropriation of the gay-themed TV show into their daily lives:

The hi-energy techno is slammed into the CD, programmed to skip any overtly 'queer' tracks. On go the muscle-tops to display toned biceps, washboard abs ... the mambo shirts, open over tanned chests ... three-quarter length trousers, just tight enough to suggest the bulge at the crotch ... Jason asks jokingly why I'm watching him so keenly as he dresses, and I struggle for words he'll understand: I am lost in the jouissance of straight masculinity.

The other group is even more aggressively heterosexual in their reaction to the 'gay' television show. Once again, Bradshaw transcribes with loving detail:

DAWG:	Aight we will watch it, yeah, and get all steamed up innit, angry, yeh? [murmurs of 'right']
RB:	*Why are you angry?*
G-BOY:	Oh my life, when we see that gayboy kissin' the other one.
DAWG:	You nearly kick the telly in, innit?
JUSTIN:	He was like, oh my eyes, 'ow can they do that, perverted, whatever...
RB [gently]:	*But you keep watching?*
G-BOY:	Yeh, 'cos you got to see 'ow bad they get, innit?
DAWG:	It's disgusting but you got to keep watchin' it.
JUSTIN:	An' then we can kick in Simon at school; that boy is a battyman.

We – and indeed Simon – might quibble with Bradshaw's appraisal of this activity as 'life-affirming' and question the assessment that 'G-Boy and his "posse" are claiming a cultural space for themselves as Other, raiding the gay text for their own radical uses.' However, taken as a whole these essays provide evidence of a reading position which, it cannot be denied, has rarely received such devoted academic treatment. If nothing else, *Straight Readings* will provoke discussion and debate, if ever a course tutor has the chutzpah to make it a set text.

A Creature Feminine: The Politics of T & A in Primetime Television, 1970–2000
edited by Patricia Fraugrois
Sunnydale: Kali Books International, 2002

reviewed by Ken Gillam and Shannon Wooden

It is especially apt for Patricia Fraugrois to have edited this volume of feminist and postfeminist criticism; after all, having written the definitive treatise on feminism, metanarrative, and television ('"Ruling with Her Pussy, Undone by Her Asp": the Cleopatra Narrative and the Made-for-TV Heroine' (1992)), Fraugrois qualifies as one of the most cogent voices in postfeminist analysis of commercial television programming.

Recent pop culture analysts have seen contemporary primetime television as too transparently gendered to warrant much critical attention (indeed, one wonders if the conservatism currently fashionable in mainstream cultural criticism is complicit with the self-determined gender-equal Pepsi generation in perpetuating a backlash which deems feminist criticism too didactic to usefully challenge the modern cultural arena, as if *Xena: Warrior Princess* has finally evened the playing field and rendered feminist inquiry no longer necessary). To make matters worse, and this desire for a critical hiatus from feminist television criticism notwithstanding, the past several years have seen many superficially clever but facile readings of largely uninterrogated 'sexism' on the small screen, the most useful of which have merely rehashed the political theory and critical frameworks offered by the likes of Laura Mulvey in the 1970s and 1980s. In this much-needed collection, Fraugrois characteristically takes television to task, offering a surprisingly insightful contribution to the world of television and feminist studies.

It is our one complaint that we don't get enough of Fraugrois herself in this collection; her introduction sketches the organizational frame and clearly summarizes the most salient moments in the essays to follow, but the Fraugrois of 'Cleopatra' is regrettably quiet. With a few notable exceptions, the essays presented in *A Creature Feminine: The Politics of T & A on Primetime Television, 1970–2000* encourage readers to look twice at familiar television texts and well-used feminist theories, to examine the relationships between characterization and the cult of 'real-world' celebrity, to consider feminist politics as subversively emerging through mainstream representations of female sexuality, and to be on guard against the supposedly 'empowering' contemporary commodifications of the female body. As Alice Stein, one of the essayists in the volume, remarks, the commercial availability of 'T & A' explicitly values the female body as market capital, but 'women's ability to purchase the means of participation in this brave new economy does not necessarily buy them control from, or autonomy within, the still-dominant patriarchy.' The still-sexist entertainment medium of television, as these essays demonstrate, continues to hold sway over feminine identity, feminist politics, and the social semantics of the female body.

The book is comprised of eleven essays in three sections. The first of these, 'Maternity, Power, and the Law of the Father', contains four essays that discuss representations of motherhood on prime-time television, leaning on Freudian, Lacanian, and Kristevan models of sexuality, maternity, and power to trouble easy readings of sitcoms, celebrities, and soap operas. Anne Bovary's 'The Negative Oedipus: Murdering the Mother in *My Two Dads* and *Full House*', employs a Freudian model of child/parent hierarchies to explore the anxieties of a motherless household with children, especially in situation comedies where the goal is humor but motherlessness arises from a woman's death. How is a dead woman funny, Bovary asks: not only does she finally demonstrate the answer to this provocative (if unsettling) question, she ultimately shows how these programs – ironically, through the trope of the dead mother – witness the triumph of motherhood, as the fathers must take on a vital role they are hardly capable of playing. Further, within her Freudian model, Bovary demonstrates how these shows subversively manifest adolescent sexuality through the control of men: symbolically murdering the mother and marrying the father, the teenagers upset the deterministic gendering of Freud's seminal theory, coming into their powerful, self-actualized selves.

Bovary's essay is immediately followed by Kristine Kilkenney's 'Cokie, Katie, or Kathie Lee: Semiotic Motherhood in a Symbolic Economy', in one of the conspicuous editorial decisions that reveal Fraugrois's astute critical eye. Though at first the two essays might seem to offer opposite representations of motherhood by virtue of their titles alone – the 'murdering' of the mother revealed as an anti-feminist structure whereby women's social and domestic power can be successfully supplanted by men, and the public celebration of motherhood and working-motherhood appearing as a progressive, pro-feminist cultural phenomenon – in fact the essays reverse this opposition. If 'Murdering the Mother' celebrates motherhood by forcing the father into the maternal role unarmed by natural, instinctual maternity, Kilkenney's analysis of three public news figures shows professional mothers in much more compromising positions between the Lacanian symbolic economy in which they build their professional personae and Kristevan semiotic motherhood. Though the essay does analyze details of each woman's public biographies in turn, Cokie, Katie, and Kathie Lee, when all is said and done, represent three 'types' of public motherhood (one suspects that Cokie is included primarily because of the potential for alliteration her name affords), women adopting various patriarchal roles to mask their desire(s) and their rebellious feminist positions as working moms.

Like 'Murdering the Mother', 'Cokie, Katie, and Kathie Lee' unsettles typical or conspicuous readings of television images. Following Kristeva's *Stabat Mater* (and, like Kristeva, brutally assaulting textual graphics in an effort to make a non-phallic 'point'), Kilkenney dismantles Kathie Lee Gifford's public persona as *'uber*-mom', arguing that during her days on *Live: with Regis and Kathie Lee*, 'Cody's Mom' instead parodied motherhood, eliding essential femininity and semiotic maternity for 'full (members)hip in the sym(bo(l)/ic/k(y)) e(con)(o'my)' that reifies unequal gender norms. As her marriage crumbled in full view of the tabloids, Kilkenney claims (and, one might add, as her company exploited child labor in the third-world), Kathie Lee reconstructed the 1950s family on morning television, with Regis Philbin unwittingly cast in the role of disaffected patriarch, or as Kilkenney puts it: 'A/not/her o(bj)ectified and op-posit-(ion)al he‹lp›mate w/hose l(ass)-it-ud-e to/ward-(off) nomi((a)nal)ism be/lies/ (not)phallic hetero-st/ru(p)ctures.' Ultimately, her *uber*-mom persona backfired with unexpected force, as the break-up of the morning show pair (ironically so that Kathie Lee could pursue 'choral' fantasies, if not chora-l ones), cast viewers in the psychologically difficult position of children of divorce. Predictably, Kilkenney demonstrates, some tried to warm up to their new 'step-mom' (one wonders whether there is birth-order research in the works), but most abandoned the show in droves.

For Katie Couric, the demands of professionalism and the semiotic, bodily desires and pleasures of essential woman/mother(hood) intersect and bizarrely transform at the site of disease. Just as with Kathie Lee, Kilkenney argues that semiotic desire(s) must be translated into the patriarchal symbolic economy for motherhood to appear in professional structures at all, but rather than electing to abandon the essential self for a prescribed 'maternal' role, Couric's experience with cancer '(dis)-(trans)for(med) the ener(gi)es of the c/hor/a in/+/to the ~~Language~~ o(f th)e ((un)dead) Fat/her'. As her husband's dying of colon cancer materially changed Couric's motherhood, it also channeled her semiotic chora-l energies into a desire for public consumption of the maternal body: her highly-publicized colonoscopy represents a uniquely maternal position of self-protection and public advocacy, as she takes her audiences beyond public health rhetoric and invites them, virtually, where no one, frankly, is interested in going.

What is missing from this section, until Maud Cannon's 'Neo-Antebellum Mammies: The Othering of Caretaking from *The Jeffersons* to *The Jetsons*', is any attention to political-historical progress or to cultural artifacts as historiographies. Though *Full House* and *My Two Dads* hit the airwaves nearly twenty years ago, little attention is paid to the role of historical moment in the manufacture of these cultural artifacts. 'Neo-Antebellum Mammies' provides a surfeit of historical information and evidence but lacks a persuasive argument tying this documentary evidence together. Still, the research in this article is exhaustive, impressive, and potentially very important to the field. Through graphic representations from the popular media of the early nineteenth century to the present day, and more impressively, through written descriptions from slave auction advertisements to *TV Guide* blurbs, Cannon demonstrates the pervasiveness of the cultural trope of 'Other as (M)other'. The most surprising reading offered is that of the robot Rosie on *The Jetsons* who represents to Cannon a potential new form of 'Othering', namely what she calls Technism: in an ominous conclusion, Cannon warns that new advancements in artificial intelligence may present new opportunities for displacing motherhood onto oppressed beings, minority races or artificial intelligence-forms.

The section closes with an unfortunately pedestrian Freudian reading of *Dynasty*, *Knots Landing*, and *Dallas*. Stanley Gique, in 'Bitch Goddess/Matriarch/*Vagina Dentata*: The Destroyer Goddess of the 80s Nighttime Soap Opera', knows his Freud but demonstrates nothing of the post-Freudian work done in scopophilic desire even as he constitutes as masculine the viewing audiences of these dramatic series, despite ratings information which indicate a large female viewing contingent. Clearly and vehemently (and occasionally almost angrily), Gique exposes the deliberate cruelty of women as represented in these nighttime vixens, arguing that 'their duplicitous and conniving ways of hurting men' render them 'as unknowable as the id, as relentless as the superego', floating signifiers of violence and unpredictability, desire, discipline, and punishment.

The second section of this collection examines the female body and feminine sexualit(ies) as represented over the past three decades of television programming. Both Lyn J. Lawrence and Ellen Van Dyke, in their essays 'Marcy Becomes Electra: Gender Dysphoria in *Peanuts* Primetime Specials' and 'Laverne and Velma as *ur*-Dyke: Outing 70s Television' respectively, investigate the not-so-deeply hidden codes for lesbianism in *Peanuts*, *Laverne and Shirley* and *Scooby Doo*, positing that the development of radical feminism seeps into the shows' otherwise heteronormative messages through an elaborate, subliminal sign system only apparent to particular, 'initiated' viewers. Van Dyke and Lawrence, perhaps too often, discover evidence that these shows act as a nexus for cryptic homosexual semiotic signs. Possibly the most famous of these signs is the large cursive L sported by Laverne of *Laverne and Shirley*. Lawrence asserts that the 'Scarlet L' acts as a diacritic, coloring the nature not only of the title character who bears it but also of the relationship between her and her co-titular roommate. We did, however, think that Lawrence was stretching when she, by association, tagged all characters whose names began with L as lesbians. While Lacey of *Cagney & Lacey* might be a closeted lesbian, we found Lawrence's argument for Lucille Ball and Laura Petry unconvincing. Perhaps the hardest assertion to believe is that the letter J is actually a backward L, so that Jo from *Facts Of Life* and Janet from *Three's Company* could be identified as lesbians.

The argument for Laverne's lesbian identity, however, is very convincing. Laverne's (closeted) butch ways extend to her trademark drink, which entails the symbolic defiling of white (mother's) milk with man's dark Pepsi-Cola, in an inherently conflicted concoction. Lawrence even teases out very fine nuances in the Laverne/Shirley relationship: noting the latter's wont to take counsel in a cat-shaped pillow named 'Boo-boo Kitty'; she insists that this is code for the passive nature of Shirley's relationship to Laverne by drawing a parallel between the site of Shirley's comfort and the fact that the submissive in male homosexual congress is derogatorily called a 'pillow-biter'. The fact that Laverne's lesbian (or liminal) identity is displaced onto an article of clothing tidily renders her 'closeted' at the end of every day, if hidden-in-plain-sight during the narrative frame of the show's individual episodes.

However, Lawrence describes Laverne not only as an aggressor in her sexual pursuits, but also as champion of woman over man. Tellingly, Laverne is a bottle-capper at the Schotz brewery: she prevents the gush of foam from phallic bottles – constraining man's 'aqua vitae'. While this is not necessarily a castrating action, it does deny the issuance of fluids; so that, as Lawrence asserts, Laverne transcends butch dyke into a space of the purely feminine and womanly. She is not the inverted male as others such as Crotchette and Beavers (1994; 1995) have put forth, nor is she hermaphroditic as Lactisse assumes. Convincingly, Lawrence finds a conventional space, that of the working-class lesbian, for a critically conflicted character.

This, however, is not the case with Marcy and Peppermint Patty in Van Dyke's essay, which showcases a resurgent academic interest in BDSM. Van Dyke argues that the Marcy character of the *Peanuts* comic strip and later television specials is the M in the SM (Sado-Masochist) relationship. Addressing Peppermint Patty (the closeted S) as 'Sir', Marcy exposes the hierarchical nature of power between the two and positions herself the weaker. Peppermint Patty, with her scratchy, sometimes gruff voice, resists Marcy's attempts to 'out' the pair. Van Dyke relates Patty's resistance to the childlike portrayal of the characters:

> They are indeed children who must answer to the power of their unintelligible parent and teachers, but Patty has discovered her own power in making Marcy submit to her sexual desires. She doesn't, though, necessarily want to expose her predilections, much like a child does not want to be caught masturbating.

Not unmindful of Adrienne Rich's enduring criticism, Van Dyke goes on to explore many of the female characters in the series. She persuasively argues that many are budding, if not mature, dominatrixes. Lucy Van Pelt, as Van Dyke points out, is easily identified as a dominant type. Particularly telling are her encounters with Charlie Brown where she is the placeholder to Brown's kicker. At the last moment she pulls the ball, which sends him flying. The football, Van Dyke maintains, symbolizes power – power she has in averting Brown's violent action through his typically patriarchal game. This power can easily transfer to sexual situations where Lucy could never be passive, but instead must control (possibly through the use of restraints and torture devices, Van Dyke asserts because of the tendency of children to be cruel). Indeed, the writer exposes the cruelty and dominance of the female characters in nearly every panel of every strip and every minute of every television special. From the 'Little Red-Headed Girl' whom Brown is enamored of to Freida with the 'naturally curly hair' to Sally Brown whose affection for Linus, the infantilized milquetoast, only further strengthens her case, Van Dyke manages to unpack the signs of unconventional sexuality.

Moving from depictions of homosexuals in the previous pieces, the next essays investigate the construction of the woman's body and interestingly negotiate the audience position. Seymour Russell's 'Reclaiming the Jiggle Factor: Commodification Without Competition from *Charlie's Angels* to *Baywatch*' does not read women's bodies as much as it celebrates them. Breasts, Russell says, have too long been condemned as objectified or objectifiable objects, and women should recognize that 'jiggle is a beautiful thing'; further they should take hold of their 'jiggle factor' and celebrate it.

We began to view Russell with some skepticism for (1) his seemingly loving descriptions of his textual examples: about Pamela Anderson in her Baywatch red tank, he says, 'Anderson's slow motion run toward the camera was evocative of feelings perhaps best described by the greatest of the Romantic poets'; and (2) his insistence that Suzanne Somers had 'missed the mark in a somewhat southerly direction' when she became a spokesperson for Thigh Master; and (3) that *Petticoat Junction* at its peak reminded him of the best of Chaucer but the worst of Marilyn Chambers. However, at the point when one begins to wonder why a scholar of Fraugrois' stature would include this essay, Russell departs from his superficial application of Kristevan terminology and convincingly sophomoric observations and assembles a virtual collage of theoretical frameworks all employed to justify his mammary celebration, the most notable of which are Lacanian and Jungian.

In a surprising move Russell co-mingles Lacanian lack and Kristevan *jouissance* in an interesting reading of feminine space. Russell persuasively insists that breasts symbolically fill the missing maternal space in men – that because men notice the lack of breasts, which necessitates the realization of their non-maternalness, breasts are already always a space for the M/Other. With this premise in place, Russell can then argue that the larger the breasts, the more man must confront M/Otherness which, therefore, gives credence to women who healthily fill out their sweaters and bikini tops. Russell further moves to include Jungian readings of the archetypicality of mammarian plenitude by performing a cross cultural reading of ancient totems in the Guappagari tribe of the Yucatan. Harnessing far-flung theory and anthropology more than make up for Russell's unabashed joy at the sight of bouncing breasts.

Be that as it may, what Russell doesn't consider are the feminist theories of the objectification of women on screen, especially Mulvey's notion that women's bodies are fragmented and voyeuristically consumed in pieces rather than evoking on-screen a whole female self. With Mulvey in mind, Alice Stein's 'Implants or Mastectomy: Self/Body Authorship, Fragmentation, and Scopophilic Desire' acknowledges the possibility for Breast Criticism as potentially liberating for women. Taking her theoretical stance in market capitalism, she argues that through plastic surgery women have the power to author their own bodies. Like the members of primitive tribes who use scarification rituals and apply pre-Cixousian cicatrixes to their bodies in an attempt to beautify themselves, a woman writing her body with silicone or saline normalizes conventional beauty standards and has added financial incentives as well.

Stein goes on to note that the viewing of the gradual change in celebrity appearance through plastic surgery positions the viewers as cannibals – consuming implants, collagen, the effluence from liposuction procedures, and the detritus from various nips and tucks. 'The "will to watch" is the "will to consume", and that consumptative force is cannibalistic,' writes Stein. She goes on to show her neo-Marxist colors when she links representation, cannibalism, and capitalism together to illustrate that, contrary to Russell's celebratory stance, breast augmentation and the 'will to be seen' place the entertainment economy within the cannibo-capitalistic jaws of the modes of signification and production by trading in and consuming female flesh.

Sympathetic to this position, Karen Berger, in the final essay of the section, investigates the confluence of Foucauldian power, anorexia, and homospectatorialism. In the essay 'Anorexia and the Homospectatorial Gaze: Investigating the Doppelgänger

Relationship Between Characters and Actors from Tracey Gold to Calista Flockhart', Berger agrees with Stein that the female body is objectified and consumed by not only men in the audience, but women as well. In fact, many television programs and commercials make it necessary for women to position themselves as lesbians to actively and properly consume the images flickering on the screen. A woman unconsciously compares the size of a celebrity's breasts, the shape of her behind or the line of her jaw – placing herself in the position to judge the relative attractiveness of the change.

The most pernicious occurrence of this move, Berger notes, is in the presence or absence of body fat. The female viewer objectifies the actor on screen, in essence masculinizing herself and thereby reinforcing patriarchal norms onto the actors. Much like the cannibo-capitalistic jaws of the modes of production where the female body is consumed, the homospectatorial gaze proceeds to force woman to consume the diminishing fat on female actors, causing a veritable symbolic liposuction that will lead to the 'clogged arteries of femininity later in life'. This surfeit of rapidly disappearing lipids (evidenced by the female actors on the popular NBC comedy *Friends*) may wreak havoc on the actors themselves when their character on screen becomes their doppelganger in real life. Tracey Gold, in the somewhat sadly titled sitcom *Growing Pains*, found, as her character was made the butt of fat jokes, herself wasting away with anorexia nervosa. Berger astutely recognizes the auto-mimetic function of representation as character and actor become not only interlocked but also juxtaposed like an X-Ray glued to an MRI slide. Calista Flockhart, perhaps the most noticeable example of a 'curtain rod', too exhibits the tendency to become more 'pencil-like – writing the abundance of her loss on the small screen in a tiny, palsied scrawl' with every season. Berger ends by speculating that the vampiric nature of the homospectatorial gaze, especially as it is implicated in the incongruous body imagery maintained by its victims, parallels the reification of the worker in vertically integrated hierarchical management structures. While we were not sure of this leap into organizational theory, the totality of the argument should prove useful to scholars and dieticians alike.

Finally, the essays in this volume examine the means of television production and the market into which the female body/self is advertised. In the final section, under the heading, 'Consumer Culture and the Commodification of Femininity', television-sanctioned femininity is predicated on pathology and self-loathing. Evelyn Sommers, in 'Piss and Vinegar: Feminine Hygiene and the Marketing of Daytime Television' negotiates the strange terrain between stress, soap, and the unclean female body, showing how the female viewer is presented with her own body as defiled, inadequate, and in sore need of advertisers' particular sweet-smelling products.

Sommers focuses on filth first and foremost, linking the societal acceptance of such a model of femininity-as-dirty to anti-feminist biblical interpretations. Once internalized, she argues, the notion of woman's impurity (most tellingly associated with odors in the nether-regions) digs a bottomless chasm in the psyche, a 'lack' of Lacanian proportions, into which a woman will pour all her expendable income and, in extreme cases, her mental health. Her desire to be clean mirrors the Lacanian desire that fuels the serial of daytime television, which critics have already noted, making the double-whammy of daytime programming and daytime advertising an addictive but ultimately unsatisfying experience. Further, her desire for cleanliness counters all other commercial desires: to be thin (which requires exercise, which produces sweat); to be domestically gifted (which requires 'dirty' tasks like gardening, cooking, and cleaning); to be sexy (which produces bodily fluids both dirty and frequently dangerous) – leaving the viewer of daytime television paralyzed, ensnared in a web of her own (socially-prescribed) yearnings.

We believe that this volume of sorely needed criticism and analysis will stand as a landmark collection – garnering much acclaim and use from those in disciplines ranging from cultural studies to women's studies. The multivalent approach to psychoanalysis and other *bricollaged* theories will be of much interest to those who may have seemed out of vogue within English departments for the last twenty years. But perhaps the enduring legacy of *A Creature Feminine* will be in its flashes of humor and good cheer, particularly from the likes of Lawrence, Russell, and Valley, not to mention Fraugrois herself, who in her introduction quotes the old standby light bulb joke: 'How many feminists does it take to screw in a lightbulb? That's not funny!' So, is there a Humor Section in a feminist bookstore? Well, maybe not a whole section, but now at least there is this one fine volume.

Captain Kangaroo and Mr. Green Jeans/Captain Kirk and Mr. Spock:
Homoeroticism as Subtext in the Post-Atomic Age
by Herman Heman
San Francisco: Gaylord Press, 1999

Howdy Doody: A Marxist Interpretation of the Manipulation
of the Proletariat
by Ivan Ivanovich
Moscow: Lenin Square Books, 2000

reviewed by Jim Riser

Captain Kangaroo and Mr. Green Jeans/Captain Kirk and Mr. Spock continues Herman Heman's study of sex and sexuality on television. For those unfamiliar with Heman's work, his first book, *Phallic Fallacies: The Myth of the Virile Western Hero* (University of Texas at Paris Press, 1991), calls into question the enduring mystique of the cowboy as the hard-loving, hard-riding hero, when he in fact spent days and even weeks in self-imposed isolation and subsequent celibacy on the lonesome prairies with only his horse or fellow cowboys for companionship. Picking up where he left off in his second volume, *Sex Sells so Sell Sex: A History of the Prostitute on Tele-vision* (University of Nevada at Pahrump Press, 1995), Heman moves from his discussion of blatant sex to latent sex as he explores the subtextual homoerotic nature of two of television's most revered shows.

Heman offers a compelling and often eye-opening analysis that is sure to challenge many of the long-established and more traditional interpretations of these programs. That he is aware of the controversy likely to arise from this latest work is clear. In the Introduction, Heman argues 'we must strive to see the world afresh, to put aside the old perspectives for the new. We have for too long tippy-toed around the subject of sexual orientation in certain programs.' Citing Emerson, he reminds us

135

that 'a foolish consistency is the hobgoblin of little minds,' and we should, therefore open our minds to new interpretations of these television classics.

Heman's scholarship is impressive, to say the least. Endless hours of viewing fading kinescope records of *Captain Kangaroo* and videotapes of *Star Trek* enable Heman to scrutinize subtleties of language, both verbal and visual, that would otherwise go unnoticed. It is exactly these subtleties that interest Heman, for it is therein that he finds the homoerotic subtext.

While Heman's most recent work may be seen as groundbreaking due to his choice of specific programs, he is by no means alone in the rapidly expanding field of subtextual studies of television. Even a cursory search of the Internet reveals a staggering number of sites devoted to this subject. Most prevalent is the widespread and divergent discussion of *Xena: Warrior Princess*. Writing of this show, Ogami defines subtext as 'lesbian innuendo ... it can be a scene, an action, a word, a line, a touch, a look, a tone of voice, or an entire episode that implies or shows Xena and Gabrielle are lovers.' Similarly, Linda Seger says, 'subtext is what the character is really saying beneath and between the lines.' Using definitions such as these, as well as drawing heavily on the relevant critical theory in Jane Tompkins' *Reader-Response Criticism: From Formalism to Post-Structuralism*, Heman presents an argument that is every bit as convincing and sometimes as equally disturbing as Swift's *Modest Proposal*.

Moreover, Heman takes great pains to refute his homophobic critics, those who say that he reads far too much into the text. Citing Kathleen E. Bennett's '*Xena: Warrior Princess*, Desire Between Women, and Interpretive Response', Heman notes, 'reader-response theory has shown that the subtexters are correct in arguing for the validity of their interpretations, because there is no objective truth to the text.' While the convincing application of critical theory gives weight and credence to his analysis, it is Heman's extensive use of evidence from the series themselves that cements his argument.

An example or two will suffice to illustrate his dexterity in analysis. On one occasion, Mr. Green Jeans – a name itself ripe with male fecundity – offers to show the Captain the latest product from his garden. Reaching into his copious pocket, Mr. Green Jeans draws forth a large potato and then tells the Captain, 'This is a potato, also known as a tuber. A tuber is a root.' In response, the Captain says, 'I certainly like the size of your root.' Heman then explains, perhaps unnecessarily, the slang meaning of 'root' as a reference to the penis. From this he extrapolates his conclusion that such exchanges between the Captain and Mr. Green Jeans are in fact *double entendres* of a homosexual nature.

Heman is equally adept at discerning the sexual symbolism in the show, as revealed in the subtext. While space here does not allow for a full repetition of those symbols – after all, that is why Heman wrote the book – the mention of a few is warranted. From Grandfather Clock with his large swinging pendulum to Tom Terrific with his phallic headdress, Heman reveals a children's program replete with sexual undertones. Of particular note is his discussion of the Banana Man, a recurring guest on the show. Writing of the Banana Man, Heman states, 'reaching repeatedly into the various pockets of his clothes, the Banana extracts a variety of fruits, including bunch after bunch of bananas. Each time he does so, he moans "wow" as if deriving sexual pleasure. This pleasurable handling of the undeniably phallic banana is certainly a latent, if not blatant, homoerotic subtext.'

Because the program aired during a time when homosexuality was very much a subculture, Captain Kangaroo and Mr. Green Jeans would, of course, have been keenly aware of the need to remain 'in the closet'. Heman suggests that the fear of discovery is also revealed in the phallocentric subtext of the show. As anyone familiar with the program knows, one of the running jokes was to have Bunny Rabbit try to steal the Captain's carrots. According to Heman, 'hiding the carrots equates to the Captain hiding his sexuality.' Despite the Captain's best efforts to thwart him, Bunny finds the hiding place and triumphantly waves the carrots about. Heman posits, 'In flashing the carrots, Bunny is in fact mocking the Captain's suppressed desire to both hide and reveal his homosexuality, to deny his sexual orientation while at the same time yearning to make it known.' He also remarks that the Banana Man's drawing forth of 'fruit' was yet another sign of conflicting desire to expose the other 'fruits' on the show.

Heman's examination of *Star Trek*'s strangely bonded pair, Captain Kirk and Mr. Spock, is equally insightful and cogent. Before discussing this second pair in particular, Heman focuses on the 'maleness' of space exploration in general. Referring to the very familiar opening voice-over for the show, Heman notes, 'the phallic penetration of virgin space is, obviously, represented by the *Enterprise*'s assigned mission "to boldly go where no *man* has gone before" (emphasis added).' Heman is quick to admit that such action is clearly heterosexual in connotation.[1] Atara Stein, in a recent article in *Genders*, argues that there is no homosexual relationship between Kirk and Spock, but finds the suggestions of one between Captain Picard and the entity Q.[2] However, as with Captain Kangaroo and Mr. Green Jeans, for Heman the homoerotic implications lie in the subtext.

The bond between Kirk and Spock has long been a subject of discussion. April Selley, in her article '"I Have Been, and Ever Shall Be, Your Friend": *Star Trek*, *The Deerslayer* and the American Romance', states, 'Kirk and Spock resist restrictive marriages with women in episodes which allow them to prove their loyalty to one another.' Speaking of the relationship between Kirk and his son David in *Star Trek II: The Wrath of Khan,* Selley comments, 'Kirk's response to David is nowhere as emotional as Kirk's response to Spock's death, indicating that the most intense relationship in the film is not that between father and son but between friend and friend.' Although Selley's comments refer to the film and not the television series, it is the series that gives rise to later intense relationships. It is exactly this intensity that Heman focuses upon. According to him, Spock's legendary restraint of emotion results not only from his Vulcan heritage but also from his equally powerful desire to conceal his homosexual relationship with Kirk. However, just as Spock at times lets his human side surface, so too does he uncover his veiled attraction for Kirk. Heman writes:

Spock makes a concerted effort to always address Kirk as 'Captain' when in the presence of others in order to maintain the illusion of distance between them as officers of different rank. On more than one occasion though, Spock, in an unguarded moment, affectionately calls Kirk 'Jim' while at the same time gently touching his arm or shoulder.

It is moments such as these that fit so precisely Ogami's earlier stated definition of subtext. Heman maintains that when barriers of rank are removed, when Spock and

Kirk treat each other as equals, the subtext reveals an irrefutable, latent homoerotic tone.

Heman contents that the most obvious of these subtextual clues is the Vulcan mind meld that Spock performs. Although Spock at various times links himself with whales, women, and various alien life forms from plants to rock-like creatures, he undoubtedly derives the most enjoyment from his episodes with Kirk. Heman explains:

> At times reluctant to establish the mind meld with other forms of life because of possible physical or psychological danger, Spock seldom hesitates to couple his being with Kirk's. Indeed, the encounter is most often marked by a reciprocal pleasure that leaves both men spent and panting in the throes of a psychic orgasm.

The homosexual bond between Kirk and Spock is, to Heman's way of thinking, as indisputable as the theory of warp drive and extends beyond the far reaches of the most distant stars.

As with Captain Kangaroo and Mr. Green Jeans, the relationship between Captain Kirk and Mr. Spock is an evocative, provocative one. All of their pent-up feelings are rarely overtly displayed, Heman reminds us, but instead lie embedded in the subtext, awaiting discovery like a hidden carrot or a far-off galaxy.

The pairing of Ivan Ivanovich's book with Heman's may at first glance seem a bit disparate, but the two do have common bonds. Like Heman, Ivanovich chooses to look beneath the surface and behind the scenes in offering his Marxist interpretation of *Howdy Doody*. Moreover, there exists an intriguing overlap of characters between *Howdy Doody* and *Captain Kangaroo*. Indeed, had it not been for *Howdy Doody*, *Captain Kangaroo* might not have been. Bob Keeshan, who played Captain Kangaroo, was, in fact, the original Clarabell the Clown on *The Howdy Doody Show*. Keeshan was fired from the show, re-hired, and then fired again in 1952. It was only after he was removed from the show in a labor dispute that he developed the role of Captain Kangaroo.

The firing of Keeshan and most of the rest of the supporting cast – to be discussed in more detail later – represents but one of the many Marxist elements that Ivanovich sees in the show. He finds in their dispute the classic 'worker/proletariat versus capitalist/suppressor' conflict central to Marxist ideals. Ivanovich uses as an epigraph for his book a quotation from Bryan Appleyard:

> It has been revealed that the television program, *The Teletubbies*, is, in fact a communist allegory intended to spread discontent and revolutionary sympathy amongst the youngsters of our great nation.

Appleyard's statement certainly has not generated the outcry about *The Teletubbies* that Jerry Farwell's accusation of that show's pandering of homosexuality did. However, for Ivanovich, Appleyard issues a warning to be heeded. Quoting the old axiom 'Those that fail to learn from history are doomed to repeat it,' Ivanovich notes that similar alarms were sounded in the early 1950s, but were eventually dismissed as the misguided and egotistical machinations of a few powerful political figures in Washington. In his Preface, Ivanovich writes: 'Joseph McCarthy and the House

Committee on Un-American Activities were undoubtedly right when they argued that Hollywood was falling under the influence of communists during the late 1940s and early 1950s.' Ivanovich finds in *Howdy Doody* the exemplum of such influence.

He begins his study with an inordinately protracted review of the Socialist/ Communist movement in the United States. Going back as far as the utopian communes such as Brook Farm and moving laboriously through the 1920s, 30s, 40s, and 50s, Ivanovich lays a background that might be useful for the neophyte but that proves tedious otherwise. The essence of the chapter is captured in its last sentences: '"Marxist" is, then, not used here as a literary theory as defined by Walter Benjamin or Georg Lukacs. Rather, it is used in a political sense as a basic struggle between economic classes.'

Ivanovich contends that the Marxist undertones of the program that made their way before the cameras were a direct result of the dispute between labor and management behind the scenes. *Howdy Doody* was a commercial success from its beginning. The producers of the show recognized its appeal when they received over 250,000 requests for buttons promoting 'Howdy for President for Kids' in 1948. Sponsorship increased and endorsements produced what for the time was significant income, $15 million in 1950 from Howdy-licensed items alone. It was precisely this economic development that resulted in what Ivanovich sees as a typical worker/ owner conflict in Marxist terms.

Bob Keeshan, the original Clarabell, and other cast members reportedly made demands for increased salary due to the financial success of the show. Interestingly, according to Buffalo Bob Smith in *Howdy and Me*, Clarabell never spoke because 'If he talks, we're going to have to pay him union scale'. Because Keeshan and the others supposedly indulged in collective bargaining, their contracts with the show were terminated in what came to be known as the 'Christmas Eve Massacre' of 1952. Ivanovich interprets this wholesale elimination of cast and crew, including the original Howdy Doody himself, as a sort of political pogrom. He writes, 'From a Marxist perspective, such action is clearly an oppressive manoeuvre on the part of the capitalistic management meant to rid the show of a rebellious faction – a unified workers' movement – bent on destabilizing the economic foundation of the network.' Buffalo Bob, Ivanovich adds, clearly aligns himself with the capitalist/management/owner faction, lining his own pockets with subsequent contracts worth over half a million dollars, while showing little sympathy for the ousted workers.

Ivanovich rounds out his discussion of the off-camera section with a brief note about the Peanut Gallery. While supposedly made up of 'average' kids given the opportunity to view the show from on stage, the Peanut Gallery was, in Ivanovich's Marxist scheme, yet another display of the contempt for the worker class by the rich and powerful. Everyday kids (the proletariat) had to wait months or even years to acquire tickets to the Peanut Gallery, just as their parents had to wait years to acquire the few material possessions they desired. Meanwhile, the sponsors (the capitalist oppressors) got half the tickets to each show, and the executives and others associated with the program got their share before the remaining few were doled out to the general public. Ivanovich asserts that it was such dealings as those with Keeshan and the Peanut Gallery that account for the Marxist undertones of the show itself.

Drawing on Appleyard's aforementioned statement about 'communist allegory', Ivanovich attempts to decipher the Marxist message the program contains. The requisite class conflict is embodied, according to Ivanovich, in the recurring struggle between Howdy and Phineas T. Bluster for control of Doodyville circus. Bluster, allegorically, represents the capitalistic forces exerting influence and control over the lives of others. Additionally, as mayor of Doodyville, Bluster represents the government with its equally abusive powers. Howdy, on the other hand, symbolizes the ordinary working-class citizen, the proletariat. Ivanovich writes:

> Dressed in his plaid shirt, bandana, and boots, Howdy Doody is a caricature of that most-American icon – the cowboy. With his 48 freckles, one for each state, Howdy epitomized rugged individualism and the desire to be free from the tyranny of an oppressive government or manipulation of a capitalistic system.

Here then, as Ivanovich argues, is the Marxist class conflict in a nutshell. Though a children's program on the surface, *Howdy Doody* was a veiled call for insurrection, for a populace uprising. Apparently, the vast audience of Baby Boomers received the call. Quoting from Buffalo Bob Smith's *Howdy and Me*, Ivanovich notes:

> Remember the Sixties? In those years between 1960 and 1970 when no Howdy Doody Time graced the air-waves, the decade erupted in protest, race riots and demonstrations ... Don't forget that Howdy knew mean-spirited Mr. Bluster for a corrupt, corrupting old goat, and stood up to him; and that Howdy's alumni exploded into adulthood with an unprecedented opposition to any authority figures they deemed unworthy of support.

The Marxist ramifications of the program, though slow in coming to fruition, seem undeniable.

Ivanovich continues his allegorical interpretation by examining the matter of voice/voicelessness in the show. He sees Buffalo Bob as a figurehead and spokesman for the capitalist sponsors of the program. In that capacity, Buffalo Bob literally lends his voice in support of wealthy promoters in order to further enrich them and himself. Conversely, Howdy has no voice of his own; he cannot speak for himself, but must mouth what Buffalo Bob says. According to Ivanovich's Marxist analysis, Howdy's inarticulate character represents the proletariat which will remain oppressed as long as it is forced to remain silent. Moreover, Ivanovich sees in Clarabell the clown an even more obvious attempt to restrain the voice of the people. Denied any voice by the repressive powers that control him, he is reduced to simple yes or no answers produced by honking horns.

Ivanovich finds in the Peanut Gallery the voice of unrest necessary to spark the overthrow of the repressive system. He writes, 'The Peanut Gallery is emblematic of the populace protest for a greater voice in the everyday events of their lives. However their outcry is subdued by Buffalo Bob, who, as representative of the capitalists, strives to quell such civil disobedience.' The irony is that in the beginning of each show they are not only allowed but also encouraged to give voice to their feelings when asked that famous line, 'What time is it?' The response, of course, is 'It's Howdy Doody time!' In issuing this reply, the Peanut Gallery, according to Ivanovich, was in fact calling for revolution, for a leader to step forth and confront the capitalistic forces personified in Phineas T. Bluster and supported by Buffalo Bob. Given the upheaval of the Sixties, the Marxist intent of the show was indeed successful.

Ivanovich closes his discussion of *Howdy Doody* with a brief summary of the then on-going court battle for ownership of the original Howdy Doody puppet. He sees the dispute as yet another indication of the capitalistic, money-oriented nature of the program and of society as a whole. Kawabonga!

Despite, or perhaps because of, the divergent nature of their works, both Heman and Ivanovich offer original and insightful interpretation of their respective subjects and present books well worth the reading.

Notes

1 For an extended discussion of heterosexual encounters in space, see my recent article 'My Space or Yours?: Gravity-Free, Guilt-Free Sex in Space', *Space Frontiers*, June 2000. Heman does not address the presence of a female leader in the person of Captain Janeway in the latest *Star Trek* series, perhaps because she does not fit neatly into his discussion of male bonding. However, a study of the relationship between Janeway and the Borg Seven of Nine might yield interesting results. It is equally interesting to note that while mating between inter-galactic species is by no means taboo, the restriction on homosexual relationships stills exists.
2 See Stein's 'Minding One's P's and Q's: Homoeroticism in *Star Trek: The Next Generation*', *Genders* 27, n.p.

theory

TV Guides: Towards Embedded Theory
by Iain John Austen
Chicago, London, and Sydney: Wiseman Associated Press, 2044

Autarchic Tele-visions
by Sarah-Jane Smythe
New York and London: TallPoppies Press, 2045

reviewed by Matthew Hills

> 'Blivit: A term from Kurt Vonnegut, denoting an incommensurable mixture of genres, styles and forms. Television is "blivitous" because it mixes fact, fiction, faking and forecasting, and it is not always clear where one form ends and another begins. Vonnegut himself characterizes it as "two pounds of shit in a one-pound bag". Blivitous media such as television produce excess meaningfulness in the connections between incommensurate textual forms.'
> John Hartley, *The Uses of Television*

Shamelessly but gloriously mixing fact, fiction, fake and forecast; this is John Hartley's indictment of television. It is a point which he develops in his magisterial book-length collection of neologisms, *Theoryspeaks*, where he describes the 'television' of television studies as emerging through a 'set of disciplining discourses which convert the messiness of intermediality into a cleanly ordered and institutionally hygienic abstraction'. In this narrative, television's essentially 'blivitous' nature – its unruly semiosis and its transmedia materializations – are prematurely brought into line by the manoeuvres of theory. However, this alignment of 'ordering' with theoretical endeavor and 'messiness' with the world 'out there' seems overly tidy itself.

143

A concern which is central to the work of Austen and Smythe is whether television's blivitous approach to culture can be analogous by academic thought, thereby disintegrating the theory/practice and order/disorder structural homology. Can theory surrender its claims to the disciplined and disciplining purism of academic authority, or is it doomed to remain cut off from 'the airwaves and opinion columns, journalistic criticism, the public committees and 'trade' books ... of public culture?'

By calling into question the role of academic work on television, both Austen and Smythe reverse the lines of influence noted by Geraghty and Lusted: 'Criticisms of Television Studies are often based on a confusion between what is studied and the act of studying, and so it is assumed that because some television is sloppy, badly researched and offensive so too is its study'. Rather than reading condemnations of television into condemnations of academic work, Austen and Smythe attempt instead to project television's cultural energy and power into 'the act of studying' television. As such, their efforts form a deliberate, politicized bid to erode any and all lines of distinction between 'television' and 'television studies'. Indeed, both writers make much of the fact that their work rejects the banner of 'television studies'; they prefer to engage in and with television culture rather than providing a 'talking heads' commentary on it:

> If tele-vision implies vision at a distance, then for too long academic work has preserved this distance and guarded the privileges of its vision. If anything, academic work has become more tele-visual than the object and practices that are discussed as 'television' in our culture-at-large. It is time to stop safeguarding the subcultural codes of authenticity that are maintained through academic tele-vision. It is time to bring this vision into catastrophic contact with the world and the culture of TV.

Austen and Smythe develop and broaden the 'turn to fan knowledge' within media studies in general. Austen, in particular, takes seriously the programs he explores, illustrating how they contain complex social philosophies which cannot be reduced to a notion of restrictive 'ideology'. One excellent example of this is Chapter 5 of *TV Guides* which discusses the fourth *X-Files* franchise (2038–present), *XF: Z-Time*. Austen shows how *Z-Time*'s central narrative presents a critique of psychologistic individualism:

> By emphasizing the telepathic powers of its human guerrillas, *Z-Time* psychically networks its protagonists. It reinforces the need for social action and social solutions to political problems, rather than relying on lone agents and hackneyed versions of individualistic heroics. Its narrative emphasis on The Network – featuring a roster of different (but recurring) lead characters who change every few episodes – also undermines any facile equation of agency with individualism. And the interlocked psyches of its characters place 'individuality' within an always-social context.

And yet at the same time, this lack of individual narrative emphasis (which appears to strike at the heart of core cultural values of consumer individualism) has been read by fans and critics of the program as the studio's reaction to supposedly exorbitant wage-demands made by previous *X-Files* stars. By presenting all the lead characters as psychologically interwoven, the studio is able to maximize the appeal of specific actors while nevertheless maintaining the narrative and economic disposability of all of them. Austen therefore highlights the multi-layered forms of cultural critique which revolve around *Z-Time*, illustrating that both fan readings and studio publicity deal explicitly with economic-industrial constraints on narrative form. Far from closing down social and cultural debate, the program's texts open up a range of complex philosophical and industrial discussions across audience demographics.

Austen also devotes a later chapter to the Cult Channel, beginning with Rob Owen's prescient prediction that it 'can't be long before the Cult TV network is created … flops would have a permanent oasis, and they could move from the networks to this specialized service within months'. Once again replacing media futurology and an abstract theoretical agenda with detailed discussion, Austen suggests that by purposefully blurring 'mainstream' and 'cult' nomenclature, the Cult Channel puts in play philosophical critiques of consumer elitism and cultural distinction.

Both Austen and Smythe seek to jettison the excesses of what they refer to as past 'paradigm wars', seeking to move beyond the sterile imposition of theoretical metanarratives and the 'cookie-cutter academic interpretations which have dogged a vibrant 21st century television culture.' Exploring the 'semiotic meritocracy' of contemporary television, these books are united in their belief that 'theory' has had its day. Indeed the term 'theory' forms a term of abuse within these titles (both of which were published as trade paperback originals; Smythe's work also boasts a comprehensive selection of forewords written by many of the actors who star in the TV shows discussed, as well as including a series of chapters co-authored by fans of these programs).

However, Austen and Smythe differ in their practical responses to the realm of televisual post-theory. Austen emphasizes the need to consider all TV as a form of 'Guide' which needs no further explication or recontextualization, and he therefore illuminates the theory which is embedded in a wide range of TV shows, touching on genres as diverse as info-tainment, edu-tainment and enter-tainment. Embedded theory, for Austen, means replacing the pseudo-criticism of prior television studies with an unquestionable respect for the forms and narratives under analysis, as well as for their audiences. Embedded theory means realizing that academics do not have a monopoly on cultural criticism, and that all audiences are always-already social critics. Austen claims to radically reconceptualize the role of the academic, who is thought of as an active 'witness' to the theoretical creativity of producers, texts and fans.

However, it could be argued that Austen overstates the extent to which his work has 'broken' with previous models and approaches. As Charlotte Brunsdon noted long ago: 'Television, as an object of study, has been produced differently by different scholars and interest groups' ('What'; see also Brunsdon, 'Whose'). In order to fetishize the novelty of his own work, Austen is forced to neglect the historical lineage and indebtedness of many of his arguments. This lack of historicized conceptualization is one of the key problems in Austen's account. As I have argued elsewhere and elsewhen:

TV Theory has been keen to silence and suppress many of its inter-texts. Writing itself out of history, it maintains a stance which emphasizes its constant 'newness' and 'nowness.' It is as though TV theory occurs in a perfect vacuum, separated from the oxygen of its predecessors and philosophical fellow travelers. Only rarely is this vacuum considered as imperfect; only rarely does TV Theory rigorously address the full range of its borrowings, logical debts and philosophical forerunners.

To take one example, the work of John Fiske (*Television Culture,* and see also *Half*) surely forms a central plank in Austen's argument but is very much under-represented, and Fiske is curiously given no place in Austen's index. Likewise, the work of John Ellis (see *Seeing* and *Taking*) is very briefly touched on in Austen's analysis of the academic as 'witness', despite the fact that this concept, and much of Austen's approach, can clearly be traced back to Ellis's work:

> Working through is a constant process of making and remaking meanings, and of exploring possibilities. It is an important process in an age that threatens to make us witness to too much information without providing us with enough explanation. Modern television does not, as it used to in the era of scarcity, provide any overall explanation, nor does it ignore or trivialize, as many have criticized it for doing.

Like Ellis before him, Austen emphasizes the cultural proximity of television, its 'closeness' to cultural concerns and ideologically-loaded issues, its contingency and co-presence. And like Fiske before him (and this is the only occasion where his work is explicitly incorporated into *TV Guides*), Austen also investigates a key distinction between the 'experience' of television and the 'learning' of TV Studies:

> John Fiske has argued that the 'suspense in television, its resolution of uncertainty, engages the viewer more intensely because its enigmas appear to be unresolved'. Fiske goes on to suggests that 'the viewer is invited to experience ... resolution, not merely to learn of it' (Fiske 1987: 97). However, this binary of experience/learning needs to be challenged. It is insufficient to take it apart it as a matter of abstract logic and deconstructive principle. Its social and cultural grounds need to be questioned so that 'experience' is aligned both with TV and theory, and so too is 'learning'.

Smythe, on the other hand, develops an even more radical approach. Moving further beyond institutionalized 'theory', she suggests that the study of television culture must be thoroughly 'autarchic', that is, it must itself seek to occupy the self-sufficient TV culture under analysis. To this end, Smythe's latest book consists entirely of words used in the scripts of the programs she analyses. Admittedly these words are used in a different order to their original appearance, but Smythe points out that this principle of rearrangement and contingent recombination is also presupposed by the channel-looping of viewers as well as by schedulers' current disregard for establishing fixed patterns of programming. Of course, Smythe stands accused of logocentrism, rendering a televisual culture purely in terms of the written word, but she also uses words as if they were pixels, forming elaborate multi-page images which coalesce into meaning only when held several meters way from the reader. Smythe is clearly very familiar with Austen's work, and on a number of occasions she accuses Austen of contradicting his own professed focus on 'embedded theory', alleging that the notion of 'embeddedness' is philosophically suspect and itself constitutes an academicizing imposition on the object of study. Smythe critiques the concept of 'embeddedness', suggesting that its emphasis on the excavation and elevation of 'theory' is a rhetorical device aimed at obscuring the possibility that what is 'found' by the critic is also created by that same critic's framework of textual excavation.

The question which is left open is whether Smythe's work can evade its own accusations. *Autarchic Tele-visions* is certainly more blivitous than Austen's contributions to TV theory, happily mixing forecast and fake. Having said this, it returns time and time again to a single quotation from the first book in Robin Nelson's epic Tele-Trilogy (*TV Drama in Transition*):

> The descriptions below go some way to illustrate a key point which I might make better (in a context other than a book) by editing together a sequence comprised of extracts from the episode of *Baywatch* under discussion with shots from the advertisements which punctuated the transmission. A verbal description of the similarities is less potent than a full graphic illustration in revealing the marked similarities between the two in visual style.

Smythe uses this quotation repeatedly to worry away at the status of verbal and written commentary on television. Nelson's sentiments – reiterated in his own later *The Death of TV Drama* and the posthumously published *TV Drama Resurrected* – underpin the entire 'logic' of Smythe's exercise, which ultimately becomes an attempt to revitalize the potency of commentary by drawing on television's cultural authority and legitimacy. And yet, Smythe's attempted appropriation of television's cultural pre-eminence is undermined by her continued use of logocentric theory. Smythe dodges this challenge on a number of occasions. She directs readers to an accompanying website which converts her theoretical agenda into a series of different televisual forms and genres, including a soap operatic version of *Autarchic Tele-visions* as well as a science fiction version. But what this manoeuvre avoids focusing on is the academic authority that Smythe's work preserves through its lead publication in book form rather than in a multi-TV format. Stamped with specific institutional and subcultural authority, Smythe's work is ultimately unable to break with the subcultural academic values that it explicitly critiques. Presenting an assault on the increasingly marginalized privilege of 'the book', *Autarchic Tele-visions*' own form of publication leads it into blatant self-contradiction. Had Smythe possessed the full courage of her convictions, she should surely have refused to publish *Autarchic Tele-visions* in book form altogether. Her proleptic thoughts on this run as follows:

> Of course, it goes without saying that I will be charged with rank hypocrisy. Surely, hopelessly unintelligent reviewers will argue, I should have refused to publish this book *as a book*. They just don't get it. Surely I should be immersing myself and my work in the world of multi-TV and online TV, despite or perhaps because of the international legislation which bans 'academic' co-present commentary that viewers can access alongside broadcast material. Certainly this legislation needs to be fought with all available means, but at the same time we need to analyze television's cultural power in all avenues that remain open to us. We must use and re-appropriate TV within academic

agendas rather than viewing it simply as 'the enemy'. Only by seeking to turn television's power against itself, creating a hybrid critical commentary, will we have any chance of winning audience-share.

Although Smythe's dismissal of the very sentiments that I am expressing here is forceful, it lacks a logical foundation. Smythe issues a rallying cry, yes, but the politics of her position are nevertheless deeply suspect. Focusing on a populist pro-TV argument, Smythe neglects the ways in which television has been regulated, controlled and disciplined not, after all, by a demonized or overly hygienic 'theory' but rather by corporate interests seeking to blunt theoretical challenges to consumerist 'common sense'. By making brands of 'theory' the enemy, Austen and Smythe conveniently neglect the structural complicity with capital that this generates. Smythe's reference to challenging the 'co-present commentary ruling', a judgment which now forms part of all introductory television histories, is pathetically cheap. It pays lip service to a notion of the politically committed academic, thus bolstering Smythe's subcultural capital amongst those whose own vision is suitably short-sighted.

Smythe's work is divided into two sections. Part One deals with television as a culturally centering discourse, demonstrating how the term 'television' has become synonymous with all screen-based technologies, replacing older terms such as 'multimedia' and being added to the term 'online' as part of the cheerful domestication of digital access. Part Two, meanwhile, tackles the 'televisualization of theory' head-on. In the opening few chapters of Part One, Smythe draws heavily on the work of Sara Gwenllian Jones (*Reading* and *How*), especially her reworking (in *Reading*) of 'Bardic' television:

> Where TV has been discussed as a bardic form, online TV is probably better thought of as hyperbardic: it apparently disperses but finally re-creates a centre for the culture that it mediates. Where bardic TV occupies the centre of its culture (see Fiske and Hartley 1978: 86), hyperbardic TV wholly constructs that centre; there is no preceding cultural centrality to be had, however much certain academics may wish this were so.

However, what marks a useful distinction in Jones' groundbreaking work, *Reading Online TV*, becomes an overused slogan in Smythe's *Autarchic Tele-visions*. She neglects the subtleties of Jones' renegotiation of the term 'hyperbardic' in her 2016 study of the cultural clash between 'online' and 'bibliographical' cultures. Jones analyses the difficulties which online TV has posed for forms of 'bibliographical' knowledge. Such knowledge stresses the authority of information via its sources rather than via its circulation as information-capital, and hence Jones argues that bibliographical culture cannot and will not recover from the digital circulation of transient information. In many ways this earlier analysis is far more nuanced than Smythe's sloganeering retread. Rather than developing Jones's work on a complex process of culture-clash and contestation, Smythe simply takes for granted the 'fact' that 'hyperbardic' TV means the death of the author (have we heard this before?) as television itself becomes the centre of cultural legitimation.

Smythe's one productive achievement in her study of 'hyperbardic' TV lies, perhaps, in her re-reading of what has become known as the Spigelian Paradox. This infamous moment in television theory was occasioned by Lynn Spigel's work on the role of the proper name in theory. Spigel's work on the subject was considered so impressive that her argument led the term 'Spigelian' to become synonymous with any excessive focus on a theorist's proper name as a marker of expertise and cultural authority. Unfortunately this 'author-centered mythos' (see Sconce 2000: 182) paradoxically led Spigel's work to occupy the same position that she had studied and decried within a decaying 'bibliographical' culture.

Smythe skillfully weaves Spigel's work into a discussion of John Durham Peters' challenging study *High Concept*. The Spigelian Paradox was supposedly finally explicated and dissolved in Peters' philosophical history of the concept of 'the concept'. Peters argues that conceptuality is essentially linked to the sincerity of the proper name. Without proper names there would be no concept of conceptuality, since the proper name forms the primal surrendering of specificity (the unique individual) to universality (the individual as semiotically identifiable and as disembodied within a system of representation). Without the proper name, the specific and the general would not be firmly experienced as rooted in one another. Without the proper name, Socratic dialogue wouldn't be Socratic, for example, and argumentative points could not be fully personalized and thus infinitely and romantically diversified. Peters concludes that it is naming, this placing of the specific within the universal, which, culturally and historically, drives conceptuality into being.

By re-reading Spigel through Peters' intervention, Smythe builds on her potentially lackluster and unoriginal 'death of the author' argument. She argues, I think convincingly, that academic subculture became excessively fascinated with its own markers of authority and expertise (i.e. the proper name rendered adjectivally) at precisely the point in time when TV was undermining bibliographical cultures based on the authority of the proper name. Critiques of academia's focus on the proper name hence drew attention to this aspect of academic cultural practice just as it was about to be dispersed and overwhelmed by the cultural energies of TV.

Indeed, it is tempting to surmise that Smythe may have been the anonymous reviewer of Spigel (2007) in the journal *Cultural Studies*. Although this would mean that Smythe had written for *Cultural Studies* at the age of 12, this is a minor empirical gripe, and shouldn't undermine the observation that many of Smythe's arguments are foreshadowed in this *Cultural Studies* review:

> Spigel's concern with the proper name seems unfounded, until one starts to wonder why concepts are always 'owned', always marked as intellectual property, so that their use, even when the author is unacknowledged, carries the ghostly implication of a naming. These archaic links between concept, name and property suggest that academic cultural practice will not survive the full onslaught of convergence, where the bonds between concept, name and property are likely to become ever weaker and ever more attenuated. Tomorrow's theory will belong to corporate and collective entities, not individual thinkers, and it will be ceaselessly refined and reworked as it flows instantaneously through the unfettered networks of creative, digitized thought.

It is in Part Two of *Autarchic Tele-visions* that Sarah-Jane Smythe focuses on the assumed repercussions of this cultural shift. It is this section of the book where

149

Smythe becomes more experimental in outlook, and rather more tiresome as far as I am concerned. Typographical trickery

does
not

an
argument
make.

NO.

Smythe's 'pixelization' of words seems like a piece of specious showmanship, and her appropriation of classic TV scripts makes for a discussion which is frankly incoherent. I am not sure that critics such as Leavis had this sort of thing in mind when they exhorted academic subculture to 'read less and watch more' in order to regain a foothold in public debate.

One of the leading post-Habermasian theorists of the public sphere, Karin Wahl-Jorgensen informs me in personal correspondence that Smythe's 'televisualization of theory' has already been denounced among 'urps' (underground radical public spherists) as the work of a 'fourth way' corporate-apologist masquerading as a critical academic. What this demonstrates is the current difficulty that we face when trying to separate out 'critical theory' from corporate-driven appropriations of the language of revolution.

Strangely, and in many ways inappropriately, I am reminded of Jeffrey Sconce's first book, which argued that twentieth-century popular culture and theory had blurred together different types of televisual 'flow', rendering them transmutable in a fantasy shared by pop and postmodernism alike:

> When the viewer turns on the television and engages its 'stream' of images, four distinct types of 'flow' appear to intersect. There is the electrical 'current' that powers the apparatus and the 'galvanic' energy that powers the body. There is the 'flow of programming' or information that occupies the medium and the 'stream of consciousness' that occupies the mind. The convergence of these rivers of flow ... produces a fantastic arena where these forces and entities can seem interchangeable. Both pop and postmodern fictions of electronic media revel in the exchange and confusion of these terms. Whether encountered in *Shocker* or *Simulations*, this logic of transmutable flow seems so naturalized as to be common sense. (1987: 199)

And yet the transmutable logic enacted in Austen and Smythe is not merely one where a stream of consciousness is fantastically exchanged for electricity, or programming for 'galvanic' energy. The 'galvanization' that Smythe and Austen argue for is one where TV finally colonizes the cultural spaces and territories of theory. The 'current' is one which flows from object of study to the act of study, not as a matter of denigration but supposedly as a recharging of academic cells.

Both these books are highly 'blivitous' in their pursuit of such an aim, but both are also highly suspect given their ultimate neglect of *substantive* cultural history and the *real* politics of academic attempts to win free speech in the marketplace and via co-present television commentary. At present, cpc remains restricted to on-screen public service advertising, fan knowledge, and 'if you like this show you'll also like…' recommendations. I remain to be convinced that aping this industrialized trivia is the way forward for television theory.

Although agreeing on a number of key points, and disagreeing as much as is necessary to preserve a sense of 'uniqueness', these two books are sure to keep the post-theory juggernaut rolling onward. They will provoke fierce debate over whether the goal of 'non-impositional academic writing' or 'autarchic composition' is either desirable or achievable. Nevertheless, on the basis of these two manifestos each author stakes a powerful claim to act as the figurehead for what has become an increasingly influential school of thought. And wherever emotivist TV fandom has overtaken critical academia, 'post-theory' will, I am sure, be *de rigueur*. Perhaps now is the time to suggest that we need far less fandom in the academy, especially fandom dressed up in politicized garb, and more good, old-fashioned criticism.

If 'theory' isn't the enemy, then 'post-theory' certainly isn't the answer.

Postnasal Drip: Post-rational Authority and Post-tenure Guilt
by Ben Picken-Schnozzel

Sliding off his banquette in a gay bar in Manhattan, Richard Hatch, the Tagi dema-gogue, attempts 'to enumerate the cacophony of odors within nose-shot': nachos, Chablis, Aramis, Newport 100s, Listerine, Preparation H, gerbil musk, antique dust, flatulence, the fragrance of leather, the unwashed pungency of British expatriates, when suddenly the inner motivational speech of the corporate trainer registered the exorbitant aroma of the Pulau Tiga sook:

> Through me passed scatologies, colossal stench, whiffs of halitosis, *and no alliance formed* ... It set up in me a palpable paranoia: this *non-alliance* was in no way something that could have acceded to the scent-ence, that might have been *before* the scent-ence: it was: *outside the scent-ence*. At the point at which the machination and treachery of strategy are replaced by the palpable probity of the paranoid proboscis, at that point, the subject of survival, whether it resides in the Australian Outback or the Department of English, moves beyond Neo-Bushian 'strategery'. It turns 'outside' strategy to inscribe the boundaries of survival (not its depths) but in the affective cologne of malodorous indifference.

This smell, Hatch recollects, 'of which Pulau Tiga was the exemplary site, was at once very cultural and very savage'; breathing in while *sans* garments on that Palua Tiga beach reminds him, *apres coup*, of consulting at Burger King. The consulting-work 'makes everything in me which is not flagrantly fragrant speak: the consulting is a clothed redolence made up of very unclothed scent-iments.'

From the unconscious of olfactory indifference, Hatch enacts a kind of affectivity outside the 'scent', completely solipsistic and sentient, but not scent-entious. Hatch contrives a poetics of the nose to contest the Luciferian lucidity of the Enlightenment project. Knowing the nose 'noes', Hatch's olfactory epistemology negates the Phallo-centric infatuation with sight, vision, language and genitalia. The shift from the positivistic affirmations of the ocular ontology (eye=I='aye-aye') as the possession of an *a priori* subject, to a mode of minimum rationality enunciated in the hirsute double-barrel negations of the nostrils' twin black holes (nose=knows='no-no'), not only changes the concept of survival theory as pleasure but also alters the very subject of post-tenure guilt. If the former is always locked into the hermeneutic circle, in the *brute visibility* of survival strategies as they tend toward totality, the latter is more a *nasalogical* process that attempts to inhale the inevitability of betrayal and decep-tion, constructing something distinctive/dis(*stink*)tive from the merely instinctive/in(*stink*)tive encounter.

Now the purpose of this Hatchian fable on odorous closure is to point to a growing tradition of the importance of 'ineffectual enunciation' in theoretical discourses that attempt to mimic modes of political and cultural posturing that are valorized by tenure committees bamboozled by the clever mystifications of privileged Brahmins 're-caste' in the role of subaltern. In other words, what is at issue is the tactics of purposive inscrutability, of re-enacting the Seinfeldian genius of replicating, *ad nauseum*, texts 'about nothing'. From that perspective, the perspective of 'ineffec-tual enunciation', theoretical discourse, to be rewarded with stardom on the lecture circuit, must be of such forbidding difficulty that it is virtually assured to have zero social or political or cultural utility. On the contrary, rational theoretical discourse that actually aims to make real differences in the lives of real people must be subjected to Foucauldian disciplinary mechanisms: circumscribed as 'unsophisti-cated', labeled as 'ungovernable', condemned as 'journalistic', and banished from the academy in tribal councils convened by the Dean. The immunity of inscrutability, then, shifts the focus from the validity of judgment as causality, or the negative dialectics of 'incompetent teaching', to the political struggle around 'clarity' (but not in the proto-Fiskian sense). Thus, there is an emphasis on the relation between arrogance and reputation in the *present* obfuscation, in the performativity of learned babble. Our attention is occupied with the relations of post-rational authority which secures professional, political, and pedagogical status through the strategy of obfus-cation in a particular temporality and from a specific endowed chair. That is part of what is entailed in being a strategic post-rational intellectual (with a hefty travel budget, minuscule teaching load, a Rolex, and a diversified stock portfolio).

This challenge to the crudeness of comprehensibility is enunciated by the radical obfuscation of Homi K. Bhabha, whose moment in survival studies is yet to come:

I can't apologize for the fact that you found my paper completely impene-trable. I did it quite consciously, I had a problem, I worked it out. And if a few people got what I was saying or some of what I'm saying, I'm happy.

The strategic speciousness of Bhabha-esque abstruseness, the olfactory agency of the nasalogical – these moments contest the limpidity of explication and the desirability of vulgar intelligibility. Why does the olfactory metaphor reek of the arbitrariness of the politics of academic careerism? What form of immunity is accessible to jargon-ridden enunciation and purposive inscrutability? What lesson in the forming of global mutual-admiration networks is whiffed in the inaccessible publications of impenetrable theory?

Nothing locates the moment of enunciatory 'void' as the necessity of survival with greater force than the final installment of Mark Burnett's *Survivor I*. In the historicity of survival narrative, Burnett's co-optation of primitivism on Pulau Tiga predates the neocolonialist travesty of *Temptation Island* while enacting a 'projective incorporation' of the Rev. W. Awdry's nostalgic (*nose*-stalgic?) revolt in the neo-imperialist melancholy of the *Thomas the Tank Engine* series. But where Awdry valorizes the benign capitalism of Sir Topham Hat, Burnett pays tribute to liberal-pluralist forms of pseudo-democratic agency articulated in 'casting the ballot'. Installed like the phallic Democlean sword, the balloting on Pulau Tiga evokes an unstable social identification where tribe members are faced with the laconic irony of either banishing the Robinsonian 'weakest link' or eliminating the most threatening (or 'fittest' in the Darwininan sense) rival. The Democlean sword of the banishment ballot generates an ambivalence in the tribal order/odor, where it is itself the source of the indefatigable smell of fear whose meaning is continually contested by the fantasmatic, fragmented, fermented motility of the perfume of alliance. But as the dominant scent of the symbolic ordering/odoring it also 'mummifies' the irrational authority of the tribal council.

It is the shadow that post-survival guilt casts on the 'object' of banishment that is the origin of a melancholia and revolt in the Tagi alliance. The melancholic discourse in the final tribal council on Pulau Tiga, rife with insistent self-exposure and the repetition of loss, displays its own weeping wounds – 'disincorporating' the authority of host Jeff Probst. Patterns of avoidance among the banished who populate the jury are those of the death reflex that, at the same time, never cease to drive the banished to resist the authority of the immunized, to usurp her necklace, and to transform the very dichotomy of the Pavlovian reward/immunity binary. This melancholic discourse of the mortified, Freud says, comes from the mental constellation of revolt: 'The melancholic are not ashamed and do not hide themselves, since everything derogatory they say about themselves is at bottom said about somebody else.' Consider the animism of trucker Susan Hawk. Hawk's lamentation and exegesis on the *Rodentia* (Kelli Wiglesworth) and *Herpeton* (Hatch) of the Tagi alliance paradoxically validates while at the same time inverts this Freudian insight: Hawk's thinly-disguised self-othering (*everything derogatory she says about somebody else is at bottom said about herself*) reveals the melancholy of a practitioner of common sense/scents struggling to survive in the entanglements of the Hatchian post-rational regime of nonsense/non-scents. Like the naivete of the assistant professor who channels energy away from obfuscation and toward teaching, Hawk had joined the banished from the extinct/ex(*stinked*) Pagong tribe who misunderstood the contest as a rational competition in which performance on reward and immunity challenges would determine the outcome of the game. Hawk's demise resulted from a strategic blunder in which she committed the *rouge*-neckian *faux pas* of indulging in affective agency by directly voicing her resentments to the immunized Wiglesworth. The banishment, then, was self-inflicted, a flaunting of the Rortyesque warning that we must always be on the 'look out for marginalization', necessarily shifting the finitude of our final vocabularies, unless of course the 'other' is in pain or humiliated.

After the territorializations of the Tagi and Pagong were reinscribed in the re-territorialization of the Rattana merger, the Pagongites would be eviscerated, one-by-one, by the inscrutable blade of the Democlean sword. What is interesting, here, is that the temporal break, or intervention, associated with the activity of balloting, happens in the id-deprived moment of subliminal syllogism. The residual and repressed rationalism of the Enlightenment project was especially evident in the voting strategy adopted by the narcissistic neurologist, Sean Kenniff. Clean-shaven from chin to shin, Kenniff negotiated the ambiguities of the banishment ritual by imposing the rationalist epistemology of alphabetical ordering on his voting decisions. Ironically, this undeniably systematic approach to avoiding the melancholy guilt of the primitive Manicheanism expressed in binary of enfranchisement/disenfranchisement left Kenniff vulnerable to accusations that alphabetical determinism was, effectively and affectively, capricious (though falling short of achieving the post-rational ideal). As a short-term (synchronic) strategy for evading survivor guilt, Kenniff's quasi-rationalism was a success; as a long-term (diachronic) strategy for survival, Kenniff's revolt against melancholia was destined to fall short.

A much more authentically post-rational voting strategy was devised by Journeyman Greg Buis, an embittered member of the subaltern Pagong who, in his final days on Pulau Tiga, would embrace the absurdities and ambiguities of the post-rational regime of nonsense/non(scents). Buis, a victim of Kenniff's alphabetical 'final solution', wisely rejected the 'eenie-meenie-minie-moe' tradition of electoral malingering because of its co-optation and contamination by racist discursive formations in the American South. Turning from the alphabetical to the numerical, Buis implicated both Wiglesworth and Hatch in their own exclusion/inclusion by instructing the two final contestants to select a number between one and ten. This shifting and sharing of responsibility, characteristic of all rituals of exclusion, but especially prominent in rendering tenure decisions, situates agency in the realm of the quantitative. Buis's numerological turn in the rendering of post-rational judgment disavows, metaleptically, how knowledge and power converge in what Foucault sees as the 'calm violence' of transference.

Hatch's selection of the number '7' would initiate a conflation of his identity with meanings embedded in this 'luckiest' of all numbers, while Wiglesworth was forced to settle with the sacred number '3' which resonated with trinities as ancient as the 'Father/Son/Holy-Ghost' of the Christian tradition to more recent triads, such as the Hendrix/Joplin/Morrison, Spielberg/Katzenberg/Geffen, Ito/Cochran/Simpson or Starr/Tripp/Lewinsky. More tellingly, new identifications forged by 'Hatch=seven' and 'Wiglesworth=three' point to a process of dehumanization that is at least as old as the Social Security Administration and the National Football League. In this co-mingling of naming and numbering we can tease out provocative connections between the original *Survivor* series and *Thomas the Tank Engine*. But the double identities of the primitive cyborgs in Awdry's utopian vision of a land where man and machine co-exist in harmonious and 'useful' nasalogical relationships displays a reversal of the dehumanization process apparent in the numerology of *Survivor I*: Thomas the tank engine, is also given the alternate identity of the Number '1' – but in this case, naming humanizes the number assigned the machine by the military-industrial complex. This dehumanizing/humanizing dynamic triggered by the naming/numbering of multiple identifications speaks to an enigma that can be further muddled by the musings of Bhabha: 'The number as sign ... can add to without adding up but may disturb the calculation' (p. 60).

To further cloud this discussion, consider how Hatch's '7' and Wiglesworth's '3' do indeed add up to '10'. But Hawk (representing a Spinal-Tapian '11') confounds the calculation in a way that demonstrates how the double-negative in nasalogical inquiry does not simply translate into a unitary grammarian positivity (see figure 1). In an oblique affront to the thesis/antithesis/synthesis of dialectical thinking, post-rational nasalectics appropriates a more convoluted triad: establishmentarianism/disestablishmentarianism/antidisestablishmentarianism. The establishmentarianism of Hatch's alliance-building strategery undermined by the disestablishmentarianism of Wiglesworth's treachery triggers an antidisestablishmentarianism in Hawk – but the negation of Wiglesworth's 'dis' coupled with the counter-negation of Hawk's 'anti' does not simply generate a synthetic affirmation of Hatch's 'establishmentarianism'. Instead, Hawk's antidisestablishmentarianism, like a cancerous wart on the end of the nose, is perched at the fuzzy border separating ontology from oncology, malignity from malignancy.

Grammarian Rationalism: Negative + Negative = Positive	Semiotic Rationalism: Signifier + Signified = Sign
Dialectical Rationalism: Thesis + Antithesis = Synthesis	Nasalogical Post-rationalism: Establishmentarianism − Disestablishmentarianism = Antidisestablishmentarianism

Figure 1: Rational Positivism vs. Post-rational Negation

Unlike *Survivor II* the literary figure of antidisestablishmentarianism as the transcription of post-rational double negation has a whimsical rendering in *Thomas the Tank Engine* that counters the melancholia and survival guilt of *Terminator 2*'s dystopian-ism. Where the antidisestablishmentarianism of Thomas is a 'cheeky' antidote to the arrogance of Gordon's rebellious disestablishmentarianism, it never poses a challenge to the establishmentarianism of Sir Topham Hat. Programmed to be a 'really useful engine', Thomas displaces the paradigm of social action as defiance and embraces hybridity as camouflage, a cyborgian survival strategy also made manifest in the servile earth movers of *Bob the Builder* and the tragic mechanicals of Kubrick/Spielberg's *A.I.* On the other nostril, Cameron's spin on post-rational survivor narrative in *Terminator 2* projects the human/organical establishmentarianism of John Connor onto a future ruled by robots. In this post-apocalyptic, post-rational universe, disestablishmentarianism is embodied in the liquidity of the T-1000 sent back to

negate the young Connor – and Schwarzenegger's mechanical Terminator, repro-
grammed to now protect Conner, gives the double-negation of antidisestablishmentarianism a robotic form. In explicating the 'inappropriate/d' (Trinh Minh-ha,
1986/7) nasalogical relations among *Survivor 1 & 2*, *Thomas the Tank Engine*, *A.I.*,
and *Terminator 1 & 2* (plus, as we shall see, *Pinocchio* and *The Wizard of Oz*), we
can, in Haraway's wording, 'unblind ourselves to the sun-worshipping stories about
the history of science and technology as a paradigm of rationalism' (1992: 297).
Haraway's insights on Mihh-ha's notion of the 'inappropriate/d' not only opens up
new ways of refiguring the heliotropisms of the Enlightenment project, but it stands
as a model of 'purposeful obfuscation' that rivals Bhabha's most vacuous work:

> To be 'inapproprate/d' does not mean '*not* to be in relation with' [emphasis
> mine to foreground the post-rational double negation] – i.e. to be in special
> reservation, with the status of the authentic, the untouched, in the allochronic
> and allotopic condition of innocence. Rather to be an 'inappropriate/d other '
> means to be in critical, deconstructive rationality, in a diffracting rather than
> a reflecting (ratio)nality – as the means of making potent connection that
> exceeds domination. To be inappropriate/d is not to fit in the *taxon*, to be
> dislocated from the available maps specifying kinds of actors and kinds of
> narratives, not to be originally fixed by difference. To be inappropriate/d is
> to be neither modern nor postmodern, but to insist on the *a*modern. (1992:
> 299)

In the context of post-tenure guilt, to be inappropriate/d also means to play the
game of 'ineffectual enunciation' without suffering from melancholia that normally
attends the act of 'selling out'. After all, as a survival strategy, to be inappropriate/d
places the academic careerist in the position of the Democlean sword, above the
fray, beyond rationality, above scrutiny/scrutibility – a kind of dangling indifference
that is poised to cut without remorse those who don't shield themselves with the
spells, incantations, and mystifications of *a*modern expertise.

  With the splitting/fusing of the inappropriate/inappropriated in Haraway/Mihn-
ha's writing/word-play, we can finally articulate what unites all of these instances
of human/machine enunciation under the umbrella of post-rational discourse. The
unifying schema is not numbering/naming. Not even double negation. It is, instead,
nasality. Though Awdry describes Thomas as a 'cheeky little engine', it is the
appendage situated between those cheeks that connects Thomas to the history of
cyborg survival narratives which, as Spielberg rightfully recognizes, harks back to
the greatest antecedent of post-rational discourse, *Pinocchio*. Sadly, while Spielberg
recognizes post-rationalism's debt to the Pinocchio story in *A.I.*, he fails to pay suitable homage to the most significant element of this seminal text – that is, Spielberg
neglects Pinocchio's nose.

  Just as the phallus fuels Freudianism, the nose guides post-rationalism. Part
orifice, part cavity, the nasal passage is an isthmus of nothingness, an exhaust duct
for hot air. Providing the basis for theoretical texts about 'nothing,' the moist void of
the nose is a chronotope in which substance is a symptom of disease and pathology.
In post-rational intellectual practice, the mucous of rationality in its fluid form is
unceremoniously expelled from the sanctuary of the nasal with the cleansing sneeze
of the double negation. Similarly, the phallic stalagmites and stalagtites of rational

encrustations are systematically plucked from the nasal cavern by post-rational theory's unrelenting pursuit of radicalism without risk. In this particular scenario, then, the booger is not so much an inappropriate/d other, as it is the infectious debris of discarded or unfashionable regimes of truth. The utility of the nose to the 'ineffectual enunciation' of post-rational theory is especially apparent in the case of post-feminism. The absent-presence of the nasal passage promises to enable a quasi-gynocentric intellectual practice that, unlike vulgar feminism, does not intend to reform or resist patriarchy. Instead, post-rational post-feminism, as expressed most starkly in the homophobia of Dr. Laura Schlesinger, deploys the performativity of assertive forms of femininity without adopting the politics of emancipation. The result is a 'projective incorporation' of the stridency associated with the Limbaughian caricature of the 'femi-nazi' – but one that negates classic feminist forms of rational action.

In *Survivor 2: The Australian Outback*, the conniving strategery of Jerri Manthey ([Man]they) gives a voice and a body to the post-feminist ideal of aggressive asser-tiveness uncontaminated by a sense of sisterhood. Above all, Manthey is 'nosy', a trait that results in the early banishment of Kel Gleason, a fellow member of Ogakor tribe voted out after she accused him of eating contraband beef jerky (a charge that was never proven). Manthey's own banishment in 'Episode 9' would not only delineate the limits of 'overt' post-feminism as a survival strategy, but it would also link *Survivor 2* to the narrative genealogy of the *Thomas the Tank Engine* Series. After Manthey's departure, Keith Famie, a professional chef whose cooking was condemned by Manthey, invoked memories of the proto-cyborgs in *The Wizard of Oz* – Tin Man and Scarecrow – who, in turn, trigger more primal images of Pinocchio's nose. Singing 'the wicked witch is dead', Famie's act of celebration/melancholia unseats the authority of overtly post-feminist nosiness. What we begin to see, forming in the present moment of this act of singing, is the ascendancy of a histor-ical, perspectival survival text that has its own unique post-rationality. That the ulti-mate champion of *Survivor 2*, Tina Wesson (a 'stealth' post-feminist), did not win a single reward or immunity challenge promotes a sense of closure that confounds the outdated rationalism of Darwinian reasoning. In other words, in authentically post-rational fashion, Wesson, like George W. Bush in the 2000 presidential election, won without winning. If we look beyond the melancholy of the banished, if we screen out the conflicts of survivor guilt, if we dare to peer into the abyss of post-rational nasality, then we can discern that in the 'inappropriate/d' Wesson's championing of strategy over performance it was Manthey who represented the Muse of Nega-tion. From the beginning, it was Manthey who was locked in battle with Wesson who stands for the Negation of Negation, the death of probability, and the sovereignty of Antidisestablishmentarianism. Manthey's time of history, in contrast goes, we are told by Famie, ding-dong, ding-dong...

The Adventure of a Lifetime: Critical Windows on
The Indiana Jones Chronicles
edited by Dale V. Vidray
(viddv.adv@press.wsu.edu—1.52M)

Dr. Jones and Mr. Indy: A Virtual Psychobiography
by Vivian Darkbloom
(darkv.djmi@pegasus.com—2.18M)

Myth, Media, and Mirrors: A Intermedial Commentary on
Indiana Jones
by Christopher J. Duffy
(dutcj.mmm@acad.publ.twisdcc.com—1M)

reviewed by Marc Dolan

With a few exceptions, scholarly study of the mass media is only seventy or eighty years old. When we look back now on the work of such early media critics as Louis Althusser, Marshall McLuhan, and Roland Barthes, it can seem provocative but primitive, much as even gifted alchemical texts must seem to a contemporary chemist. Even when we review the work of those scholars' immediate successors, the academics of the 1970s, 1980s, and 1990s, it may still seem crude and incomplete to us. It misses perceptions that we consider obvious, if only because we have lived through the last quarter-of-a-century of cultural transformation. No doubt our work will seem antediluvian, too, to those who write 25 years after us, as we settle into the middle of this still unfamiliar century. As scholars in a market capitalist society, we inevitably sketch the blueprints for our own obsolescence.

And yet, as in any field of intellectual endeavor, there are still some questions that continue to nag us. No matter how frequently we revise our methodologies and terminologies, the biggest problems still refuse to yield to our best efforts. In media and cultural studies, one of the most persistent problems has always been that of the distribution of power. Simply put, who controls a mass medium in a capitalist society: the conceptual artists, the physical artists, the capitalists, the managers, the distributors, or the consumers? Or is it, as an unreconstructed deconstructionist might argue, the medium itself and its inevitable *abyme*? These questions haunted cultural critics before Althusser, McLuhan, and Barthes, before television or online culture, and even before radio or motion pictures. Still the theories we hold out to our students today are no more conclusive or irrefutable than the earliest suggestions of Karl Marx and Matthew Arnold. We can be no more certain why a particular dramatic series receives more subscribers when its hero is reconfigured as multiracial than Marx or Arnold could be certain why Dickens' readers wept so hard for Little Nell.

This question of power arises once again with the near-simultaneous availability of three new works of scholarship, each devoted in a very distinct way to the most successful narrative series of the last quarter-of-a-century: *The Indiana Jones Chronicles*. This series, which made its way by a frustratingly intermittent route from feature film to broadcast television to cable transmission and finally to online narrative subscription, is a marvelously fecund subject for cultural criticism. It captures in microcosm a number of the most notable changes that American media and culture have undergone over the last several decades. Still, the approaches we find in Vivian Darkbloom's *Dr. Jones and Mr. Indy* and Christopher J. Duffy s *Myth, Media, and Mirrors*, as well as in most of the essays in *The Adventure of a Lifetime*, Dale V. Vidray's hyperanthology surrounding the series, seem decidedly at odds. Even after ten or fifteen years of study, viewers bent on cultural criticism seem unable to decide why this character took the specific path that he did from conventional twentieth-century adventure-hero to trailblazing twenty-first-century user-avatar. Taken together, all these readings might even suggest that our culture is little more than mere viewer projection, and our cultural critics little more than highly specialized types of viewers.

Henry Jones, Jr. (better known as 'Indiana') began life as the cinematic offspring of two of the most successful young filmmakers of the 1970s, George Lucas and Steven Spielberg. Originally, Lucas and Spielberg envisioned the Indiana Jones films as big-budget glorifications of the cheesy Saturday afternoon motion picture serials that they had adored in their youth. From the beginning, though, the three films that they made about their swashbuckling archaeologist were far more successful than those earlier serials had ever been. Condemned as racist and imperialist by some viewers and embraced as a return to good old-fashioned entertainment by others, *Raiders of the Lost Ark* (1981), *Indiana Jones and the Temple of Doom* (1984), and *Indiana Jones and the Last Crusade* (1989) left a lasting impression on a whole generation of American filmgoers. Over the last forty or fifty years, both the individual sequences and the overall feeling of these films have been frequently imitated but never equaled.

But in late 1989, just after the third film went out of release, producer George Lucas got an idea. That last film had begun with a prelude, set in Utah in 1912, in which rising screen-icon River Phoenix had played a thirteen-year-old Indy on what was presented as the character's first real adventure. Response to the prelude had been fairly positive, and there was something of a vogue in the late 1980s for 'Young' or 'Teen' versions of established heroes. (The most notable example of this phenomenon was Barry Levinson's highly uncharacteristic *Young Sherlock Holmes* (1986), which Spielberg's Amblin Entertainment also produced.) In Hollywood's terms, it seemed logical for Lucas to spin off the younger character, especially since both Spielberg and Harrison Ford, the lead actor in the films, had signaled that they were done for good with the older version. Lucas did want to spin Young Indy off on his own, but he also wanted to take the 'Teen Hero' phenomenon in a very different sort of direction. 'I have an educational foundation working on interactive products,' he told an interviewer at one point in the early 1990s, 'and I got this idea to get kids involved in history through the Young Indiana Jones character.' In other words, rather than simply showing a younger Indiana Jones leaping across chasms and running from snakes like his elder counterpart, Lucas wanted to show him growing up with the twentieth century. He wanted Young Indy to meet artists and scientists and even revolutionaries, and to grow gradually into the hero audiences had come to know.

Interestingly enough, Lucas wanted to do all this on broadcast television. For those who only know the old broadcast networks through the conventional histories of the late twentieth century, the producer's choice of medium may seem a bit surprising, but even more surprising may be the networks' interest in return. The late 1980s and early 1990s were a very odd time in broadcast television. Networks were actually courting all kinds of filmmakers, from John Sayles to David Lynch to Steven Spielberg himself, in the hopes of winning back viewers to their failing primetime schedules. Moreover, the attraction was more than reciprocal. In the case of all the filmmakers but Sayles perhaps, these creators quite often had charitable memories of the television programs they had watched in their youth. In the specific case of Lucas, his Young Indiana Jones project had clear forerunners in the young adult programming of his own childhood and adolescence. It resembled such forgotten programs of the 1950s and 1960s as CBS's *You Are There*, NBC's Kennedy-era *Profiles in Courage*, and a number of the old historical Disney programs that had appeared on both ABC and NBC.

For a number of the contributors to Vidray's project, the story of the *Chronicles* begins and ends there, in the mind of George Lucas, and there is certainly some evidence to support this auteurist view. Even now, more than a half-dozen years after Lucas' death, his incredibly detailed outline of the fictional life of Jones continues to set the general pattern for many of the series' most recent individual episodes. His idea to ground the original broadcast episodes in three separate eras – the emerging modern world of 1908–1910, the war-and-revolution-torn landscape of the late 1910s, and the narrating and sometimes even satirical perspective of the early 1990s – must also receive considerable credit, especially since none of those eras fell even close to the one in which contemporary audience-members were used to seeing the series' central character. Most of all, Lucas's stated intention to make a regular broadcast television series with feature-film production values must especially be credited as a visionary act. Indeed, the techniques that Lucasfilm pioneered for use in the broadcast version became essential to the series' eventual prolongation in other, as-yet uninvented media.

But despite the arguments of these diehard auteurists, it seems fairly obvious that even *The Young Indiana Jones Chronicles* was a collaborative effort. Principal photography for the seventeen hours that were meant to serve as the series' first season took place over forty-four weeks in late 1991 and early 1992 and was a remarkable achievement in and of itself. Not since the late 1960s/early 1970s fad for shooting adventure series like *I Spy*, *It Takes a Thief*, and the short-lived *Shirley's World* on location around the globe had anything on this scale even been attempted. The original theory was to shoot in as many actual locations as possible, insofar as those locations still conformed to the necessary historical periods. The series also employed well-known actors like Jean Pierre Aumont, Max van Sydow, James Gammon, and Vanessa Redgrave and generally respected directors like Bille August, Terry Jones, Deepa Mehta, Gavin Millar, and Nicholas Roeg to bring those periods to life. In addition, however, Lucas planned to save money on crowds and other miscellaneous costs by using the sorts of digital visual effects in postproduction that were then being developed at Lucas' Skywalker Ranch. Episodes were shot on location or in studio space in London and then sent back to Northern California for editing, postproduction, and scoring. Principal photography on each episode usually took about two to three weeks. That rate that would not have been remarkable for most dramatic series of that period, but it was nothing short of astonishing for a series whose every episode painstakingly recreated a different specific time and place.

Even more notable than the production process, perhaps, was all that had gone on before production began. In part to minimize expensive readjustments to tightly scheduled location shooting, the scripts for all 17 hours of the original season were written and revised before any film was shot. While producer Rick McCallum scouted locations in China, India, The Czech Republic, Kenya, and other countries that fit the individual phases of the season's outline, seven screenwriters back in California worked collaboratively – at one point, even communally – on the seventeen screenplays that fleshed out that outline. (This original group of seven included such prior and later successes as Frank Darabont, Jonathan Hales, Jonathan Hensleigh, and Rosemary Anne Sisson.) After the scripts were completed, each writer provided detailed commentary on every other writer's completed work.

While such close collaboration among writers was not necessarily unusual in the old broadcast era, few if any other unlimited series of that period had a whole season's scripts completed before any shooting on that season had even begun. Because of this practice, there was a remarkable unity and development to that first round of episodes. As Lucas envisioned, the first season featured six hours of adventures from a two-year world tour by Young Indy's family. During this tour, an eight to ten-year-old version of the character got to meet Edgar Degas, Gertrude Stein, Sigmund Freud, Teddy Roosevelt, Annie Besant, and Jiddu Krishnamurti. The first season also included eleven hours focusing on an older Indy's increasing involvement in the events of World War One. During these episodes, he moved from observing the Mexican Revolution and the British women's suffrage movement to fighting in the trenches at the Somme and Verdun, from serving in the Belgian Colonial forces in German East Africa and the Congo to engaging in espionage and diplomacy in Austria, Spain, and pre-Bolshevik Russia.

These elder episodes were also filled with encounters with famous historical figures (including Francisco Villa, Sylvia Pankhurst, Siegfried Sassoon, Henri Petain, Mata Hari, Albert Schweitzer, and Vladimir Lenin), but more important they also made sense as drama. Perhaps it was the result of the writers' close collaboration, but you could see the protagonist of these episodes change as he went on, moving from enthusiast to soldier to officer to operative. Like several of the episodes that featured the eight to ten-year-old version of the character, these episodes from Indy's sixteenth and seventeenth years were remarkably critical of both their protagonist and of the historical figures whom he met. You saw the character fail, pursue false dreams or goals, and learn from his mistakes – or repeat them – in future episodes. In some ways, these first 17 hours, especially the latter 11, were more convincing as fiction than they were as history.

Had they been shown in their entirety (and, perhaps, in their narrative sequence), these earliest episodes might have met with a very different reaction. But in the spring of 1992, around the time that principal photography for the first intended season was ending, the earliest completed episodes of *The Young Indiana Jones Chronicles* began appearing on ABC. The results were disastrous, at least in terms of audience ratings. The two broadcasts of the series' two-hour pilot drew fairly large numbers of interested viewers, but almost immediately after that the series began sinking in the ratings week by week. While Darkbloom remains understandably silent on this subject, the contributors to Vidray's project review a number of the more frequently cited explanations for the series' early failures. Arthur Donaldson, for example, points to the lack of success that greeted a number of other excellent historical series of that period, including such now-neglected classics as *I'll Fly Away* and *Homefront*. Donaldson ultimately attributes these failures to the same denial of history and responsibility that characterized the corporate downsizing of that era. By contrast, Rafe Albright hews to a paleo-independent approach, insisting that the specific failure of Lucas's series was simply an inevitable clash between a visionary creator and a mindless bureaucracy. Sally Kosinski, however, offers a refreshingly simple explanation for the series' early decline in viewership. 'It was dreadful,' Kosinski bluntly reports...

> ... at least in the form that the audience originally saw it. The younger incarnation of the character was boring, the elder incarnation (who narrated these episodes) was annoying, and most of the episodes consisted of nothing more than Young Indy watching other people doing marginally interesting things. Audiences also were not helped by the fact that the series jumped around so much in time and place: from Cairo to Mexico to London to Kenya, and from 1908 to 1916 to 1909 and back to 1916 again. That sort of leaping was permissible later, once the outline of Jones' life was clear, but in the beginning it alienated the casual viewer. In general, the early broadcast episodes were little more than a concept in search of ideas. Only later, in its online mythos, did *The Indiana Jones Chronicles* finally discover the real heart of its narrative. As the story evolved there, users could grasp its central theme: how the cynicism of the World War One era was transformed into the heroism of the World War Two years.

Kosinski's questionable interpretation of early twentieth-century history aside, her reading does provide us with an interesting variation on Christopher J. Duffy's intermedial approach. According to Duffy, the pilot and the first five broadcast episodes failed because of the way Young Indy was marketed: Three years after the highly successful release of *Indiana Jones and the Last Crusade*, *The Young Indiana Jones Chronicles* was sold in all of its advertising (if not in its press releases) as a continuation of the film series' accent on adventure. So when viewers watched the pilot in March of 1992, they saw all the explosions that were featured in the ads, as well as the trips through old Egyptian tombs. But they were also stopped cold by long speeches by characters whom they may not have known were historical figures. When confronted with a conversation between Howard Carter and an eight-year-old Indy, how were most viewers supposed to know that one of them was a 'real' archaeologist and the other one was 'fictional'? They may only have known that

163

T. E. Lawrence was 'real' but only because they had seen an old and very long movie about him.

ABC had originally ordered a two-hour pilot and thirteen episodes of the series, and that had grown to seventeen hours of material when two of the originally outlined episodes had been expanded into two-part stories by their authors. This left the series just five hours shy of the twenty-two episode full-season order that was customary for dramatic series at that time. But ABC only aired the pilot and five episodes in the spring of 1992 before it yanked the series off its schedule and sent Lucas's operation back to regroup. The series was renewed but kept on a short leash: nine new episodes were ordered, along with three two-hour movies. The implication was that the show would either sink or swim in its second run on the air.

Duffy and several of Vidray's contributors spend much time speculating about what specific demands the network might have made with reference to the form and content of the series' second season. Until Lucas' papers become available to scholars in 2069, however, speculation is all that such theories can be. Still, whoever's idea it might have been, the shift in focus in this second round of episodes is undeniable. Nearly all these scholars agree, for example, that the network's demand for three two-hour movies was particularly ill-advised, since the pilot may very well have been the dramatically weakest episode of all. Even the television critics of the series' original era noted that at least two of these three 'movies' were just two episodes of the series that had been tacked together with a makeshift narrative transition. Clearly, the executives at ABC had confused the pilot's priority with its 'feature' status and had credited the latter rather than the former with the series' initially high ratings.

Far more interesting conclusions may be drawn, however, from the content of the episodes that were intended for the second season. They seemed to shy away somewhat from the series' originally educational intention, turning more to pure action, suspense, and adventure (particularly in the Princeton, German East Africa, and Northern Italy episodes). Moreover, the chronological and geographical focus of the series also shifted slightly in this second round of stories. Only one new episode featured the youngest version of the character. The teenage version's adventures were expanded out in both directions so that a greater emphasis could be placed on American history and historical figures rather than indigenous European, African, or Asian material. Considerable attention was given to emerging nationalist movements in 1916 Ireland, 1917 Beersheba, and 1918 Istanbul, as well as to the conflict between self-determination and imperialism at the 1919 Paris Peace Conference. This material blended well with similar issues that had been highlighted in the first season's Mexico, London, German East Africa, and Petrograd episodes. But much of the seriousness and continuity of that first round of episodes seemed lost in the second season, even if its repeated focus on performance and spectacle offered a fascinating counterpart to the first season's exploration of bureaucracy and authority.

No matter how many adjustments Lucas and his team may have made for the second season, however, it seems in retrospect as if ABC had already made up its mind. The network dumped four of the remaining ten hours from the first season on the air just before their real fall season began, and they then preempted Young Indy twice for political advertisements by a third-party candidate for President by the lusterless name of H. Ross Perot. Then the series vanished until the dog days of

March, when it came back in a third slot for another six weeks. Finally, after official cancellation, the network aired the last remaining two hour 'movie' and seven of the remaining one-hour episodes in June and July, when the ratings for the series' time slot no longer mattered. Even in that last round of airings, Lucasfilm was still making noticeable changes: the elder narrator was dropped in three of the final episodes, and newsreel footage was substituted at the opening of one of those episodes to great effect. None of this, however, made the slightest difference. In July of 1993, the series had its last airing on United States broadcast television, and that, it seemed, would be the end of that.

At this point in the series' history, its executive producer had a definite problem. He had built a fairly efficient machine for turning out good-looking and frequently intelligent television episodes, but the US television market seemed impossible to crack. Overseas, the series was doing quite well. In a few countries, it had even placed in the top ten. But in late 1993, Lucas had four unaired episodes in the can, and one or two dozen more episodes sketched out on paper, but no domestic venue in which to transmit them. Even if he could find a venue, what he still needed most was the luxury of time, especially with a series that (as Kosinski suggests) needed a certain amount of narrative familiarity to draw in its most likely potential viewers.

As Evan James points out in *Falling to Pieces*, his engrossing history of the final decades of the dominance of broadcast television, what doomed the networks of the late twentieth century may very well have been their limited methods. The decline of truly mass culture in the 1970s had seen an increase in instant quantification of audience reaction without any comparable increase in qualitative data. The ratings systems of this era allowed executives to parse their audiences down to the smallest possible demographic subsubgrouping, to know who was watching what and for precisely how long. However, their methods for gauging the relative interest of those audiences in the programs they were watching were surprisingly primitive, at least by current standards. Anyone who doubts this need only read James' chapter on 'The Reign of the Focus Group'. By his account, late-twentieth-century entertainers possessed only the most rudimentary concepts of cultural stimulus and response.

Once Lucas' series had been sunk by the commercial limitations of this broadcast mentality, he turned, like many other producers of his era, to cable transmission as a possible market. Perhaps because the form of his series seemed so old-fashioned, even if its critique of twentieth-century Western world dominance was not, Lucas was able to sell four 'two-hour movies' to evangelist Pat Robertson's Family Channel, where they aired between fall 1994 and spring 1996. Once that agreement ended, Lucas intended to add three or four new hours of material to the forty hours that had already been shot in order to prepare the complete series for release on video-cassette. In essence, he and his associates had now done what they had set out to do: they had produced about fifty hours of narrative for film and television that charted the growth of a single central character. Now that it was done, he intended to release the entire series on video so that it could be enjoyed by all the viewers who had not been able to catch it before.

By that point, though, Lucas had turned back to his other popular saga: the *Star Wars* stories. In 1997, Lucasfilm released the 'Special Edition' of Episodes 4 through 6 of that series, which were paradoxically followed by the 'prequel trilogy' of Episodes 1 through 3 (released in 1999, 2002, and 2005, respectively). In all these cinematic instances, Lucas used digital techniques that had been pioneered during

165

work on his TV series. However, in all the excitement over the rebirth of *Star Wars* after nearly 15 dormant years, Young Indy seemed to get lost in the shuffle. The extra footage was shot, but no Young Indy videos materialized for four or five years. Even then, only half of the projected 22 videos were released. The remainder were dumped on cable outlets, and the promised 'complete' series on videocassette was never achieved.

If some of Vidray's contributors see Lucas's early 1990s conception of Young Indy as the pivotal phase in its eventual development, Duffy, by contrast, emphasizes this moment in the early 2000s when Lucas was preparing the series for video release. As he points out, if Lucas had struck when the iron was hot, when the series was cancelled by ABC, the 'complete' series would probably have gone to the last generation of VHS-heavy neighborhood video stores. If that had happened, it is more than likely that it would have quickly and finally passed into oblivion. That kind of purchasing environment was no more hospitable to the producer's collected series than broadcast or even cable had been to its individual episodes.

Duffy persuasively argues that it was the coincidence of Lucas' plans with the rise of the equally short-lived DVD format, with its proto-hypertextual branching and menus, that led to the series' eventual longevity. As would have been the case with a complete video release, of course, in this form all the episodes were simultaneously available. What made the DVD format superior to VHS in this case, however, was that viewers could access their own 'footnotes' or even 'flashbacks' in order to review the historical and narrative context for what the characters were saying or doing. Starting with the second round of ABC episodes, Lucasfilm had made *Study Guides* available free of charge to interested parents and teachers, but many viewers were not aware of their existence. Now those *Study Guides* were part of the actual program and could be clicked on like old-fashioned closed-captions at the bottom of the screen.

The success of Young Indy when released on DVD in 2003 was not spectacular, but it did surprise many who had written off the series as Lucas' folly. Two years later, when Howard Stringer revived Tele-TV (his unsuccessful 1990s video-on demand project) as the now-famous online service Content-on-Demand, *The Young Indiana Jones Chronicles* appeared on its menus from the very first day. Services like COD, after all, were interested in large blocks of entertainment product. Audiences might wish to order some films or programs again and again, particularly those programs aimed at children or families. However, content providers like Stringer already understood that such a service would profit even more from holding the rights to distribute so-called 'sets' of entertainment. A service that offered all of Clint Eastwood's movies, for example, or all the episodes for the ten *Star Trek* series, could anticipate so-called 'branching orders', with each purchase leading to the next. A well-stocked service like COD could thus make sure that consumers who had seen one piece of a 'set' and liked it would not have to look too far to find another.

Oddly enough, when COD came knocking at Lucasfilm's door, what they had wanted was the *Star Wars* and *Indiana Jones* movies, because those seemed like good candidates for both repeat business and 'set' consumption. As a term of the agreement, though, George Lucas insisted that all TV work in both 'universes' must be included in the deal. And so in late 2005 all 44 hours of *The Young Indiana Jones Chronicles* became available to COD customers, even though the distribution lease for those episodes had actually been little more than an afterthought. In many ways,

COD seemed like the ideal environment for Lucas's series, especially as more and more innovations brought this service even closer to Lucas's ideal of interactivity than the DVD format had done. Of course, some of what had originally been wholly educational had now become ever so slightly commercial. In the new superimpos-able *Study Guides*, viewers were directed not only to general historical information but to verbal and visual product that was offered by other online services and that was sometimes only loosely related to the episode at hand. But the information was available nevertheless, and it was now available in a more immediate and much less cumbersome form than it had originally been offered to the series' broadcast audiences. Watching an episode about Paul Robeson, for example, viewers could stop, go to a Robeson site, listen to a recording of 'Steal Away' that he made six years after the 'events' that they were watching, and then go back to the point in the action where they had stopped.

Most recent scholars agree that the popularity of the series in this newest medium was not as immediate as its producers and distributors have generally claimed. At Lucas's insistence, *The Young Indiana Jones Chronicles* was listed in three of COD's subdirectories: Action/Adventure, Historical, and Young Adult. As on broadcast and cable television, the series definitively failed as Action/Adventure. In 2005, just as in 1992, a viewer who sat purposefully down to have an Action/Adventure did not want to also hear extensive discussions about early twentieth-century Turkish national-ism. The much briefer and less substantive speeches made by the Afghan rebels in Sylvester Stallone's consistently unpopular *Rambo III* (1988) probably represented the outer limit of the acceptable politics-to-explosions ratio for most of these adven-ture-minded viewers.

But even as Young Indy continued to fail in that one category, something inter-esting happened with the other two sets of listings. In any given online community, there was very little interest in the series, up to a point. Then one user would begin to watch an increasing number of episodes, followed by other users whom purchasing software like *Firefly 12.2* could track as belonging to the same purchase niche. Follow-up questionnaires by COD's marketing division established that the popu-larity of the series was increasing by extraordinarily slow word-of-mouth. Its popu-larity chiefly dwelled at two ends of the age spectrum: with families with small chil-dren, and with those in retirement. The popularity in this latter group was especially growing. (As Margot Ng points out in her contribution to Vidray's project, this may have been because of the series' occasionally strident anti-imperialist ideology. It was far more acceptable to the elderly baby boomers of 2005 than it had been to the 'greatest generation' senior citizens of the early 1990s.) If it had not been for the new medium's emphasis on 'staggered' rather than simultaneous viewership, however, COD's market analysts might not have even noticed this drawn-out development, any more than their counterparts at the broadcast or cable networks would have.

But however it happened, the series' audience grew, and it grew quickly enough (at least for the medium in which it now appeared) to justify its continued listing. By the fall of 2007, it had become enough of a cult object to be cited as a 'Special Delivery' in the customary monthly message to COD subscribers. By then, chat groups formed around the series had grown to unprecedented levels – almost triple what they had been at the height of the series' broadcast popularity. As with many other 'Special Deliveries', COD eventually integrated salient selections from these critical exchanges with episode deliveries, so that they could be read as part of the episode's text. Most of Vidray's contributors compare the role of these chat groups to that played by early online critics in the rise and fall of such other 1990s series as *Twin Peaks*, *The X-Files*, and *Buffy the Vampire Slayer*. Duffy, however, makes a slightly more intriguing comparison. He sees the roots of this new hybrid form in the old comic book culture of the mid-twentieth-century. In the 1960s, 1970s, and 1980s, one of the most popular features of the superhero comics published by the now-defunct DC and Marvel divisions of TimeWarnerTurnerDisneySonyColumbiaCorp were their letter columns, or 'lettercols', as the fans used to call them. These pages usually occupied a full seventh of the monthly space in a comic book. In them, fans debated whether The Incredible Hulk could beat Hercules in a fight in zero gravity, or whether a story in which Superman had switched places with his dog had been a 'real' story or only 'imaginary'. And indeed, just as with the comic books that Duffy cites, once all of Young Indy became available online, viewers began to debate which episodes were 'historical' or 'apocryphal'; which, in other words, added up to a 'real' fictional life.

Certainly, the best proof of Duffy's crossmedia comparison is Darkbloom's admittedly bizarre work of amateur rather than academic scholarship, which has evolved from his own enthusiastic postings on the series. It purports to be nothing less than a psychological profile of the 'true' Indiana Jones. Darkbloom sees Jones' life as a study in psychic splitting, a conflict between the academic and the adventurous, the devout and the cynical. In this virtual biographer's view, this conflict was only resolved with the mysterious late twentieth-century accident that somehow resulted in the loss of Jones' right eye. At first blush, Darkbloom's argument might seem preposterous. However, its will to retroactive unity is no less extreme than Kosinski's (which seeks to unify the entire series into a single interpretation of twentieth-century history) or that of Albright and several other of Vidray's auteurists (who disregard as inferior or unessential all episodes that cannot be viewed as clear products of Lucas's singular aesthetic consciousness).

As I myself have theorized elsewhere, this will to unity across cultural instances is an inevitable result of the wide availability of cultural product. In earlier centuries, when cultural artifacts were comparatively rare, there was less of an attempt to unify such product. Even in the late nineteenth century, when Arthur Conan Doyle's ur-detective Sherlock Holmes first appeared in a series of magazine short stories, while loyal readers may have wanted Holmes to rise from the dead and take part in further published adventures, they did not spend as much time as their twentieth-century counterparts trying to smooth out the intertextual narrative inconsistencies that ran across and through all those published adventures. Once the stories became available during the early twentieth century in countless cheap and expensive editions, however, fan clubs like the Baker Street Irregulars began to form. Their members spent countless hours trying to figure out why Dr. Watson's Jezail bullet seemed to move from his left leg to his right, or why Mrs. Watson called her husband James instead of John at the beginning of 'The Adventure of the Man with the Twisted Lip'.

Such nitpicking and obsessive-compulsive reception always results from cultural familiarity. It especially comes with private ownership of reproduced and reproducible cultural artifacts, which makes familiarity as easy as taking down a book or a print from the shelf. Certainly in the history of televised narrative, cult viewership really began in earnest with the mid-twentieth-century system of episodic redelivery called 'syndication', which predated videotape and videodisc collections by at least two decades and predated our current systems of order and subscription by almost half a century. When viewers could see episodes of *The Honeymooners*, *Star Trek*, or even a relative curiosity like *Gilligan's Island* again and again, they could attempt with each new viewing to memorize, codify, and unify their narrative. Cult viewership became even greater with the wide availability of videocassette recorders, which made it possible for fans to 'reread' these texts as easily and with as much attention to detail as they could reread a Sherlock Holmes story or a comic book. Now, even before syndication and formal videocassette release, aficionados of a particular series could connect the accumulating pieces of their evolving reading at their own leisure.

As Duffy points out, with the arrival in the summer of 2008 of new, digitally generated episodes of the renamed *The Indiana Jones Chronicles*, the phenomenon of cult-viewership reached its furthest state of evolution. With the combined technologies of series subscription and digital emendation, both character fans like Vivian Dark-bloom and academic fans like Sally Kosinski could now to a certain extent 'rewrite' the narrative of their favorite series. After reading posted synopses of projected episodes, they could vote to see specific synopses developed into episodes because they showed more of the character or story they wanted to see. As Duffy also notes, the most startling results of this practice may be the relatively low popularity of the Raiders material (which seems to work best as a separate film) and the enormous popularity of the new anthropological episodes (including the current favorite at the time of this writing, Indy's encounters in 1925 New York with Franz Boas, Ruth Benedict, and Zora Neale Hurston).

This formal reconception of the series also made sense from Lucas' point of view, since the new technology made his original concepts even more plausible, at least on a visual scale. After pioneering digital composition in the late 1980s and early 1990s for a number of projects (including the original Indy series), Lucasfilm's Industrial Light and Magic had taken this practice to a further level in the late 1990s and early 2000s with the revised and new episodes of *Star Wars*. In the late 2000s, the revived Indy series took that relatively limited process even further still. With slight digital emendation, the series' composite hero now looked convincingly consistent, as he aged through the four phases of the series' four actors. And with all the unused footage and alternate takes that had been amassed during the series' five years of physical shooting, Lucasfilm's live animators had enough material available to them to spin out almost any episode they wanted, with minimal location shooting to establish new backgrounds.

From the beginning, of course, digital composition and live animation have proved to be highly controversial processes. Certainly, they would not prove suitable for all types of visual narrative. The *Chronicles*, however, would seem like a fair candidate for the use of such techniques, since the long-gone world in which its stories take place can exist in its entirety nowhere on earth. Nevertheless, several of Vidray's contributors complain that this practice has created a soulless kind of cultural product, one hatched in machines by emotionless data. Even the initial use of live actors on a so-called 'grid stage' (to provide physical and aural orientation for subsequent animation and generation of material) seems insufficient for many of Vidray's younger contributors. Dan Rombauer, to choose only one example, insists that 'art is always an act of creative collaboration, not of assembly-line production. Only when all the artists are gathered in one place does true creativity ever occur.'

The strongest dissenting voice on this point from within Vidray's project is that of LaVonda Torres, a scholar whose historical (if not methodological) perspective has a great deal in common with Christopher Duffy's. Torres has some misgivings about digital composition, especially about its minimized contribution from live actors, but she also contends that technology alone does not make a cultural product inhuman. 'As with all of Lucas' work', Torres suggests,

> it is the writing that makes it human or inhuman, not the many tools that turn the writing into audiovisual narrative form. Anyone who contends that the emended episodes of the *Chronicles* are by definition more inhuman than those shot and edited during the original broadcast and cable runs need only compare 'Barcelona—May 1917' (shot in the fall of 1991 and first shown a year later on ABC) with 'Sao Paolo—January 1936' (first generated and distributed by COD in the summer of 2012). Whether they were generated by computers or not, the latter episode's Indy and Claude Levi-Strauss sound more like actual human beings, not to mention like actual working anthropologists. By contrast, the former episode's Edward Diaghliev and Pablo Picasso sound like cardboard cutouts in a badly acted farce. Those scholars, especially the younger ones, who idealize the days of pre-digitized production should go back and see many of the films that were released when I was in high school. *Porky's*, *Hardbodies*, and that endless series of *Police Academy* movies did not require digitized settings and actors to be unimaginably soulless. All they really needed was cynicism and greed.

Even those scholars who prefer the semi-digitized episodes of the *Chronicles* to the fully digitized ones, however, still end their essays, as Torres does, by casting a relatively glad eye toward the future of the series. Since Lucas' original cap of fifty or sixty hours of material has been retained for the most part, the available 'life' of his most famous creation tends to shift around a little from year to year, with fans continually circulating bootlegged discs of episodes that have currently been 'lost' from the series' continuity. Vidray's most vocal auteurist contributors hold out for a return to Lucas's original outline, without even the re-emphases that they believe ABC forced on the producer before they would greenlight the episodes for the second broadcast season. Darkbloom, on the other hand, argues for a strict chain of stories that reinforces his own narrative conception of the character's seventy-year battle to be a serious scholar rather than an adventurer. Kosinski, for her part, argues for an evenly paced series of episodes that chart a clear progression from Indy's disillusionment while fighting in World War One to his renewed fights for self-determination in World War Two and after. Duffy, predictably, says the process is the point, whether it is ordinary viewers like Darkbloom who are engaging in its phases or more rarified academics like Dale Vidray's contributors. 'This is a narrative,' Duffy concludes, 'that has found its proper form, one that couldn't really work in any earlier media. To 'fix' it in one piece would be to distort it. Its amorphousness is ultimately its truest feature'.

As several of these scholars predictably suggest, the journey Indiana Jones has taken from film to broadcast and cable television and then on to online narrative subscription may be the wildest adventure of his entire career. As they also demonstrate, the specific details of that intermedial journey can provide fodder for any model of cultural change that a scholar or viewer might wish to embrace. Taken in all its forms and stages, for example, *The Indiana Jones Chronicles* has been an observable product of a state-apparatus of clearcut ideology – but it has also undermined that ideology, by producing a 'hero' who exists to be taught how wrong he and his world really are. The series has also been a case-study in the importance of polysemy in marketing mass media – although, in a way, the less polysemic the series became the more successful it ultimately was. And it has been a remarkable testament to the power of a single artistic vision – even though that vision ultimately succeeded most when its audience was allowed to rewrite the series' text.

When academic study of the mass media first began in earnest, scholars were most worried, in the wake of the demagoguery of the 1930s and 1940s, about those media's potential for producing a race of ideologically identical zombies. When the field was transformed into cultural studies in the 1980s and 1990s, the worry likewise shifted toward a fear of excessively atomistic consumers. These consumers, scholars worried, perpetuated a solitary, isolated environment with their personal stereos and their elaborate home theatres, which let culture be as private as it has ever been. Scholars of our own day understand a little better that both views describe parts of our cultural experience. The privacy of extensively personalized consumer culture can often prove to be a common experience, one that thoroughly and insidiously socializes not only its most avid consumers but also its harshest and most skeptical critics.

These issues become essential when one considers the eventful history of *The Indiana Jones Chronicles*, because that history hinges on the problem of audience socialization and/or audience power. For all the critics who may decry the rise of subscriptive narrative series, this system still seems superior to the old broadcast and cable networks' methods of product delivery, superior indeed in every way but that of economic access. This issue aside, audience-members of our own day are not merely receiving whatever dissimilar executives think that they may like. They are ordering the programs that they think sound intriguing, and they are debating what is good or bad in those programs, what is consistent or inconsistent, and what is dynamic or static in narrative. Their reactions, in turn, help shape the series' larger narrative. In the specific case of *The Indiana Jones Chronicles*, by interacting and arguing over what should be the 'proper' narrative, audiences are quite often arguing and thinking about the nature of twentieth-century history, as Kosinski would probably be the first to observe. Indeed, the fact that so many of them are willing to embrace the relatively thoughtful and deferential protagonist that the series' original broadcast viewers seemed to have rejected may be one of the more encouraging signs in recent American culture.

Ironically enough, all these recent changes have only brought George Lucas' series back to its original goals of education and interactivity – but they have brought it back in a way that the producer himself probably never could have imagined. In the end, even he may have learned an important lesson about culture. It was also learned by the heads of the old broadcast and cable networks, maybe even by the scholars we allegedly revere, the same men and women we unconsciously rewrite so that they may become even truer precursors of ourselves. Power exists only in the present, and the past and the future are rewritten to serve it. That lesson bears on every point in the cultural process: from conception to development to production to delivery and finally to reception, which comes last of all. At any individual point in the process, a modern cultural artifact may be controlled and shaped by its producers, its writers, its performers, or its executives. In the end, however, it is always controlled by its audience, who can rewrite it in almost any way that they wish. Audiences outlive every other part of the process, because their role is the only one that can always be going on. As *The Indiana Jones Chronicles* ultimately proves, audiences may be the most creative and influential artists of all.

afterword

Robert J. Thompson
Director, The Center for the Study of Popular Television
Syracuse University

In the event you haven't noticed it, the books that are reviewed in the preceding collection of essays do not really exist. But they might have existed, and many just like them do. The field of Television Studies, and more traditional academic disciplines, is rife with volumes that exhibit the same turgid, hyper-analytical, self-absorbed prose that the authors sling so joyously in the pieces you've just read.

Should we allow these young scholars to get away with this? The reviewers in this anthology could very handily have written the books they have invented. Ten years ago they might have. But these multi-diploma intellectuals found that just as they had become fluent in the specialized but often impenetrable style and vocabulary of contemporary cultural criticism, they also found themselves part of a small but significant avant-garde wing of the academy that had begun to see this kind of writing as exclusionary and laughable.

All dressed up with no place to go, what were they to do? The essays in this collection provided one solution. Heavily dosed with both academic indoctrination and anti-academic raised consciousnesses, they could write what they knew behind the distancing protection of end-of-century irony. They could make the points and strut the virtuosity that their big-ticket educations had made possible without having to take full responsibility for any of it. 'We know this all sounds a little silly,' these pieces announce. 'We're hip to the seams of the ivory tower.' But still they write. How dare they? Electing to present reviews of imaginary monographs and edited collections, of course, is a further extension of their hubris. This form allows them to subject us to their drive-by critiques without undergoing the inconvenience of actually writing an entire book on the subject.

Yet when I heard some of these pieces presented at an academic conference, and when I read the manuscript of the entire collection, I noticed that I kept learning things about the television shows being discussed. I was reminded of something that I haven't thought much about since I got tenure: the specialized language of contemporary criticism, for all its abuses, can be of very great value. The sophisticated jargon of the modern humanities needs to be taught and used with care, not eliminated. These bogus reviews, it seemed to me, exposed a legion of problems present in current styles of academic inquiry, while at the same time providing some examples of how those same styles of inquiry can, in responsible hands, be very illuminating.

It isn't surprising that essays making fun of academic discourse are part of an emerging genre of scholarly writing. Profspeak is, after all, such an easy target. However, as I write this – a sincere review of a real book containing ironic reviews of fake books – I wonder if the whole thing isn't getting a little out of hand. But I don't think so.

The idea of reviewing imaginary books might be the best thing to happen to clarity, conciseness, and economy of expression in academic writing since *The Elements of Style*. The books reviewed in this collection don't deserve to be written. The reviews do. There are enough ideas in each one to sustain an essay, not a volume. If every assistant professor proposing to write a book considered first that a review of that book might do just as nicely, libraries would have more shelf space, the world would have more sylvan glades, and dissertations would have shorter bibliographies.

general bibliography

Barthes, Roland (1982) 'The World of Wrestling', in Susan Sontag (ed.) *A Barthes Reader*. New York: Hill and Wang, 18–30.

Baudrillard, Jean (1989) *America* (Trans. Chris Turner). London: Verso.

_____ (1990) *Cool Memories* (Trans. Chris Turner). London: Verso.

Begley, Sharon and Adam Rogers (1996) 'Morphogenic Field Day', *Newsweek*, 3 June, 37.

Bennett, Mark (1996) *TV Sets: Fantasy Blueprints of Classic TV Homes*. New York: TV Books.

Berko, Lili (1988) 'Simulation and High Concept Imagery: The Case of Max Headroom', *Wide Angle*, 10, 4, 60–1.

'Best Hero' (1996) *Soap Opera Digest*, 27, 27, 31 December, 42.

Bhabha, Homi K (1992) 'Postcolonial authority and postmodern guilt', in Grossberg *et al. Cultural Studies*. New York: Routledge, 56–68.

Boorstin, Daniel (1961) *The Image: A Guide to Pseudo-Events in American Life*. New York: Atheneum.

_____ (1965) *The Americans: The National Experience*. New York: Random.

Borges, Jorge Luis (1999) 'Kafka and His Predecessors', in Eliot Weinberger (ed.) *Selected Non-Fictions*. New York: Viking, 613–15.

'Call for Papers' (1996) *Village Voice*, 25 June.

Campbell, Richard (1993) *Sixty Minutes*. Urbana: University of Illinois Press.

Deleuze, Gilles and Felix Guatari (1986). *A Thousand Plateaus: Capitalism and Schizophrenia* (Trans. Brian Massumi). Minneapolis: University of Minnesota Press.

Douglas, Lawrence (1996) 'Scholarship as Satire: A Tale of Misapprehension', in *The Chronicle of Higher Education*, 17 May, A56.

Douglas, Lawrence and Alexander George (1994) 'Freud's Phonographic Memory and the Case of the Missing Kiddush Cups', in *Tikkun* January/February, 74–8.

Eco, Umberto (1983) 'Postscript', in *The Name of the Rose* (Trans. William Weaver). New York: Harcourt Brace Jovanovich.

_____ (1992) 'How to Be a TV Host', in *How to Travel with a Salmon & Other Essays* (Trans. William Weaver). New York: Harcourt Brace & Company, 50–6.

_____ (1993) 'The Phenomenology of Mike Bongiorno', in *Misreadings* (Trans. William Weaver). New York: Harcourt Brace & Company, 156–64.

'Falwell's Newspaper Claims "Teletubbies" Character is Gay' (1999), in *CNN Interactive*. 10 Feb 1999. 23 May 2001. Available online: http://gabrielmedia.org/news/falwell_teletubbies.html

Fiske, John (1987) *Television Culture*. London and New York: Routledge.

'Four Generations of Americans Demand Sitcom Reparations', *The Onion*. Available online: http://www.theonion.com/onion3725/sitcom_reparations.html

Freud, Sigmund (1917) 'Mourning and melancholia', in *Collected Papers* Vol. 4. New York: Basic Books.

Fukuyama, Francis (1992). *The End of History and The Last Man*. New York: The Free Press.

Gaines, Jane (1990) *Fabrications: Costume and the Female Body*. London: Routledge.

Genette, Gerard (1983) *Narrative Discourse: An Essay in Method*. Ithaca, NY: Cornell University Press.

Geraghty, Christine and David Lusted (1998) 'General Introduction' to *The Television Studies Book*. London: Arnold.

Grossberg, Lawrence, Cary Nelson, and Paula A. Treichler (eds) (1992) *Cultural Studies*. New York: Routledge.

Hamilton, Edith and Huntington Cairns (eds) (1961) *Collected Dialogues of Plato*. Princeton: Princeton University Press.

Haraway, Donna (1992) 'The Promises of Monsters: A Regenerative Politics for Inappropriate/d Others', in Grossberg *et al. Cultural Studies*, 295–337.

Highet, Gilbert (1962) *The Anatomy of Satire*. Princeton: Princeton University Press.

Hillman, James (1979) *The Dream and the Underworld*. New York: Harper and Row.

Hofstadter, Douglas (1979) *Gödel, Escher, Bach: An Eternal Golden Braid*. New York: Basic Books.

Hutcheon, Linda (1985) *A Theory of Parody: The Teachings of Twentieth-Century Art Forms*. New York: Methuen.

Jameson, Fredric (1991) 'Criticism in History', in Charles Kaplan and William Anderson (eds) *Criticism: Major Statements* (3rd edn.). New York: St. Martin's, 574–94.

Jonson, Ben (1977) *Bartholmew Fair*. Edited by G. R. Hibbard. New York: Norton.

Jung, Carl G. (1959) *Flying Saucers: A Modern Myth of Things Seen in the Skies*. London: Routledge & Kegan Paul.

____ (1968) 'Approaching the Unconscious', in *Man and His Symbols*. New York: Dell, 1–94.

King, Barry (1989) 'The Burden of Max Headroom', in *Screen*, 30, Winter/Spring, 122–38.

Lem, Stanislaw (1971) *A Perfect Vacuum* (Trans. Michael Kandel). New York: Harcourt Brace Jovanovich.

____ (1981) *Imaginary Magnitude* (Trans. Marc E. Heine). New York: Harcourt Brace Jovanovich.

____ (1984) 'Todorov's Fantastic Theory of Literature', in Franz Rottensteiner (ed.) *Microworlds*. New York: Harcourt Brace Jovanovich, 209–32.

Meglin, Nick and John Ficarra (1999) *Mad About TV*. New York: Mad Books.

Miller, Mark Crispin (1987) 'Deride and Conquer', in Todd Gitlin (ed.) *Watching Television: A Pantheon Guide to Popular Culture*. New York: Pantheon, 183–228.

Minh-ha, Trinh T. (1989) *Woman, Native, Other: Writing Post-coloniality and Feminism*. Bloomington: Indiana University Press.

Morris, Emund (2000). *Dutch: A Memoir of Ronald Reagan*. New York: Random House.

Mulvey, Laura (1975) 'Visual Pleasure and Narrative Cinema', *Screen* 16, 3: 6–18

Nabokov, Vladimir (1962) *Pale Fire*. New York: Vintage.

Newcomb, Horace and Paul M. Hirsch (1987) 'Television as a Cultural Forum', in Horace Newcomb (ed.) *Television: The Critical View* (4th edn.). New York: Oxford University Press, 455–70.

Nochimson, Martha (1993) *No End to Her: Soap Opera and the Female Subject*. Berkeley: University of California Press.

O'Brien, Glenn (1987) 'Like Art', in *Artforum International*, 25, 6.

Ogami (2001) *Subtext*, 4 April. Available online: http://pegasus.cc.ucf.edu/~jeb66038/subtext.htm#TOP

'Report: Mankind's Knowledge of TV Trivia Doubling Every Three Years', *The Onion*. Available online: http://onion.com/onion3705/knowledge_of_tv_trivia.html

'Report: TV Helps Build Valuable Looking Skills', *The Onion*. Available online: http://www.theonion.com/onnion3539/looking_skills.html

Rose, Margaret A. (1993) *Parody: Ancient, Modern, and Post-Modern*. New York: Cambridge University Press.

Scholes, Robert (1982) *Semiotics and Interpretation*. New Haven: Yale University Press.

Sconce, Jeffrey (2000) *Haunted Media: Electronic Presence from Telegraphy to Television*. Durham and London: Duke University Press.

Seger, Linda (1990) *Creating Unforgettable Characters*. Boston: Holt.

Selley, April (1986) '"I Have Been, and Ever Shall Be, Your Friend": *Star Trek*, *The Deerslayer* and American Romance', in *Journal of Popular Culture*, 20, 89–104.

Silverman, Kaja (1988) *The Acoustic Mirror: The Female Voice in Psychoanalysis and Cinema*. Bloomington: Indiana University Press.

Sokal, Alan D. (1996) 'Transgressing the Boundaries: Toward a Transformative Hermeneutic of Quantum Gravity', in *Social Text*, 46/47, 14.1–2, 217–52.

Thompson, William Irwin (1971) *At the Edge of History: Speculations on the Transformation of Culture*. New York: Harper and Row.

'Tinky Winky Comes Out of the Closet' (1999) *NLJ Online*. Feb 1999. 23 May 2001. Available online:
http://www.liberty.edu/chancellor/nlj/feb99/politics2.html

Todorov, Tzvetan (1969) *Grammaire du Decameron*. The Hague: Mouton.

Tomlinson, John (1991) *Cultural Imperialism*. Baltimore: Johns Hopkins University Press.

Tompkins, Jane (1981) *Reader-Response Criticism: From Formalism to Post-Structuralism*. Baltimore: Johns Hopkins University Press.

Von Franz, M-L. (1972) 'The Process of Individuation', in Carl G. Jung (ed.) *Man and His Symbols*. New York: Dell, 375–88.

Zenka, Lorraine (1995) *Days of Our Lives: The Complete Family Album*. New York: HarperCollins.

faux bibliography

The editors have made every effort to track down complete bibliographical information for each book and article referred to in *Teleparody*. For some, however, we succeeded only in identifying the author and title. We suspect that some of these scholarly works may in fact be imaginary.

Addison, Justin (2000) *Cultural Displacement and the Hegemony of Wealth in The Beverly Hillbillies*. Bugtussle, AK: Ozark State College Press.

Anglophone, Andrew (2000a) '"The Los Angelization of Planet Earth": *Baywatch* and the Dream of a Common Language', Anglophone 1–17.

_____ (ed.) (2000b) *Californication and Cultural Imperialism: Baywatch and the Creation of World Culture*. Point Sur: Malibu University Press.

Anonymous. *If You Were Married to Him, You'd Take Them Too.*

Anonymous (2008) 'Naming Names? A Review of Spigel (2007)', *Cultural Studies*, 22.3.

Anopheles, Aristotle (1997) *Tele(ological)tubbies*. Athens: A & M University Press.

Austen, Iain John (2044) *TV Guides: Towards Embedded Theory*. Chicago, London, and Sydney: Wiseman Associated Press.

Basore, Karen (2000) 'All Things to All People: The Question of *Baywatch*'s Genre', Anglophone, 229–40.

Bauer, Dale M. (1988) *Feminist Dialogics: A Theory of Failed Commuinty*. Albany: State University of New York Press.

Beljang, Lucius and Wyblad Glisnic. *Mush Brains! Unite.*

_____ *The Nexus of Mash(ed) Potatoes and Turkey Hash: Comfort Food for the Over-Stimulated Television Generation.*

Bell, Artemis (1996) 'Boys Just Wanna Have Fun', Lavery 1–19.

Bennett, Kathleen E. '*Xena: Warrior Princess*, Desire Between Women, and Interpretive Response'.

Berger, Karen. 'Anorexia and the Homospectatorial Gaze: Investigating the Doppelganger Relationship Between Characters and Actors from Tracey Gold to Calista Flockhart', Fraugrois 189–218.

Bhose, Arvind (2000) '*Max Headroom* in the Age of Mechanical Reproduction', Dumfries 104–28.

Bonkin, Stephen (2000) 'The Monstrous Feminine in *South Park*', Levine 149–62.

Bortman, Chauncy (1986) 'He'll be Back, Mark My Words', *Trends for Television's Future*, 14, 135–70.

_____ (1988) *I'm Still Predictin', He's Still A Comin': Ray Gardner and the Trumpet's Call.*

_____ with Robert Dylan (1991) 'The Times May Be A Changin' but Ray's Pieces Aren't Blowin' in the Wind'. *Conspiracy Theories and the Insane*. L. O. Stone (ed.).

Bovary, Anne (2000) 'The Negative Oedipus: Murdering the Mother in *My Two Dads* and *Full House*,' Fraugrois, 12–26.

Bradshaw, Richard (2000) *Straight Readings: Resistance, Reappropriation, and Heterosexuality*. London: Peacock.

Brantley, Will (1996) 'Eroteneutics', Lavery 38–57

_____ *Marine to Marine: Ethnicity, Race, and Diegetic Desires*.

Brigance, Linda (2000) 'Amoral Moralism: *Baywatch*, Public Discourse, and the Didactic Text', Anglophone 241–61.

Brunsdon, Charlotte (2003) 'Whose Black Box? Why Television Studies Still Needs to Get a Life', *Screen*, 44, 1.

Campbell, Richard (2000) '*Baywatch* as Commodity: Marketing the World's Most Popular Show', Anglophone, 86–110.

Cannon, Maud (2000) 'Neo-Antebellum Mammies: The Othering of Caretaking from *The Jeffersons* to *The Jetsons*', Fraugrois, 41–55.

Carroll, Deborah. *The Politics of Disembodiment in My Mother the Car.*

Coloring the Teletubbies. Smith-Binney Publications.

Culpa, Felix. '*There You Go Again! Again!*': The Politics of Repetition and the Repetition of Politics*. Bora Bora Institute of Technology Press.

Cursive-Waters, Taryn P. (2000) *Visual Pleasure and Nasal Elevation: A Television Teleology*. Boise, ID: Proboscis Books.

Darkbloom, Vivian. *Dr. Jones and Mr. Indy: A Virtual Psychobiography* (darkv.djmi@pegasus.com—2.18M).

Delaponcé, Claude (2000) ''The Unconscious is Structured as a L-l-l-language': Max as Mirror Stage', Dumfries 18–30.

Delsing, James (1993) 'Dressed up in *Dragnet*', in *Detective Fiction Quarterly*, 15, 3, July: 174–7.

Di Turno, James (2005) *From Gidget to the End of History: Sally Field and the American Century.* Volumes I and II. New York: Situation Press.

—— *Timmy's Down the Well, Again: The Life of the Lassies.*

Dimsdale, Art. *A Bird in the Hand: Homoerotic Subtexts of the Bush Presidencies.*

—— *From Marilyn to Monica: Shiny Perishing Republic.*

—— (2010) *On Temptation Island: The View from the Hot Tub.* New York: Danaides & Baedecker.

Dross, André, ed. (1997) *Subverting Desires: Spectacles of the Simpson Year.* Bucksnort, TN: Volunteer State Press.

DuBois-Herkemer, L'Wanetta. 'The Subtext of Eugenics and the Conspiracy of Silence in Beatrix Potter's 'Jemima Puddle-Duck', *The Journal of Postmodern Philology.*

—— (2000) 'Theory, Theora Jones, and the Second Sex', Dumfries 202–40.

Dufy, Christopher J. *Myth, Media, and Mirrors: A Intermedial Commentary on Indiana Jones* (dutcj.mmm@acad.publ.twisdcc.com—1M).

Dumfries, Martyn (2000a) 'Afterword.' Dumfries: 241–44.

—— (2000b) 'Ben Cheviot: Hegelian World-Spirit Incarnate?' Dumfries: 181–201.

—— *The Brontës' Secret Authorship of the Barchester Novels* (forthcoming).

—— *The Faked Deaths of the Brontës: An Examination of the Insurance Records.* Routledgerdemain.

—— (2000c) ed. *Zipping the Great Minds: Max Headroom's BigTime Philosophy.* Gary, Indiana: DeLancie Presbyterian UP.

Dunne, Michael (2000d) 'Saving Gilligan: Meta- and Inter-Textuality in *Baywatch*', Anglophone, 193–210.

Eagleton, S. D. (1955) *Leavis, Labor, and Lucille Ball.*

Ellis, John (2009) *Taking Another Glance at Television in the Academy.* London: I. B. Tauris.

Fiske, John (2037) *A Half-century of Television Culture: Anniversary Edition*, Martin Sedgewick (ed.). London: Sage-Routledge.

Foreman, Janis (2000) 'Introduction', Addison 1–13.

—— *The Munsters as Mirror of Societal Dysfunction.*

Fraugrois, Patricia. 'Introduction', Fraugrois: 1–10.

—— (1992) '"Ruling with Her Pussy, Undone by Her Asp": the Cleopatra Narrative and the Made-for-TV Heroine'.

—— (ed.) (2000) *A Creature Feminine: The Politics of T & A in Primetime Television, 1970–2000.* Sunnydale: Kali Books International.

Fredericks, Jameson. 'Dark (K)night of the Frankfurt School: Adorno, Mass Culture, and *The Today Show.*

Fritz, Paddy and Joseph Serf. 'I am not a Number. I am a Teletubby': *The Prisoner and Teletubbies.* Village Publications.

—— *Spongebob Squarepants and the Geometry of Style.* Atlantis University Press.

Galehouse, Sigmund (1992) 'Tangled in a Webb', *Cultural Perspectives on the 1980's*, 3, 2, April, 118–9.

Gardner, D. Raymond (1996) *Acronym for Alterity: AMC and the Subaltern.* Carolina: Berngergy Press Ltd.

Gebstadter, Egbert R. (1979) *Copper, Silver, Gold: An Indestructible Metal Alloy.* Perth: Acidic Books.

Gendron, Charisse (1996) 'Romancing the Family Simon', Lavery 20–37.

Gentilhommé, Stephanié (2000) 'Decoding *Baywatch*: A Cross-Cultural, Ethnographic Study', Anglophone, 124–44.

Gique, Stanley (2000) 'Bitch Goddess/Matriarch/*Vagina Dentata*: The Destroyer Goddess of the 80s Nighttime Soap Opera', Fraugrois, 56–77.

Goldthwaite, Charles (2000) '*Baywatch* and Television Wrestling: A Narratological Comparison', Anglophone 219–28.

Grace, Mary Elizabeth (1999) *Tinky Winky, I Wuv You!* Scholastic Books.

Graham, Allison (1996) 'What Did You Do in the War, Rick?', Lavery 58–78.

Hague, Jill (2000) 'Surf and Surfeit: The Role of Music in *Baywatch*', Anglophone 110–23.

Hartley, John (2010) *Theoryspeaks: Neologisms and the Blivitous Science Fiction-alization of Media*. Cambridge: Cambridge University Press.

Hatch, Richard (2001) Unpublished internal dialogue channeled by Baron Von Schnott.

Havelock, Xerxes. *Good Cop, Bad Cop: CHiPs and Plato's Model of the Soul.*

_____ *Nichomachaen Ethics and Miami Vices.*

_____ *Ponch, Jon, and Phaedrus' Chariot.*

_____ (1998) *'This is the City-State': The Idea of the Guardian in the TV LAPD.* Springfield: Full Court Press.

Heman, Herman (1999) *Captain Kangaroo and Mr. Green Jeans/Captain Kirk and Mr. Spock: Homoeroticism as Subtext in the Post-Atomic Age.* San Francisco: Gaylord Press.

_____ (1991) *Phallic Fallacies: The Myth of the Virile Western Hero.* Paris: University of Texas at Paris Press.

_____ (1995) *Sex Sells so Sell Sex: A History of the Prostitute on Television.* Pahrump: University of Nevada at Pahrump Press.

Hills, Matt (2005) *An Imperfect Vacuum: Theorizing TV with and without History.* London: Sage-Routledge.

Ivanovich, Ivan (2000) *Howdy Doody: A Marxist Interpretation of the Manipulation of the Proletariat.* Moscow: Lenin Square Books.

James, Evan. *Falling to Pieces.*

Jones, Lugnut (2000) *Foreign Objects in the Ring: Professional Wrestling and the Politics of Engagement.* New York: Pile Driver Press.

Jones, Sara Gwenllian (2016) *How Long Does My Bibliography Have to Be? Essays on Media Knowledge in the Information Age.* Oxford: Oxford University Press.

_____ (2015) *Reading Online T.V.* Oxford: Oxford University Press.

Kilkenney, Kristine (2000) 'Cokie, Katie, or Kathie Lee: Semiotic Motherhood in a Symbolic Economy', Fraugrois 27–40.

King, Rebecca (2000) 'David Hasselhoff: A Semiotic Approach to One of the World's Most Recognized Images', Anglophone, 60–85.

Kubek, Elizabeth (2000) 'Mirrors of Sand: *Baywatch* from a Lacanian Perspective', Anglophone, 168–92.

Lavery, David (1996) *Boys Will Be Boys: Critical Approaches to Simon and Simon.* Bucksnort, TN: Middle Tennessee Normal University Press.

Lawrence, Lyn J. (2000) 'Marcy Becomes Electra: Gender Dysphoria in *Peanuts* Primetime Specials', Fraugrois, 79–89.

Leavis, Englebert (2032) *Read Less, Watch More.* Durham and London: Duke University Press.

Lefkowitz, Anastasia I. (2000) 'Blank Reg and Heideggerean Authenticity.' Dumfries 151–69.

Levine, Lavender (2000a) 'Cartmen out of the Closet: Screw You, I'm Going Homo', Levine, 25–41.

_____ (ed.) Seinfeld, Master of His Domain: Jerry Seinfeld and Sado-masochism.

_____ (2000b) *They Deconstructed South Park: You Bastards!* Liverpool: Routleger-demain.

Lloydminster, Jake. 'Max/Edison Carter: So Who's the Ding-an-sich.' Dumfries 1–17

Lutz, Alfred (2000) 'Bakhtin Goes to the Beach: Dialogism and *Baywatch*', Anglophone, 145–68.

Marton, Carol (2000) 'Deborah Schwartz: A *Baywatch* Auteur', Anglophone, 210–18.

Masters, Bonnie-LeeAnne (2000) '20 Minutes into Althusser's Future', Dumfries, 141–50.

Minkoff-Reilly, M. (2001) *'Fear no more the heat of the baby-faced sun': Teletubbies and Early Modern Drama.* Dismal State University Press.

Neamo, Victoria (2001) *Don't You Be My Neighbor: Dystopian Visions in Mister Rogers' Neighborhood*, Moose Pass: Arctic University Press.

Nelson, Robin (2004) *The Death of TV Drama and Other Theoretical Melodramas.* London: Palgrave.

_____ (2006) *TV Drama Resurrected.* Tokyo and Basingstoke: Global (formerly Palgrave).

O'Connell, Rosie (1995) 'I love de two of yas', *Women, Television, and Society*, 14, 14–37.

_____ *Marx, K-Mart and Mark (ya know, Erica's long-lost brother, de one who had AIDS or something): When Consumer Culture and Pine Valley Collide.*

O'Reilly, Dan Chinh-Wah. 'If You Meet Max Headroom on the Road, Kill Him!'

Pendant, Sasha (2000) 'Twistati: Kenny as Frustrated Orator', Levine 1–13.

Peters, John Durham (2002) *High Concept: Representing Thought and Mediating the 'Concept',* Cambridge and London: Harvard University Press.

Phillips, Vanessa (2000) 'Salisbury (what's at) Stake: Cafeteria Carnivores at *South Park* Elementary', Levine, 42–65.

Pilgerstock, Renate (2000) 'Being and Nothingness – to the Max', Dumfries, 71–103

Porlock, Percy (1998) *We All Live in a Stately-Pleasure Dome: The Magical History of Teletubbies.* Liverpool UP.

Pupkin-Bickle, R. (1983) '"Start Spreading the News": Representing Manhattan in the Films of Allen, Cassavetes, Lewis, Scorsese, and LaGuardia', Dissertation, University of California at Sunnydale.

_____ (1996) *Tropes of Turbulence.* London and New Delhi: Parsley Publications.

Radway, Martha Stewart (1988) *Reading the Roll, Man.*

Ramsbotham, Roy Smythe (2000) 'Max, Marx and Sparks', Dumfries, 45–70.

ReSalvo, Lucia (1996) '"Don't Tell Anybody": The Effect of Childhood Sexual Abuse upon A. J. Simon', Lavery, 79–135.

Rhode, Sally (2000) 'Stan's Projectile Vomiting: The Retchedness of Femininity in *South Park*', Levine, 14–24.

Riser, Jim (2000) 'My Space or Yours?: Gravity-Free, Guilt-Free Sex in Space', *Space Frontiers*, June.

Rood, Rafe (1996) 'Afterword', Lavery, 136–44.

187

Rosenberg, Sheila (1999) *The Piano and the Trolley: The Rhizomatic Mister Rogers*, Sunnydale: Sunnydale UP.

_____(2000) 'Tan Lines and Identity: A Psychohistorical Reading of *Baywatch*', Anglophone, 18–33.

Runciman, Simon G., Jr. 'Live and Direct from Plato's *Republic*', Dumfries 129–40.

Russell, Seymour (2000) 'Reclaiming the Jiggle Factor: Commodification Without Competition from *Charlie's Angels* to *Baywatch*,' Fraugrois, 121–55.

Scott, Wilhelm (1989) 'Positivist Teleology, My Ass', *Professional Forecaster*, 12, 65–83.

Sherwin, Edward. 'Requiem for a Lightweight', *American Thinker*.

Silvera, Charlene (1992) 'Good Cop, Bum Rap,' in *Omnia: A Journal of All Things Philosophical and Social*, 17, 3, June: 159–62.

'Smith', Babs Bush. *Me and Modernity: Marginalization at the Edges of Kennebunkport*.

Smith, Buffalo Bob (1990) *Howdy and Me: Buffalo Bob's Own Story*. New York: Plume.

'Smith', Hillary Rodham Clinton (1996) *Daytime Dialogism: Erica's Eroica in the Pine Valley Village* Washington, D.C.: Presidential Partner Press.

'Smith', Jackie Kennedy. *Discipline and Punish: Adultery in America*.

'Smith', Lady Bird Johnson. *Genderbubbles: Lawrence Welk's Penchant for Cross Dressing*.

'Smith', Mamie Eisenhower. *What's War Got to Do with It: Ike and Tina in the Vietnam Years*.

'Smith', Nancy Davis Reagan. *The Rules: Listen to Me!*

'Smith', Pat Nixon. *Helpful Hints for Around the (White)House*.

Smythe, Sarah-Jayne (2045) *Autarchic Tele-visions*. New York and London: TallPoppies Press.

Socalled, Alan. *My Own Inadequacy: Transgressing the Boundaries of Mister Rogers Neighborhood*.

Sommers, Evelyn (2000) 'Piss and Vinegar: Feminine Hygiene and the Marketing of Daytime Television', Fraugrois, 219–58.

Spigel, Lynn (2007) *The Making of Theoretical Elites: Proper Names in Media Theory*. Durham and London: Duke UP.

Steffansen, Jan. 'Zik Zak, Telelections, and the Vu-Age Church; or, Baudrillard Proved Right Yet Again', *Old Left Review*.

Stein, Alice (2000) 'Implants or Mastectomy: Self/Body Authorship, Fragmentation, and Scopophilic Desire', Fraugrois, 156–88.

Steinhauer, Karl-Helmut 2000 'Bryce Lynch: Beyond Good and Evil', Dumfries, 170–80.

Stern, Jerome (1996) *Equinicity: Contending Discourses in Mister Ed*. Murfreesboro, TN: The Augean Press.

Summar, David (2000) 'Surf and Simulation: Baudrillard and *Baywatch*', Anglophone, 34–46.

Thorgoode, Quentin (2000) 'Syntax á la Max: A Wittgensteinian View', Dumfries, 31–44.

Todorov, I. B. *Aerosmith and Otherness: An Answer to Said* (forthcoming)

_____ (1996) *Beavis, Butt-head, and Bakhtin.* Leeds: Antisocial Texts.

_____ (1992) *Deconstructing Dennis (the Menace).*

_____ (1995) *Fabio and Fabulation.*

_____ (1994) *Materializing Madonna.*

_____ (1993) *Signs, Signification, and Sushi.*

_____ *Who Invited All These Tacky People?* (forthcoming).

_____ *Xena and Xenophobia* (forthcoming).

Umlaut, Gerund (1999) *Entschuligen Sie, bitte, wie komme ich zum Land Teletubby?* Berlin: die Presse einfältig Universität.

Valence, Sir Lawrence (2000) 'Blame Canada: The Only Good Canuck is a Dead Canuck', Levine, 162–180.

Van Dyke, Ellen (2000) 'Laverne and Velma as *ur*-Dyke: Outing 70s Television', Fraugrois, 90–120.

Van Loon, Herschel '*Max* and Maimonides'.

Vidray, Dale V. (ed.) *The Adventure of a Lifetime: Critical Windows on The Indiana Jones Chronicles* (viddv.adv@press.wsu.edu—1.52M).

Wahl-Jorgensen, Karin (2007) *Tele-journalism: Public Spheres, Private Stories and Political Systems.* New York: Columbia University Press.

Waller, Gregory A. (1993) *The Weather Channel is Our Whitman.* Lexington, Kentucky: privately published.

Ward, Burt (1995) *My Life in Tights.* Boulder: Martin Keating.

Wetvac, Gyatra (2000) 'Cartman's Quest for Capital: Mo' Money, Mo' Problems', Levine, 66–148.

Wilcox, Rhonda V. (2000) 'The Postmodern Inane: *Baywatch* and the Insipid', Anglophone, 262–88.

Williams, Lisa (2000) 'T and A: Gazing *Baywatch*', Anglophone, 47–59.

Wilson, Timmy (2000) *Po! Laa-Laa! Fall Down Again,* Mother Goose Press.

Wortham-Quinn, Kristen Susan (2000) *The Semiotics of Days of Our Lives: The Possession of Marlena Evans as a Pedagogical Means of Interpretation.* Salem: Coma Books.

Wynette, Georgina and Tom E. Jones (1991) 'Did He Really Stop Loving Her Today? Necrophilia and Male Masochism in Country Music', *Lefty Frizzell Newsletter*, 35, 14–25.

_____ (1995) *Mapping Meteorology, Signifying Storms, Deploying Doppler.* Minneapolis: Southern Minnesota University Press.

Xu, Vera (1999) *Boat Shoes and Sweaters: Ontologies of Mister Rogers' Closet.*

index